T0007084

Waiting for Mister Rogers

Waiting for Mister Rogers

TEACHING WITH ATTACHMENT, ATTUNEMENT, AND INTENTION

Wysteria Edwards, BA, Ed.M

NEW YORK

LONDON • NASHVILLE • MELBOURNE • VANCOUVER

Waiting for Mister Rogers

Teaching with Attachment, Attunement, and Intention

© 2023 Wysteria Edwards, BA, Ed.M

All rights reserved. No portion of this book may be reproduced, stored in a retrieval system, or transmitted in any form or by any means—electronic, mechanical, photocopy, recording, scanning, or other—except for brief quotations in critical reviews or articles, without the prior written permission of the publisher.

Published in New York, New York, by Morgan James Publishing. Morgan James is a trademark of Morgan James, LLC. www.MorganJamesPublishing.com

Proudly distributed by Ingram Publisher Services.

Morgan James BOGO™

A **FREE** ebook edition is available for you or a friend with the purchase of this print book.

CLEARLY SIGN YOUR NAME ABOVE

Instructions to claim your free ebook edition:
1. Visit MorganJamesBOGO.com
2. Sign your name CLEARLY in the space above
3. Complete the form and submit a photo of this entire page
4. You or your friend can download the ebook to your preferred device

ISBN 9781636981031 paperback
ISBN 9781636981048 ebook
Library of Congress Control Number: 2022949591

Cover & Interior Design by:
Christopher Kirk
www.GFSstudio.com

Morgan James is a proud partner of Habitat for Humanity Peninsula and Greater Williamsburg. Partners in building since 2006.

Get involved today! Visit: www.morgan-james-publishing.com/giving-back

Waiting for Mister Rogers

TEACHING WITH ATTACHMENT, ATTUNEMENT, AND INTENTION

Wysteria Edwards, BA, Ed.M

NEW YORK

LONDON • NASHVILLE • MELBOURNE • VANCOUVER

Waiting for Mister Rogers

Teaching with Attachment, Attunement, and Intention

© 2023 Wysteria Edwards, BA, Ed.M

All rights reserved. No portion of this book may be reproduced, stored in a retrieval system, or transmitted in any form or by any means—electronic, mechanical, photocopy, recording, scanning, or other—except for brief quotations in critical reviews or articles, without the prior written permission of the publisher.

Published in New York, New York, by Morgan James Publishing. Morgan James is a trademark of Morgan James, LLC. www.MorganJamesPublishing.com

Proudly distributed by Ingram Publisher Services.

A **FREE** ebook edition is available for you or a friend with the purchase of this print book.

CLEARLY SIGN YOUR NAME ABOVE

Instructions to claim your free ebook edition:
1. Visit MorganJamesBOGO.com
2. Sign your name CLEARLY in the space above
3. Complete the form and submit a photo of this entire page
4. You or your friend can download the ebook to your preferred device

ISBN 9781636981031 paperback
ISBN 9781636981048 ebook
Library of Congress Control Number:
2022949591

Cover & Interior Design by:
Christopher Kirk
www.GFSstudio.com

Morgan James is a proud partner of Habitat for Humanity Peninsula and Greater Williamsburg. Partners in building since 2006.

Get involved today! Visit: www.morgan-james-publishing.com/giving-back

For Blue Eyes—you changed everything.

Contents

Author's feet on Neighborhood Trolley symbol located in Latrobe, PA. 2019.

Introduction

I must be an emotional archaeologist because I keep looking
for the roots of things, particularly the roots of behavior
and why I feel certain ways about certain things.
—Fred Rogers

I climb the stairs with quiet reverence, aware of my heart pounding with anticipation. It reminds me of turning the corner into our living room on Christmas morning as a child, knowing something wonderful awaits but unsure what it will be. Do you remember that feeling? The exhibit emerges at the top of the stairs with a large photo of Fred Rogers next to a glass case. Inside, four sweaters hang above a pair of worn Sperry Top tennis shoes and scuffed loafers. I suck in my breath, expecting to cry over the magnitude of what I'm seeing, but don't. Approaching, I hear people talking, only to realize it's a monitor playing scenes from the *Neighborhood*. I'm completely alone. Just me and Mister Rogers. No one else in the world is with me.

I refuse to rush this moment. His puppets smile back at me from behind glass: King Friday, Queen Sara Saturday, Prince Tuesday, X the Owl, and Daniel Striped Tiger. *Oh, Daniel. There he is!* Inching closer, I observe his right paw where the fur, once fluffy and thick, is worn down, exposing only the burlap base. How often Fred Rogers offered that paw to children or Betty

Aberlin to hold in affection—worn down through countless loving intentions and gestures.

I move closer to the sweaters knitted by his mother each year for Christmas. She would affectionately say, "I know which one you want, Freddy. The one with the zipper." A new color each time but knitted in love, and now four hang in front of me: red, blue, purple, and green. (A quilter, I study the handiwork and notice the pieces of yarn that have frayed from wear.) His tennis shoes modestly lay flat from years of wear and being packed around in a bag for his appearances, filming, and photo shoots. The loafers contain orthotics, and I smile at the thought of him wanting to be comfortable on the set. I take in every scuff and scrape.

And then I hear it. As clear as if you were speaking to me, in the voice of Fred Rogers: "Well, there you are, Wystie. What took you so long? I've been waiting for you."

Without hesitation, I speak aloud. "I had to wade through a lot of crap to get here, Fred." Startled by the sound of my own voice, I laugh. Glancing back to Daniel, I finally realize the truth: I've come searching for the humanity of Mister Rogers. How did Fred Rogers show up every day and do what mattered? People didn't always understand or believe in what he knew was right. But he did it anyway. What did that take? And how could that be me? Blue Eyes was counting on me.

Before the trip, I remember telling my counselor about my frustrations with being intentional and doing such emotional heavy lifting. "I feel like I'm waiting for Mister Rogers to show up and tell me what to do."

She replied, "That's the name of your book, Wystie. Waiting for Mister Rogers."

It's so much easier to wait for someone with more wisdom and insight, isn't it? We doubt that we could be just what the situation or person needs. And I can't tell you how many times during the last three years I've seen people comment on social media about how Mister Rogers is needed today. But there was a time when even Fred Rogers had his doubts. In the aftermath of 9/11, as he prepared for a public service announcement, he, too, wondered if he was enough.

The highly competent, award-winning American icon was unsure what he could say to the world in the wake of such catastrophic violence. It wasn't as if his words would ease the loss of life, the fear of the unknown, the confusion of being "at war with terror." He had retired only one year prior, after entering the door on a simple set close to a thousand times, changing into his sweater and sneakers, singing familiar songs, teaching lessons, and manipulating his mechanical trolley into the Neighborhood of Make-Believe.

As *Neighborhood* producer Margy Whitmer recalled,

> Right after 9/11 we decided to do these public service announcements for parents, teachers and for adults. We were getting ready in the studio, and I went downstairs to his office. . . . I walked in and Fred was just, I can't even explain it. He was just so sad, so questioning. He said, "Why are we doing these? They aren't going to do any good." I panicked because he was always the one who took care of us. And I thought, "How am I going to convince him this is worthwhile?" So I said to him, "Fred, how can you say that?" I said, "Don't you understand how important you are? You know that millions of people love you, and their kids love you. They listen to you. You've got to do these!" And so, we had a time together where we just calmed down, and I said, "I'm going to go downstairs [to the studio], and I'll see you in five minutes. You can do this; it's so important. People listen to you; they care what you have to say." And so, we did them, and that's when I remember him using the phrase, "look for the helpers."[1]

Leaders, teachers, parents, and caregivers get weary and doubt. Even Mister Rogers needed to be reminded of what he meant to Americans who trusted his voice and opinion. Everyone needs emotional first aid, as we've all been overwhelmed and broken. We're still waiting for Mister Rogers to tell us that we're loved, and that we have the courage to know what to do next. That's what the best of prophets are—voices of conscience in an age that cries out for righteous and loving leadership. Now it's our turn to remember what he taught us, to go back to doing what we know in our hearts is right for children. He was right all along!

---

1 Swift Fox Media, "Our Assignment from Fred Rogers (2020) Award-Winning Documentary," July 29, 2020, YouTube video, https://www.youtube.com/watch?v=0ijzTmatpdM&t=989s.

****

When I was a boy, and I would see scary things in the news,
my mother would say to me, "Look for the helpers.
You will always find people who are helping."
—Fred Rogers

Security brings comfort and emotional healing. The fact that you want to care for children in an age that dismisses pain, values fast-paced methods, and condones apathy is courageous. Loving and teaching children requires understanding our own stories of harm and heartache, while guiding with empathy. It's not about perfection, but intention. For the man who still doubted himself, Fred Rogers, never saw himself as significant, only as a friend to children and families. Reluctant leaders are the best leaders because they recognize failure is part of learning. Fred Rogers was a reluctant leader, but he took what he had and repeatedly used it to help children.

****

"I pulled these for you on the topics you sent me." The archivist motions to the pile. "Let me know if you need anything else." A jolt of excitement tightens in my chest as I see handwritten notes atop the typed sermon. It's his handwriting!

I sit down, exhaling slowly, and take in my surroundings. Adrenaline surges through me as I place my hand on the pile, unable to begin. Discarded desks are piled in one corner of the long room amid tattered boxes of puppets, posters, framed photos, memorabilia, and old *Neighborhood* advertisements. *Mister Rogers' Neighborhood* letterhead pokes out of manila file folders with fluorescent newsletters from 1994, and an interactive exhibit displays the Fred Rogers Center (now Institute) logo on the wall. A rocking chair prop I recognize from Cornflake S. Pecially's factory sits casually on an empty table. Just inside the archive door, I see the painting Big Bird created while visiting the Neighborhood of Make-Believe, and the large book Fred Rogers reads in the introduction to the opera *Josephine the Short-Neck Giraffe*. We watched the opera last week as a class, and now that very book is within my reach. It's surreal. What will my kindergarteners think? Growing up in the theater, I understand they are only props, but the child within me wants to jump up and down and shout to the world, "Do you realize what this is?"

Fred Rogers had two types of script. When he was writing in his swirling cursive, it slanted to the right, often incomprehensibly, reflecting his racing thoughts while in conversations with his mentor, Dr. Margaret McFarland. There are scribbles, add-ins, connections to his puppets, and abbreviations I have to decipher with the archivist's help. However, when writing to friends and colleagues, his handwriting shifted to include large swooping *f*s, giving the letter his own artistic flair. In a world saturated with text messages and emails, we can go a lifetime without seeing a person's handwriting. But I can picture him sitting on the couch in his office at the WQED studio or at his Crooked House on Nantucket Island, drafting a letter that speaks to families with his predictable honesty.

My grandmother spoke of penmanship often and prided herself on receiving high marks for her handwriting in high school. She wrote letters and cards to everyone. Scribbling down her thoughts inside her Al-Anon book and mini spiral notepads, she joined my grandfather in his recovery from alcoholism. Her notes on sermons and affirmations are a treasure to me today. And I myself have filled more than forty notebooks recording my own emotional recovery for the past six years. Choosing to put pen to paper is an act of courage and vulnerability.

Fred Rogers frequently wrote letters for the newsletter and scripts for the *Neighborhood* in longhand before giving them to his secretary to be typed. He always kept two things handy: yellow legal pads and blue Flair pens (during my writing of this book, I deliberately used the same technique to feel closer to him). Many of his papers are water stained and wrinkled, which I suspect is from being carried back and forth in his bag to the pool where he swam laps each morning. Fred Rogers, like myself, found comfort in habits and materials.

Clearly, Rogers valued the ever-evolving process of learning. How often do we fight being in the middle of something, wanting to hurry up and "arrive"? Not Fred Rogers. He liked to take his time, innately understanding that keeping an open mind and heart helps us receive more from what the world is communicating. Books on world religions and philosophy filled his nightstand, and despite being a man who spent over fifty years working in television, he viewed reading as a more worthy pastime. Although the world made fun of Mister Rogers for being simple, a caricature, the real man was deeply complex and rich in his openness to new experiences, ideas, and details. How else could a man take advanced theories of child development and synthesize them into something a preschooler could understand?

As I open a green file folder, two pages of his cursive scroll stare back at me.

"Dear Families," he begins with such familiarity. There are notes in the margins with omissions and insertions, but it was clearly drafted with deep thought and reverence for his congregation of viewers. Since Fred Rogers aimed to be inclusive, one never heard religious talk but experienced religious values. As his wife, Joanne Rogers, remembered, "He walked the walk." Such pastoring came through in how he spoke to his television neighbors on and off camera, the way he treated his staff, and the self-discipline he showed in his personal life. It reminds me of when I was an undergraduate about to enter the teaching profession and my professor Dr. Doris Liebert reminded us: "You don't just belong to yourself. After you teach in the public eye, you are a member of your school, the community where you live, and God. People will look to you and at you. Being an educator is a sacred profession." What we stand for should be apparent in how we treat people, young and old.

For years the public asked Rogers for a book on parenting. Puppetry came naturally for him, but he often found his work on-screen in the television house nerve-wracking. Although trained in child development, Rogers viewed himself as a minister, composer, and television creative, not an expert. He was a perfectionist and worked diligently to fine-tune everything he did and every word he spoke to his television audience. Rogers thus valued the "process of learning," believing that he was always in the middle of everything, never fully arriving. In his opinion, he wrote, a book would be too much of one thing. Of course, a few years later, he did publish several works on parenting, play, and divorce in response to the voiced needs of his viewers.

"Too much of one thing" makes me laugh, as I feel the same way about life. I don't have just one hobby or idea. I have hundreds, all flying through my mind simultaneously. When children complain about being bored, I adopt the philosophy of "assign yourself" something interesting to do. As Brené Brown so aptly puts it, "Boredom is your imagination calling out to you."[2] I think that's why kindergarten is the perfect place for me. It moves quickly, pauses for wonder and reflection, easily distracted by a ladybug, a hangnail, or a cloud shaped like an elephant.

Fred Rogers often spoke about all he learned from children. His ability to be childlike, not childish, made him a receiver of all they had to share. My connection to him deepens as I find a fellow pilgrim on the journey of celebrating childlike wonder, with an ability to connect at each child's level. Growing was important work to Fred Rogers, and he counted himself lucky to be trusted as a part of children's experiences.

****

Teachers, parents, and caregivers forget the honor it is to fill the space of a secure and loving model for young children. What would happen if we were to embrace that calling with gratitude and determination? Fred Rogers' steadfast resolve, love, and appreciation for the significant role he played in the lives of countless children reach out to me like an embrace as the rain pours down outside the window. He signs off the letter in calm, slanted cursive: "Most sincerely, Fred Rogers."

I stare down at the closing, sucking in my breath as tears run down my cheeks. My fingertips trace over the signature in reverence. It's overwhelmingly beautiful to me. He'd held *this* paper in his hands, and now it is in mine, telling me what I want to know—Fred Rogers was real. He made mistakes and crossed them out. He had dreams, fears, and limitations and desired to be his authentic self. Somehow, seeing it laid out in his handwriting gives me more courage. He, too, longed to help create a new and better world through working, helping, and teaching children, much like you and me. In the wise words of W.E.B. Dubois, "Children learn more from what you are than what you teach."

We demonstrate love and security to children in our care through our humanity. But it takes you and me getting vulnerable. We will have to look inside and see if anything is holding us back and remain curious and courageous. Brené Brown

---

2   Brené Brown, *Atlas of the Heart* (New York: Random House, 2022).

explains: "We cultivate love when we allow our most vulnerable and powerful selves to be deeply seen and known and when we honor the spiritual connection that grows from that offering with trust, respect, kindness, and affection. Love is not something we give or get; it is something that we nurture and grow, a connection that can only be cultivated between two people when it exists within each of them—we can only love others as much as we love ourselves."[3]

What if all your experiences, good and bad, were used to serve and guide the children you teach? Fred Rogers spoke about this concept in a 2000 commencement speech at Saint Vincent College three years before he died. "I'll never forget the sense of wholeness I felt," he said, "when I finally realized what, in fact, I really was: not just a writer or a language buff or a student of human development or a telecommunicator, but I was someone who could use every talent that had ever been given to me in the service of children and their families."[4]

****

What would happen if we were to stop hiding behind curriculums, platitudes, pedagogies, and contracts? It's easier to blame and make excuses about parent involvement, home environments, lack of resources, or anything else than to look within ourselves and acknowledge that *we* could be the problem. It takes massive self-awareness. Do we have the courage to listen to our own hearts regarding those who matter most, our students?

We are all capable of loving children like Mister Rogers did—but it's a daily choice. If we model love, children will learn how to love and make the world a better place. "We need more real love. Gritty, dangerous, wild-eyed, justice-seeking love."[5] That's what changes the world—not coloring inside the lines, being like everyone else, and avoiding making waves. Isn't that what Mister Rogers did? It wasn't always popular, contrary to his acceptance today. Loving radically and dangerously wasn't normal then, or now. We say we want to be inclusive, but

---

3   Brown, *Atlas of the Heart.*
4   Fred M. Rogers, "About Fred," Fred Rogers Center for Early Learning and Children's Media, 2018, https://www.fredrogerscenter.org/about-fred.
5   Brown, *Atlas of the Heart.*

we aren't. "Shame, blame, disrespect, betrayal, and the withholding of affection damage the roots from which love grows. Love can survive these injuries only if they're acknowledged, healed, and rare."[6] Broken connection destroys our trust and erodes our best efforts in all relationships.

Against the wall behind my desk leans a framed poster. It's a 1998 calendar printed by Family Communications, Inc. Various promotional photographs from the *Neighborhood* are showcased—Big Bird's visit; famous athletes; Rogers waving from a plane, baking with Chef Brockett, sitting in construction equipment, and meeting a child in a wheelchair smiling—along with this quote from Fred Rogers: "Although children's 'outsides' may have changed . . . their inner needs have remained very much the same. Society seems to be pushing children to grow faster, but their developmental tasks have remained constant. No matter what lies ahead, children always need to know that they are loved and capable of loving. Anything that adults can do to help in this discovery will be our greatest gift to the future."

What keeps you coming back day after day to teach the children in your care? A paycheck? I hope not. Self-proclaimed "Irritational Speaker" Joe Martin said regarding teachers: "Some of you have the fire. Some of you used to have the fire. And some of you need to be fired."[7] Which one are you?

If you aren't wholeheartedly crazy, gritty, dangerously in love with meeting the emotional needs of children, please leave education. We all know someone in our school buildings who doesn't want to be there, looks unpleasant in the hallway, talks during meetings regardless of whether others are listening, spreads rumors about others, complains about children, and is exclusive and hostile. Be painfully real with yourself, and if this is you, please leave teaching. We don't need any more children hating school or thinking that's what learning is like. I've honestly prayed that many people would leave my buildings over the years, and it's worked. Do it or be brutally honest. I dare you! I often say, "The world doesn't need more jerks." Are you being one?

Fred Rogers understood that teaching and caregiving is often selfless, unrelenting work. He said:

---

6   Brown, *Atlas of the Heart.*
7   Dr. Joe Martin, 2022, http://www.drjoemartin.com/.

Do you ever wonder if you've made a difference in this life? Whether any of those children who have come to your care have remembered anything you did for them—any ways you cared for them? I believe that by the time a child grows up, that child's first teacher and second teacher and all the child's important adults will have become incorporated into that child's development. That's the way it is with all children, and although they might not remember clearly, those of us who were the educators of their early lives will always be a part of who they are. Just like those who meant so much to us when we were children will always be part of who we are.[8]

****

When I entered the Fred Rogers Archive in October of 2019, it was the culmination of my three years of recovery from a behavioral addiction that almost destroyed my life.

My attachment to my husband, Matthew, was secure, but something bled to the surface in 2000 when I had my first son, Jonathan, and deepened after the birth of our second, Benjamin, in 2003. Postpartum depression went untreated for five years as I fought off the stereotypes of being one more crazy person in my family. I longed to bond with my boys but found an invisible wall surrounding my heart. No matter what I tried, I couldn't find a way over it. What was wrong with me? I was an educator, for goodness' sake! Shouldn't I be able to meet my own children's needs and cope? *As if just being an educator would somehow make me maternal.* But I was young and naive. After all, I could pour my heart into the lives of other people's children!

Something was preventing me from fully engaging with my boys at an emotional level, and because of this, they terrified me. Every time they struggled or misbehaved, I saw it as confirmation I was a "bad mother." Jonathan's emotional struggles overwhelmed me, and my reactions were uncontrolled and childlike.

---

8   Fred Rogers, *You Are Special: Words of Wisdom from America's Most Beloved Neighbor* (New York: Viking, 1994).

The reality of the situation wasn't lost on me. I was responsible for preparing him for life, yet I lacked the ability to control the emotions engulfing me. Even after I was medicated for depression, self-loathing, shame, and "not-enough-ness" raged within me. I constantly compared myself to other mothers and educators. Being maternal wasn't coming naturally, and it shocked me. Finding an escape in the success of my playwriting, I'd be away from home for weeks while my devoted husband raised the boys. It was easy to attach to the wrong people, and I found myself attaching to men who were cruel and selfish.

It all came crashing down in 2016, three years before I entered the *Neighborhood* archive.

As I sat weeping in a chair in my counselor's office that first visit, I cried, "What is wrong with me? Why do I keep sabotaging my life?"

It was a rhetorical question, but her response came quickly. "You have insecure attachment, Wystie. But we can fix it with attachment repair and attunement."

Depression was only a symptom of the deeper wound in my soul. I would've done anything at that point. (Often, you must hit the end of yourself before you're willing to make a profound change.) And now my wound had a name: insecure attachment.

What is insecure attachment? How was it playing a part in my fulfillment as a mother and educator? Simply, insecure attachment is a broken connection with safety and trust, resulting from developmental trauma and heartbreak. When I speak about trauma throughout this book, I will be referring not just to accidents or events that are out of our control but to everyday moments that overwhelm our system and make us unable to "brace for impact."

According to attachment experts, insecure attachment (or broken connection) and trauma are synonymous. In relational traumas, the body, brain, and nervous system react by making us lose trust in our "feelings, thoughts, and body. In this way, trauma is a form of tremendous fear, loss of control, and profound helplessness."[9] Diane Poole Heller, PhD, an author and therapist who specializes in adult attachment workshops, argues that broken connection affects every facet of our lives: "Broken connection to our body; broken connection to our sense of

---

9   Diane Poole Heller, *The Power of Attachment: How to Create Deep and Lasting Intimate Relationships* (Boulder, CO: Sounds True, 2019).

self; broken connection to others, especially those we love; broken connection to feeling centered or grounded to the planet; broken connection to God, Source, Life Force, well-being, or however we might describe or relate to our inherent sense of spirituality, open-hearted awareness, and beingness."[10]

We need to know that there are people in this world who "get us" and with whom we resonate. Heller argues that that won't be everyone, as the world is full of broken connections: "We aren't good at articulating our wants and needs."[11] It is traumatic to feel unknown by yourself and those you love, as if you cannot fully show up and cannot be seen, heard, or valued. Dan Siegel, founding director of the Mindful Awareness Research Center of UCLA, says our brains are naturally wired and attuned to understanding when we resonate with someone or not. Our brains are "hypersensitive to inconsistencies and authenticity."[12] For example, if I were to ask a roomful of educators to describe how they feel looking at a photo of Mister Rogers, more than 90 percent of those in the room would say words like *safe*, *known*, and *loved*. Why is that?

That's what this book is all about.

Fred Rogers lived his life and worked hard to create authentic, consistent resonance and connection with other human beings. We felt it not because he was a good actor—he never claimed to be one—but because the connection was genuine, and because such genuine connection fostered secure attachment in the hearts of millions of children for decades. The problem was that he didn't know every child.

But we do. They are in our homes and classrooms every day, and it's up to us to generate attachments that foster resilience to the trauma life will certainly give them.

We each grew up with a sense that our caregivers got us, or they didn't. Period. We can tell ourselves otherwise, but our insecure attachments play out in our ability to trust children, colleagues, and ourselves. This includes our reactions to the behaviors and opinions around us. We need to investigate our own stories for patterns and themes, because identifying these places that need healing and integration enables us to offer greater empathy, deeper compassion, and an understanding of the brokenness that's in our classrooms.

---

10 Heller, *The Power of Attachment*.
11 Heller, *The Power of Attachment*.
12 Heller, *The Power of Attachment*.

This is how we become like Mister Rogers. We care about the broken-hearted. If we can't trust, we can't love, learn, and grow. Fred Rogers believed that all of life was better standing with people who loved you. Although solitude is necessary to enjoy one's own company, reflect, and connect with God, life is meant to be lived with our neighbors.

****

My own broken connection with trust was blocking me as a mother and educator, but it healed with intention as I chose to engage my story. How we make sense of our brokenness has a tremendous impact on our brain's rewiring of the experiences. Each experience can confirm our aloneness or our interconnectedness to the human race. The good news is that healing is possible for everyone.

"I need to tell you something," I said to David Newell (a.k.a. Mr. McFeely on *Mister Rogers' Neighborhood*) during our first meeting in 2019.

"What's that?" he said.

"Each time Fred looked into the camera and attuned the way he did, he was healing kids' brains."

"Is that right?" he said.

"Yes. He was right all along. They've just finally proved it."

If you care about young children's social and emotional experiences, you can thank Fred Rogers. He was a pioneer in the "inner world of children," paving the way for people like you and me, and he worked to make truths as simple as possible to understand. A creative genius, Rogers synthesized current research discovered by progressives like Dr. Benjamin Spock, Erik Erikson, Dr. T. Berry Brazelton, and later, his mentor and regular contributor to the *Neighborhood*, Dr. Margaret McFarland. Before their time, people didn't think much about childhood's inner world or emotions.

McFarland pointed out Rogers' keen ability to recall his own childhood and use it to connect with children, as she observed him, as a student, using puppets: "The children confided to Fred and his puppets many important things."[13]

---

13 Maxwell King, *The Good Neighbor: The Life and Work of Fred Rogers* (New York: Abrams Press, 2019).

****

Early attachment wounds follow us into adulthood, wrecking our interpersonal relationships. After years of studying this subject, I'm convinced that all adversity, violence, and brokenness connects back to our broken attachments in childhood. Your early attachment figures had more influence on your brain development than any other person in the first years of your life. Were they attuned to your needs? What did your body and nervous system experience in their presence?

Years of childhood abuse left my mother broken and conflicted. There's no doubt she loved me, but her fragmented mind was traumatized. Her family of origin let her play the codependent "peacekeeper" and the queen of another chance. Old patterns and unprocessed trauma created a hot-and-cold/smother-or-distracted parenting style. It distorted how I saw the world and our enmeshed relationship. The toxicity spilled over into my romantic ideals, how I viewed sexuality and connection, and eventually my inability to attune to (pay attention to the deeper needs of) my children.

Over the course of three years, I studied my story, returning to moments of harm and heartache as my "wise adult self" and with my counselor acting as the safe, attuned guide. I learned how to reparent myself, love the little girl I'd abandoned for the sake of my mother's emotions, and set boundaries. Before the truth can set us free, we must realize what lies hold us hostage. I thought I had emerged from my large family unscathed and free from abuse. What a lie!

Our wounds are probably not our fault, but our healing and choices are. Everyone in our lives is imperfect; therefore, they fail us. Period. We must look deeper into who we are, and where we came from. (It's been a raw, messy process that led me back to myself and to the heart of Mister Rogers.) It's time to stop making excuses, to stop dismissing emotional traumas by comparing them to false narratives, and to acknowledge the pain of being ignored, belittled, forgotten, lost, mislabeled, ridiculed, bullied, and so on. **Instead of treating the wound's symptoms, it's imperative to return, remember, reparent, attune (pay attention), and be the person we needed while growing up.** That's the beginning of love.

Teaching with attachment, attunement, and intention is a mindset, and it's possible to foster secure attachments in every child. I've witnessed healing and miracles in myself and my students—but it is intentional work. We need to wrestle with our own mess and not keep letting it spill onto the next generation. In *Waiting for Mister Rogers*, you'll learn about what every child needs to be secure and how you can begin the process toward security in your own life.

Fred Rogers suffered from insecure attachment but used it as a catalyst to ensure other children would know security through his life's work.

Let that also be true for you and me.

****

This book is my love letter to you about creating a secure attachment for the children you teach. It's the result of what I've learned as I encountered simple and deep love, slowed down, and became intentional. I've learned some of my best lessons the hard way, never without a bit (or a bunch) of humility. You'll read about my colossal failures and my "Thank you, God" successes. I'm choosing to be vulnerable because "attitudes are caught, not taught."

But first, let me state here a few caveats and important thoughts:

- I'm not a neuroscientist or child psychologist, although I've spent my fair share of time in counseling and at the feet of many great mentors.
- Though I spent time in the Fred Rogers Archive reading his personal papers, I'm not an expert on Fred Rogers but an apprentice of his genius in life and death.
- I believe all insecure attachments can heal with the right tools and attention, and all adversity begins with broken connections and hearts. "To be human is to suffer insults and injuries, failures of love, and episodes of disconnect. To be human is to suffer trauma both big and small."[14]
- Every story is unique, but our interconnectedness as a human race is found in naming, pondering, articulating, and blessing the broken connections within us.

---

14 Dan B. Allender and Cathy Loerzel, *Redeeming Heartache: How Past Suffering Reveals Our True Calling* (Grand Rapids, MI: Zondervan, 2021).

- After living through a global pandemic, we have a lot of things backward in education. It's time to go back to what all children need to thrive and grow—connection.
- Children need physical touch and affection, and our world is terrified of touch.
- Looking at our personal story is the bravest work we'll ever do. Such intentionality unlocks hidden power for deeper connection in the classroom.
- Learning, growing, and honesty are messy and feel uncomfortable. We all grow at different speeds and are responsible for our own journeys.

Fred Rogers walked through the set door of his *Neighborhood* house more than 895 times to model secure attachment for us. It's possible! We can give our students the same attachment repair and attunement through daily intentions. Returning to the *Neighborhood* is all about remembering what he taught us long ago: Love is an intentional choice. It takes showing up. We don't have to have all the answers. Let's turn the handle, step inside, and remember childhood.

****

After five months of the COVID pandemic, my friend Bri gave me a fantastic gift for my birthday. She rented a tandem kayak so we could float on the river for two hours and catch up without interruptions. I was ready to relax, chat, and take in the beauty around us.

Much to our surprise, the river was bare, with only a few paddleboarders coming in at the shore as we waded into the water and jumped in our boat. We found a steady rhythm, chatting about her son Kaden (who was in my class before the pandemic) and the progress of the writing of this book.

I pulled out my phone to snap a few shots to post on Instagram when a text pinged: "Bailey had a heart attack at the park yesterday." As our kayak bobbed on the river, I worked to process the news. Bailey had been in my class two years ago, and my mind flashed to the little girl who wore a T-shirt adorned with angel wings on her first day of kindergarten. Every day she'd bring art projects for a friend or her favorite toys so her friends could enjoy them too. She's from a large family whose mother runs an at-home preschool.

Earlier that spring, Bailey had a routine procedure to look at a heart murmur they'd said was not life-threatening . . . but a heart attack? The news left me feeling numb and short of breath. Her little sister Katie entered kindergarten at four because she had aced the entrance exam. It was a test on the district's part, but she'd risen to the challenge and soared above most other students in the first month of school. Katie was also a student in my class before the pandemic, and I instantly thought about her. Bailey had been life-flighted to Seattle, so I knew she was safe, but I was frantic to hear how Katie was dealing with the trauma.

"If a traumatic situation can be resolved in a fairly short time, there will be less debris."[15] Let's take time to attune, contain a child through affection and conversation, and remain available for big questions and feelings. We mitigate the trauma sticking in their nervous system and weaken its lasting impact.

Although I couldn't make the hurt go away, I could ensure that it made sense for Katie. How was it being handled? I texted Katie's mom: "I just heard the news. How can I help?"

She responded quickly: "Please pray. We're in Seattle, and Bailey is stable, but Katie's struggling. She witnessed the whole thing."

There had been a massive seizure, and they had to resuscitate her on the tennis court. The questions raced through my mind as I willed myself not to panic. *Remain calm. Don't jump into the chaos.*

Did Katie understand what had happened? Had anyone processed the horror with her? She must have felt utterly helpless watching Bailey, who was her entire world, in distress. The sisters were inseparable. I remember when my dad threw out his back doing some plumbing one winter. When the paramedics came, they looked like giants to my five- year-old self while they wheeled him out on a stretcher. The sensations burned into my young body: fear, confusion, uncertainty. Would he be okay? Was he ever coming back? Was he going to die?

It's only natural to focus on the patient in an emergency, but we often forget those taking it in on the sidelines. Witnessing trauma is equally damaging, which we'll see in more depth as we discuss adverse childhood experiences (ACEs) and

---

15 Allender and Loerzel, *Redeeming Heartache.*

trauma through the eyes of a child in a later chapter. Katie needed to be able to talk to someone she trusted.

"Where's Katie right now?" I asked her mom.

"She's at the house with my in-laws."

"Send me your address. I'll go to her."

"That makes me feel so much better. Thank you." I was honored that she saw me as a safe place for her daughter in such a crazy moment.

"Tell her I'm on my way," I said, and pushed my phone back into my pocket.

Frantically, we paddled to shore and returned our life jackets. Nothing else mattered but getting to Katie. Thirty minutes later, I was on my way to their house. As I drove, I thought about Fred Rogers and all I'd learned from him about helping children in difficult times.

Thinking about Fred always makes me calm, and as my tires bumped rhythmically over the blacktop, I could hear him saying, "You know what to do. I'm so proud of you for loving the children in your care."

Part One:
Where Are You, Mister Rogers?

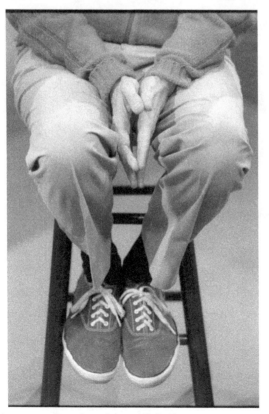

Lynn Johnson Collection

A collection of stick puppets of the *Neighborhood* made by the author for the classroom. *Used with permission.*

Chapter 1:
Returning to the Neighborhood
"It's a Beautiful Day in the Neighborhood"

Anyone who does anything to help a child in his life is a hero to me.
—Fred Rogers

don't ride a trolley to get here. I pull my chair to the middle of the room and face the screen. The overhead lights are dimmed, with only the soft glow of the fish tank illuminating the calm-down area. When I had put the tank together, the girl in the pet store looked at the photo on my phone and said, "I think my mom liked that guy." That guy being Mister Rogers. It was important to me to replicate his fish tank to add more comfort to my classroom. Since then, it's become a space where my autistic student sits for breaks and others soothe their sadness.

Watching *Mister Rogers' Neighborhood* with my kindergarten students is a nonnegotiable part of our day. It's garnished miracles and changed my life. As they eat their Ritz crackers, I take a deep breath. Breathing deeply keeps us present and grounded in the moment. Every day, I pull up a chair to watch as a gift to myself and my students, and I invite in anything that love wants to teach me.

Where some teachers would see thirty minutes as a break to prepare the next activity, I'm making an intentional choice to sit down. To stop. It comes from a place deep inside me that misses a time when the world wasn't as violent, fast-paced, sophisticated, and insecure. Do you remember?

There was a time when people understood the power of a written letter and an intentional conversation, when families sat down and talked at the dinner table. I miss being a little girl. I miss my grandma, who made me feel safe as she snuggled up to read to me and stroke my hair. I knew I was the only one who mattered at that moment in her eyes and presence. In her love, I wasn't afraid but safe and warm. She represented a pause in my life, my safe place.

Returning to the *Neighborhood* is about coming home to the children we once were. In a place where time stands still, we watch a kind man in a cardigan sweater. And it's my return to the real me I'd lost along the way of trying to understand self-worth, trust, and security.

Perhaps we abandoned ourselves long ago due to being left alone with all that we didn't understand. I've learned so many things I didn't know I didn't know. Learning and discovering the truth will set us free. The *Neighborhood* is where I come back, with my sweet "Baby Girl" inside, and sit with all my stories of harm and heartache. It's time to be intentional. It's time to pause, focus our attention, and grow in love.

Shea Tuttle, the author of *Exactly as You Are*, writes:

> Over the years, I grew out of *Mister Rogers' Neighborhood*. I forgot the storylines and many of the songs. But I remembered the man, and I remembered how he and his program made me feel: completely seen, completely loved. I cannot recall the precise origin of my affection for Mister Rogers, and I cannot quite explain its intensity. I just know that he is indescribably special to me; I feel as if I have always known him like he was part of my becoming. It is not simple nostalgia, fleeting, and saccharine. It is deeper than nostalgia. It is formation. It is Love.[16]

Mister Rogers climbed into our implicit memories as children, becoming a secure base, a home. "When I see Mister Rogers' face, I feel instant relief," a friend commented on my social media post. People would come up to Fred Rogers on

---

16 Shea Tuttle, *Exactly as You Are: The Life and Faith of Mister Rogers* (Grand Rapids, MI: Eerdmans, 2019).

the street when they recognized his face and say, "Thank you for my childhood." He counted it an honor to go through life with "the face" that meant such a great deal to many people. We all crave relief from emotional heavy lifting, a place or person that feels like home. We don't have to recall our affection for Mister Rogers; he's simply there. He's tucked away in our childhood schema, woven into the tapestries of our stories. He told us the truth ever so long ago, and we believed it. Memories unconscious and unintentional on our part, but always deeply intentional on his. In Mister Rogers' love, we are unique, valuable, capable, celebrated, received, and accepted. But some children need that same relief when they see your face and mine. What do they feel when they see you in their mind's eye or each morning entering the classroom? It's a humbling but important question.

I bring my students to his love every day because it fosters healthy attachment and convinces them that good people exist in this world. I want them to experience friendship, grace, and kindness and to talk about the big feelings in their hearts. Every song was written by a man dedicated to doing what was right, regardless of the world's understanding or acceptance. People tried, without success, to get the man in the cardigan to update things, catch up with the times, and refresh the show. Yet gritty, unrelenting love is intentional and dedicated. His wife, Joanne Rogers, writes:

> Even when the world around him was changing, becoming fast-paced and materialistic, even hectic and violent, at times, even when he seemed to be going against the current and some were urging him to pick up the pace of his program, Fred was determined to stay the course. Anyone who was close to him knew about his "steel backbone." A lot of people might be surprised to think of him that way, but he was strong-willed and determined. The mentors he trusted supported his decision to continue on what he knew was the right path to be himself.[17]

You must know what you stand for and where you will plant your feet. Are there any nonnegotiables for you regarding the children you love and lead?

---

17   Fred Rogers, *The Mister Rogers Parenting Resource Book* (Philadelphia, PA: Courage Books, 2005).

Watching the *Neighborhood* became mine when I got tired of watching children emotionally bleeding out in front of me. I had a choice to make, and you do too. What will we do? Continue gathering the latest information, the repackaged, relabeled, complex, and shallow interpretations of old wounds? Radical love unnerves the best scientists, pragmatists, and analytics who crave data and assurances. How do you measure hope, love, peace, and kindness? We can say we are loving children, but what does love look like? What does it sound like?

As author and activist Bell Hooks cautions, "Remember, care is a dimension of love, but simply giving care does not mean we are loving." Just doing the job of teaching doesn't change lives—but the intentional, simple, and deep commitment to the wellness of the human heart and spirit does. And it begins with yourself. Love yourself first, because your thoughts lead to your emotions and actions. In a moment of desperation to help a child, I reached out for something in the *Neighborhood* that became a lifeline for myself too.

It all makes sense. The home we're searching for—the belonging—is within us. Home is the combination of all that we know is true and right. Home is where our authentic selves live. Brené Brown defines belonging this way: "True belonging is the spiritual practice of believing in and belonging to yourself so deeply that you can share your most authentic self with the world and find sacredness in both being a part of something and standing alone in the wilderness. True belonging doesn't require you to change who you are; it requires you to be who you are."[18]

We access our inner home, just like opening the door to Mister Rogers' TV house, by stepping inside and studying our story. And, yes, it will often feel like the wilderness. But if we don't remember, the price is great. We won't reach children emotionally or heal broken attachments.

When Fred Rogers said he liked us "exactly as you are," he meant the whole of each of us. How we look and all that we feel. Honest love. Yes, even the dirty, mangled, uncertain, delightful, successful, broken, and abused parts. The *all* of us. Through his intentional choices, that was the gift he left, and we can use it as a model for loving children: simple and deep love.

---

18 Brown, *Atlas of the Heart.*

****

So, I click play, sit down in my chair, and wait. As the familiar melody begins, Mister Rogers enters through the wooden door smiling, showing up again to help me. My privilege is facilitating healing in broken places and hearts, with him as a guide and model.

My students surround me as they finish their snacks. Each one gets as close to me as they can. Instantly, they become more gentle, quiet, and engaged. It is my daily glimpse of glory.

"Hi, neighbor," he says to the camera.

"Hi, Mister Rogers!" they eagerly greet him.

When we first began this journey with him, they preferred time with Mister Rogers over the Neighborhood of Make-Believe. I assumed the puppets and costumes were too simple for them as they squirmed and conversed among themselves more. But when Mister Rogers came back on the screen, they were frozen, captivated by connection and intention. They just wanted to be near him. He looked directly into the camera as if he could truly see them, authentic and vulnerable. Author Shea Tuttle recalls, "Mister Rogers would summon Trolley, the cheerful red streetcar who guided the transition into Make-Believe, and I from my corner of the couch would let out a sigh—I preferred the segments of the show in Mister Rogers' company to the interlude in Make-Believe—but only a small sigh, because I knew that, in just a few minutes, Trolley would faithfully return me to that living room and Mister Rogers."[19]

I bring my students to the *Neighborhood* because it's emotionally safe. It's the best I can give when the little girl inside me is still healing, too, and the world gets messier and fast-paced. We grow together every time. The energy in the room shifts, and they are free of all the things that complicate a modern child's world. (It's funny how, as a child, I longed to be grown-up, and now all I want is to go back to a simpler time when I believed in puppets and automated trolleys.)

My students watch in awe as Mister Rogers makes music with old soda bottles, blowing over the top of the water. They're transfixed by the food coloring

---

19 Tuttle, *Exactly as You Are.*

mixing in the water; they barely move as blue drops twist and turn inside. Bob Trow creates a pulley to open the door in a workshop, and we watch as yellow wax is made into colored crayons.

But it only takes a day or two before the Neighborhood of Make-Believe holds their attention, generating questions and wonderment. They don't notice the outdated clothes or the simplicity of the puppets. "Does that surprise you?" former *Neighborhood* director Paul Lally asks when I interview him for my podcast in November of 2020. "It has always worked, and it still does. That's the beauty of it, Wystie."[20]

When Daniel Striped Tiger sings about being forgotten by Lady Aberlin, my student Julian, whose mother recently had a baby, begins to cry, and we comfort him. My class recognized that his new role had left him feeling isolated. Within the first month of viewing the program, parents began to communicate that their children asked to watch Mister Rogers at home instead of meaningless cartoons and YouTube videos. The shift was quick and purposeful, and it filtered into every facet of our learning.

I don't need a curriculum for this or a set of questions for debriefing. I let Fred do what he did best and trust it.

As I shared my findings with my mentor, she challenged me to look for God and love within every episode. What did God want to tell me? What was love needing to say to my students? Love would change everything if I remained open. But there was a condition: I wasn't to multitask but should instead model for my students, watching with wonder and attunement. Accepting the challenge, I was amazed and delighted by the show's most intricate connections to my curriculum, to recent conflicts on the playground or in the classroom, and to my own healing. Questions that only moments before had never been spoken aloud were answered by Fred Rogers.

****

"It's what is going on inside a person that matters," he says, and I'm a three-year-old again.

---

20 Paul Lally, "Fred's Friend," interview with author, November 15, 2020, in *Simple and Deep*, podcast, https://www.wysteriaedwards.com/simple-and-deep-podcast.

"Where are you, Mister Rogers? I'm waiting for you, right here in this little chair. You said you'd be back again tomorrow and willing to spend time with me. Please, look me in the eyes and help me understand that I still matter in this crazy, mixed-up world," the child inside me pleads.

"Help me, Mister Rogers, to be love to children who are emotionally bleeding out in front of me!" the teacher in me cries. "The needs are too great, and I'm still small in so many ways."

"Can I just sit here and be quiet with you, Mister Rogers?" the little girl inside me asks.

An equal mix of emotions has emerged on this journey back to the *Neighborhood*. Mister Rogers and I have become partners in preserving childhood. The world vies to squelch the time between birth and consumer, and it's like turning backward in a strong river and choosing to dam the onslaught of pressures heading my students' way. I believe there needs to be more time for them to breathe easy, to be children longer, to wonder and dream.

****

We often don't realize when life is rewriting our story. Each day is part of a more significant journey we can't see until we look back in hindsight. You might call it the universe, but I call it God, love. As I struggled to find my way back over the bridge to secure attachment, it was as if I was healing backward, like the rings of an onion. Healing included learning how to be present with all the feelings in my body, tolerating the sensations, and reacting with compassion instead of judgment. I needed tender nurturing and attunement. My insecure attachment left me with unresolved longing, yearning, and a feeling I could never have what I wanted. I often thought about how I didn't deserve the love of my husband and children. They were "too good" or "too right" for me. Somehow, having Matthew and the boys, I'd tricked the world and slid by with the best. Hypervigilant to the possibility of shattering and loss, my brain wasn't used to peace and goodness. It was the duality of keeping what I had and wondering if there was something I'd missed along the way. I can only compare it to the feelings of "unrequited love." Had I gone down the right path and made all the correct choices? Such thinking kept me in constant panic and anxiety with profound moments of depression and despair. "The problem with identifying with deprivation is that when love truly presents itself, we may find ourselves rejecting it because it feels unfamiliar and disorienting."[21]

Healing from broken connection requires work, work that's intentional and sometimes uncomfortable. Let me share with you a few areas and concepts I worked hard to explore and embrace.

Discovering my authentic self. Who was I? What mattered to me? What did I stand for and want out of this life?

Integrating my experiences. What stories had made me who I am, and how did I make sense of them? Where was I holding on to narratives that weren't my own? In the case of ambivalent attachment, I had enmeshed with my mother, and it was as if we were braided into the same story. I didn't know where I started or where she ended. Part of healing was unwinding my own identity (autonomy) and recognizing that I had integrated her stories of abuse and neglect, swallowing them deep into my soul. My counselor frequently said, "That's your mother's memory, not yours." This was one of the most painful processes of my healing, as it forced me to emotionally emancipate myself from my mother, the person I had clung to my entire life. The separation was necessary, but it broke her heart. Without her realizing, I'd been appointed her emotional caretaker, and I needed to connect to my sense of self and meet my own needs. "A child who takes care of a parent often forges a lifelong pattern of overextension and creates a blueprint for habitually feeling overwhelmed."[22] This is where it was extremely helpful for me to have a wise and attuned counselor who reminded me that, one day, only wholeness and freedom would be left.

Grounding into each present moment. I learned how to honor myself while being in the presence of others. This is a big step if we're used to being swallowed by emotions, experiences, or needs. "Often in anxious attachment, we lose ourselves . . . due to [the] learned habit of over-focusing on others for external regulation."[23] I was tremendously skilled at reading a room with this hyperfocus

21 Diane Poole Heller, "Dare Module 1 Student Manual," Trauma Solutions, April 7, 2008, https://dianepooleheller.com/dare-module-1/.

22 Mark Wolynn, *It Didn't Start with You: How Inherited Family Trauma Shapes Who We Are and How to End the Cycle* (New York: Penguin Books, 2017).

23 Heller, "Dare Module 1 Student Manual."

but susceptible to falling victim to the circumstances and feelings of others. This knowledge blew my mind when I realized that my inability to self-regulate was why I couldn't help my son Jonathan when he was dysregulated. I didn't have this healthily wired into my brain.

The problem with having an underdeveloped sense of self is that it often results in codependency with a warped view of what "love" does or doesn't do. I'd been raised to believe that love never ever gives up on you, regardless of how crappy you act or how much you damage or scar those around you, and everyone is more important than your own emotional well-being. Such warped thinking made it easier for me to be abused and exploited and was a recipe for relational disaster. Mix in a bit of dogma or religious thinking, and, *wham*, I was stuck in a cycle of shame and guilt.

Giving and receiving. I am a work in progress. I may not be where I want to be, but I'm certainly not where I used to be. *Thank you, God.* The goal is to allow others to give love and receive help when offered. This included hearing hard truths from my counselor, husband, children, and others. How did I do receiving their love? I worked on what Dr. Heller calls the "1% more" concept.[24] Heller argues that asking ourselves questions gives us clues to our childhood attachment blueprints. Such questions to ask might include:

- What was my mind telling me at that moment? My emotions?
- Did I immediately fear loss—telling myself that I was bound to be abandoned, dropped, or fooled?
- Did my body block contact nutrition? Was I avoiding physical contact with my children, husband, and others?

Heller says: "Giving and receiving is a complicated issue for those of us with ambivalent or anxious attachment because in childhood, we were never sure our needs would be met or if a parent would be available. So we react to the unpredictability and consequent insecurity until the original wound is healed. Be kind to yourself when you explore this loaded territory."[25]

---

24   Heller, "Dare Module 1 Student Manual."
25   Heller, "Dare Module 1 Student Manual."

I evaluated where I could stay in moments 1 percent longer without running, distracting, or dissociating. Then I evaluated what I received: goodness, love, information, the gift of remaining present, opportunities for deeper connection—the list went on and on. At what moments was I most receptive to new information and conversation versus other times during the day? Where did I find difficulty in receiving help or feedback?

Noticing the caring behaviors of others deepened my understanding of what made my life simple, deep, and beautiful. Fred Rogers said, "Mutual caring relationships require kindness and patience, tolerance, optimism, joy in the other's achievements, confidence in oneself, and the ability to give without undue thought of gain."[26]

Beauty is everywhere if we are open to it. I found goodness in the way my youngest son, Ben, emerged to welcome me home and would balance his arms on the top of the car and say, "Hi, Mama." If I tapped my hand, my German shepherd would fall backward on the bed so she could nuzzle into me, smiling. The beauty in ways my husband demonstrated his love for me, protecting our finances with sound decisions, calling every morning to say he loved me, even though we'd only left each other thirty minutes prior. The sound of my daddy leaving a message on my voice mail: "Hi, Scooter, it's your dad. Just calling to tell you that I love you." I noticed my custodian's joy and pride in cleaning our building and the patience of a teacher sitting in the hallway to calm a suffering child. The rain contained peace and comfort more than before, and the sunshine communicated hope and expectation. I rolled my windows down while driving and enjoyed being alive. Music became the soundtrack for my healing and heartache as journals cataloged my dance with my younger self and the woman I was becoming. Appreciation replaced mistrust. Fred Rogers believed "appreciation is a holy thing. . . . When we look for what's best in a person we happen to be with at the moment, we're doing what God does all the time. So in loving and appreciating our neighbor, we participate in something sacred."[27]

Slowly, I began to trust my instincts, meet my own emotional needs, and define truth my way. The teachers and guides in my discovery were everyone and

---

26 Heller, "Dare Module 1 Student Manual."
27 Rogers, *You Are Special.*

everything. I experienced, for example, the most incredible summer storm while I was in Atlanta. The haze of the summer day clashed with the cool air, creating a murky fog. Suddenly, rain poured from the clouds, intense and unrelenting. People scattered for cover like ants. High above the streets, I threw my hotel patio door open, letting the wind whip through my room. Tears streamed down my face as I surrendered all I'd been holding on to. To this day, if it's raining, I want to be in it. Let it soak deep into me, because that's where I found love and me. I came home to the little girl inside me whom I'd abandoned long ago.

I belong to Wysteria, and she belongs to me. I have strengths and weaknesses, and it's not often I don't share my opinion and love with ferocity. I'm fully alive when creating, singing, teaching, and connecting. I'm a collection of every person I've met and every experience I've had. I'm Lyle's granddaughter, who thinks broken people are holy. I'm Eileen's granddaughter, who believes that people need more love. I'm my daddy's Scooter, who delights in strangers' company and understands that hard work includes sacrifice. I'm Nancy's daughter, who sees that stories need to be told, acknowledged, and healed. I'm Matthew's wife, who's experienced the man's grace who said, "I knew you'd find your way home again." I'm Jonathan's mom, who has taught me that love pulls us from the darkness to the light, even when we don't have all the answers. I'm Benjamin's "Mama," who obsesses over my passions, champions the underdogs, and never underestimates the power of a good snuggle. I am loved. I am enough.

Thank you to every person who ever failed, betrayed, and abandoned me. I've learned how to dance atop the disappointments and heartaches. To those who stood in my way or told me no, this is my way of letting you know that even evil and unkindness can be repaid with gratitude. I'm a fighter against the emotional suffering of broken attachment in children—for as long as there's breath in my body. My life is simple, deep, and beautiful.

The need for reassurance. I mistrusted people's motives and intentions. My "ability to believe that a relationship was stable and intact, despite the presence of setbacks, conflict, or disagreements"[28] wasn't solid. I experienced extreme anxiety in

---

28 Corrina Horne, "What Is Object Constancy and How Does It Affect People?," BetterHelp, April 11, 2022, https://www.betterhelp.com/advice/general/what-is-object-constancy-and-how-does-it-affect-people/.

relationships of all types and lived in constant fear of abandonment. After becoming a mother, I became concerned about losing my husband to death or divorce. I was terrified that I didn't have the skill set or ability to cope independently as an adult. As I learned that I could trust myself, my marriage, and other close friendships, I gained more freedom. When children can't trust their caregivers for consistent love and acceptance, they may struggle to trust others fully in adulthood.

Learning to say "goodbye" well. Fred Rogers said, "Often when you think you're at the end of something, you're at the beginning of something else." I've always struggled with goodbyes and would ask for reassurance if the momentum of a relationship or friendship changed. "Ambivalent people tend to feel upset when alone and not in close proximity to the important people in their lives."[29] I began to understand my need to look to others to help me regulate my emotional states and how to feel and take cues from others. Before, I'd have difficulties when relationships ended without "closure" (as if such a thing exists) and struggled when I didn't get the last word in an argument. Every action of someone was interpreted, and I was hypersensitive to word choice and emotionally entangled with friends in constant crisis. Look at the company you keep, and it will tell you how you're doing emotionally.

Decluttering and redefining wellness. I began to declutter every area of my life, starting with people who no longer served me or believed in my emotional wellness. I established boundaries and knew where I ended and others began. Instead of ignoring my emotional triggers and reactions, I leaned in and became curious. I used daily affirmation and mindfulness practices, meditation and prayer, journaling, podcasts and sermons, music and worship, and collected wisdom on social media boards that encouraged me. I also made weekly counseling appointments my top priority; focusing on my emotional healing also benefited those I loved.

Rupture and repair. I worked on understanding how I behaved when my stress response was activated during conflicts, understood the value of communicating what I needed, and actively listened to others without fear of abandonment. It wasn't easy to allow my children to talk about the damage I'd caused and hold the emotional space, but I survived it.

---

29 Heller, *The Power of Attachment.*

Practicing kindness. Loving others became easier when I began to recognize broken connections in them. As I extended kindness to myself, I empathized with others and held their stories of harm and heartache without absorbing their emotions. Attuning to myself and the child inside helped me self-soothe, connect to my core values, and establish a true sense of self.

****

> With everything that has happened to you, you can either
> feel sorry for yourself or treat what has happened as a gift.
> Everything is either an opportunity to grow or an obstacle
> to keep you from growing. You get to choose.
> **—Wayne Dyer**

Sitting in a diner with my mentor Phyllis, I cried my eyes out, and she understood without much explanation. (That's the wonderful thing about resonance, when a person really gets you.) We'd spent time building a small school together, we'd walked through the beginnings of my addiction, and my children viewed her as another grandmother. I often cried in my car where I was alone and with my counselor, but there were things I kept between myself and God. I was still wrestling, and it felt good to pour my heart out to someone who wouldn't judge me.

She took my face in both her hands. "Wystie, it's time to leave your school. Now you're abusing yourself with your job."

"I can't leave," I cried. "They need me, and I promised myself I'd always teach there."

"I know, but it's time. Can you imagine going home every night and not worrying if your kiddos are eating? What about your own boys? They'll be grown before you know it."

I knew she was right, and although the thought brought angst, there was peace right behind it. Assurance wrapped around my heart. I had no idea where I would go, but I needed to start looking at teacher vacancies in other buildings.

I'd worked in poverty for a substantial portion of my career—the smells, the need, and what was necessary to survive as a teacher wasn't lost on me. I'd stuffed backpacks with clothes at Christmas and stocked up on extra snacks, toothbrushes, undies, and dry shampoo. Vaseline for chafed skin, journals full of documentation, pillows and quilts to take naps because parents fought all night, and CPS on speed dial. I surrounded them with as much goodness and safety as I could muster while overspending, overcommitting, and gradually suffering from secondary trauma.

It was time for me to make a hard choice because I had hit burnout. Not a failure, just worn out and needing to mother myself. Educators are the worst at taking care of themselves. One of the most valuable lessons I've learned is that I am only one human, and my abilities can't meet every need, especially if I'm losing my own way. It takes a village to raise children, and we have to take care of ourselves and each other. So I switched schools, one of the hardest things I've ever had to do. It was time to change my course.

Fred Rogers told the following story in his Dartmouth commencement speech in 2002:

> There's a story . . . about the Special Olympics. For the hundred-yard dash, there were nine contestants, all of them so-called physically or mentally disabled. All nine of them assembled at the starting line and, at the sound of the gun, they took off. But one little boy didn't get very far. He stumbled and fell and hurt his knee and began to cry. The other eight children heard the boy crying. They slowed down, turned around, and ran back to him—*every one of them ran back to him*. The little boy got up, and he and the rest of the runners linked their arms together and joyfully walked to the finish line. They all finished the race at the same time. And when they did, everyone in the stadium stood up and clapped and whistled and cheered for a long, long time. And you know why? Because deep down we know that what matters in this life is more than winning for ourselves. What really matters is helping others win, too, even if it means slowing down and changing our course now and then.[30]

---

30 Fred M. Rogers, "Fred Rogers' 2002 Dartmouth College Commencement Address," May 2002, YouTube video, https://youtu.be/907yEkALaAY.

Moving to the other side of town felt like I was on another planet. (I had no idea that schools had a PTA! And parent volunteers come in to read with kids? Huh? What?!) As the school supplies piled up on my classroom table, I was floored. Where was I going to store all those boxes of Kleenex? I began to plan how I'd shuffle extras back to my old school. (Yes, I did think about that.) The first weekend I slept like a baby. I had no idea I was that tired. Emotional weariness is a thief. If you live with it long enough, it feels like a second layer of skin.

I missed my old school, but gradually I became more present and available for my own family. And as my boys experienced high school, I realized what a gift I'd given myself by taking Phyllis' advice and caring for my own heart. **Teaching is a job, not a life.** I was more effective when it wasn't the air I was breathing 24/7, and the contents of my rolling cart stayed in the classroom each weekend.

****

I'm emotionally in a good place as I watch Blue Eyes walk down the hall toward me at the kindergarten meet-and-greet. His mother, eight months pregnant, shuffles a short distance behind him. His blond hair is so light it looks white, and he has crystal-blue eyes and numerous freckles sprinkled across his nose. Puffing out his chest, he reminds me of rapper Eminem, trying to sag his jeans and bump other students with his chest. He doesn't realize he's freshly five and not twenty-three. One little boy begins to cry as his mother grabs the paperwork, obviously uncomfortable with the chest bump. She gives me a hasty goodbye and moves to leave as Blue Eyes turns his back, already forgetting the damage he's caused.

Blue Eyes' mother begins to relay the story that his father, recently paroled from jail on drug charges, will most likely relapse. "Just keep your eyes open, and let me know if he seems high," she tells me. *Fabulous.* Blue Eyes walks around the room looking in cabinets, ramming cars together, and doing karate chops in the carpet area. His energy feels out of place with the other children, who instantly seem like he could swallow them whole. His mother yells his name, causing him to stop and whine, "What?!" when she cusses for him to get over to her. Motioning to her stomach, I inquire about her due date. "October," she tells me, and I make a mental note to write "drop day" on the calendar near his name—because it won't be pretty.

This one is different, my heart whispers to me.

"Tag! I'm so not it," my colleague says, watching him walk away.

"Nope. That one is all mine," I reply.

****

The soul is healed by being with children.
—Fyodor Dostoevsky

"Mister Rogers is a show for babies!"

I sit and look back at him, amazed. Two months into the school year, Blue Eyes is still determined to convince the world how tough he is, not needing anyone. Now he's attacking Mister Rogers.

A week earlier, I'd hit my limit. Unpredictable and bright, Blue Eyes could easily grow up to be someone who will pull off the biggest federal scam ever, only to retire in the Cayman Islands rich and undetectable. The street smarts on that kid are unparalleled, and I'm trying to stay at least one step ahead of him.

He's just one of many struggling with behavior. I also have Michael, who suffers from severe, undiagnosed ADHD with ambivalent attachment and whose parents are divorcing. Michael needs to know where I am at every minute of the day, refuses to stay in his seat, does kung fu everywhere, and has little difficulty telling me, "I'm really, really angry at you, Mrs. Edwards," when I tell him no for the fifth time in a row. He's convinced he will wear me down, which never works, much to his exasperation. After all, I'm a stubborn only child, and I always win.

Meanwhile, Blue Eyes intimidates the other children. They avoid standing next to him in line and switch to a different center if he sits down to join them. Each time I kneel at his level and try to instruct him, he looks over my shoulder and yells, "I don't care!" startling the rest of the room into silence. He keeps me on my toes, and I regularly pray for him on my knees before school starts.

Ask any teacher, and they will tell you about a child like him—the ones we categorize as the walking wounded. Child psychologists would label them

ADD, ADHD, conduct disordered, and oppositional defiant. They're the students who test every bit of our love, patience, grit, boundaries—and why some teachers need wine or chocolate at the end of the day. He wants me to fail him, waits for me to prove I'm like everybody else: unpredictable, quick to leave, impatient, and conditional. Something begins to shift in me the year he becomes my kindergartener.

Call it a sweet storm of surrender or a perfect storm of "enough," but I was *totally done* watching kids like him tank. He had nine out of eleven of the adverse childhood experiences (ACEs), including family member incarceration, witnessing violence, watching his mother being abused, drug use, mental illness, physical and emotional neglect, and physical and emotional abuse. I had no idea where to start repairing his behavior.

Teaching him is like going to Vegas with all the money you own. *I'll take this behavior intervention for $500 and this positive reinforcement tool for $1,000. Yes, it worked for a day! I'm amazing!* The next day, we do the same things, and my interventions and reinforcements flop. Why?

Because children aren't problems to solve: They're emotional, reactive human beings. We can *influence* behavior, but we need to be repairing what is actually missing—secure attachment, connection. And connection is created through "felt safety," not programs.

Blue Eyes has *disorganized attachment.* (I'll cover this and the other three attachment styles in chapter 4.) His home life has been domestic violence, incarceration, drug use, mental illness, emotional neglect, and avoidantly attached parenting. No matter what he does or who he's with, he never feels emotionally safe. His body is in constant fight or flight—which daily threatens to trigger me back to my own childhood and my own *ambivalent (anxious) attachment.* If I'm not careful, I begin to take his behavior personally, fixate on his every move, and base my worth as a teacher on whether he's having a good day. He struggles with object permanence and object consistency because he's experienced inconsistent and unreliable caregiving; thus, it thwarts my ability to override his doubts and insecurity. Children with insecure attachments didn't learn as infants, for example, that if their mother leaves the room, she stays the same and returns. To these students, nothing is predictable or permanent, except unpredictability.

Every day we must start out brand new. I'm determined to demonstrate consistent presence and love while rewiring the brain's attachment system. Neuroscience has proved that we generate new neuro networks and connections, and heal the brain's attachment system, through repetitive and positive interactions.

But attachment repair isn't for the weak, and most days I feel like an emotional punching bag. If I want any reassurance or happy feelings, Blue Eyes isn't my kid. He's ruthless, and in fact, he makes it easy *not* to like him. "That's why it's so helpful that those with wounds related to consistency get to experience . . . more reassurance about commitment, permanence, and reliability."[31]

Each time he leaves for the day, he experiences departure stress, not knowing if I'll be here when he returns or whether the new man—his dad—will keep him safe. He gets overstimulated during centers and brain breaks, often over- and underreacting to various moments. He dances too big but won't participate if his peers are enthusiastic, and karate kicks his way to the carpet excitedly, watching the other children run away in fear.

Power is exhilarating to a little boy who feels helpless in every other way. His behavior screams, *Go away!* But as I turn to leave the class at PE, he yells to me, "Where are you going?"

Oddly, he can act kind and quickly articulate classroom rules and responsibilities, charming a stranger who enters our space. "The sweet blond boy told me where to sit," a practicum student explains and motions to Blue Eyes. (And I fight the urge to roll my eyes.)

"He's manipulative," a colleague states after specials.

"Guess who's down at the office, again," a duty from the playground informs me.

Yes, my boy is in constant motion, as unpredictable as he is wonderfully confusing to his teacher. *But I can do this! Help me, God!*

****

Inside of every great educator is
a child that needed a better teacher.
—Unknown

---

31 Heller, *The Power of Attachment*.

"Greyson, is he hurting your hand?" I ask, observing the boys playing one afternoon at the block center.

Greyson had set up the houses and wheeled a firetruck around the structures, but taking his Hot Wheels, Blue Eyes had begun to crash his car into Greyson's hand: "Eeeeeerk!" Making a crashing sound, Blue Eyes repeatedly bashes his car into Greyson, but the little boy says nothing. It's a balance when working with children, as we want to facilitate them in interpersonal conflicts yet give them the space to try problem-solving on their own. But Greyson looks down, not speaking, clearly intimidated. Blue Eyes is like a cat poking at a mouse it's caught, delighting in watching the squirming and the fear.

"Greyson, tell him, 'That's hurting my hand. Please stop hitting your truck into me.'"

He tries to say the words and mumbles something, but I don't recognize anything intelligible. Blue Eyes watches his opponent crumble and then moves all of Greyson's houses closer to himself. As far as he's concerned, he's won and is claiming his prize.

I get down on the floor between the boys to work through the conflict, only to be met with the classic Blue Eyes rebuttal at the top of his lungs: "I DON'T CARE!"

Throwing down a Hot Wheels car, Blue Eyes runs to his table, kicks the leg, sits down, and buries his face in anger.

Greyson watches in stunned amazement, then looks up at me, perplexed. I let out a sigh. Epic fail.

****

Little by little we human beings are confronted with situations
that give us more and more clues that we are not perfect.
—Fred Rogers

"He said, 'Mister Rogers is for babies,'" I whine to my counselor in my afternoon appointment. Blue Eyes stories have become a regular topic in my therapy, and I've grown accustomed to her pause-and-wait. The chair I'm seated in is sunken in from countless bodies bringing in their heaviness, and the arm cushions are also dented. Because my counselor has secure attachment, she can pass it on to me.

That's the key—we must be conduits of peace for our students. But today, I feel like a failure again. *Why can't I get through to him? Aren't I doing everything right?*

A month earlier, I made a choice. Blue Eyes and Michael were in such a crisis I had to find a solution: for them, and for the other twenty children who waited a lot on their behaviors. There is a forgotten group in our classroom—those students who aren't in chaos—who wait for the instruction to begin. My little Mary is one of them. She was the perfect one to sit next to Blue Eyes because of her *secure attachment*.

Fred Rogers identified six necessities for learning: a sense of self-worth, a sense of trust, curiosity/wonder, the capacity to look and listen carefully, the capacity to play, and times of solitude. The necessities of learning are supported by a secure attachment with our primary caregivers in the first few years of life. If a child suffers from an *insecure attachment* (see chapter 4), the higher cognitive reasoning and problem-solving levels won't be developed or accessible in their brains. And we must teach children at their developmental age, not their actual age. This is a difficult problem when they're constantly being compared to their peers through state testing, classroom assessments, and school-wide data.

Author and human potential thought leader Bryant McGill said, "Our children can be our greatest teachers if we are humble enough to receive their lessons."

What lessons are our children from hard places trying to teach us? "Somebody failed me. I was ignored, abused, yelled at, abandoned, neglected, invisible, a burden, belittled, demeaned, annoying, ridiculed . . ." The list could go on and on.

I rack my brain, looking for strategies for Blue Eyes, and become overwhelmed. Where do I start? Do I look at his behaviors? His ACEs score? Motivations of behavior? Begin documenting for our School Assistance Team to do a possible 504 accommodation for behavior? In kindergarten, we are often the first to key in on a difficulty for a child, if they didn't attend pre-school. Then, as we collect mountains of data, we hear, "Let's wait until next year and see what happens," and the wheel continues to spin. Sound familiar? These systems aren't working, the needs are too great, and the workers are too few. Since COVID, it's become nearly impossible to find an opening with a good children's counselor, and specialists have long waiting lists. Blue Eyes is in crisis *now*. What do you do with a little boy who has experienced such losses and broken connections and is so angry at the world?

One night, I pour my frustrations out into a journal.

What do I do with a little boy?

A boy who pushes every nerve,
emotion and trigger
within my body?

Who acts like he is the only one
who matters in the moment?

A little boy who
ignores the social cues of his peers,
masks his behaviors with cursing,
and attempts false bravado.

I listen.

I have compassion.
I choose to be kind.

When I feel angry,
I will remember . . .

he just wants me to see him.
He needs me to tell him
a hundred times
I value him.

Yes, he is listening, and
he thinks he's a mistake.

What do I do with a little boy?
The one others avoid because of "bad choices"?

A little boy,
whose peers don't pick for a partner,
complain about while standing in line,
and is often hitting, pinching, or spitting.

A little boy
who is "in trouble"—
with or without me.

Full of energy, yet never satisfied with any outcome.
The one I worry about when taking a day off.
I listen to what he says without words.
I give compassion, even when I don't understand.
I refuse to give up.
I tell him when I see him growing.
I instruct with care and firm boundaries.
Why?
He is precious.
He doesn't understand the world as I do.
He is on his own journey.

I will count myself lucky
to be called his teacher.

What do I do with a little boy,
who pushes every one of my buttons?

I let him fall . . .
into love,
into understanding,
into kindness.

I will be the one . . .

to surprise him,
challenge him,
listen to him.
Tell him, "You are enough."

He can have a voice with me.
Be heard.
Be seen.

I won't leave, even when it isn't pretty.
I won't stop
looking,
loving,
believing.

I will let him encounter grace.

I sit crying for a long while, aching for some respite and answers for my precious students, and then I see his face: Mister Rogers. What did we have when I was little? We had Mister Rogers! Peace floods my system, and I know I can trust *Mister Rogers' Neighborhood* to be a safe place for my boys, little Blue Eyes and Michael.

"Isn't Mister Rogers kind of dated now? You think they'll respond to it?" my colleague asks me when I tell him what I'm planning to do.

Of course they'll respond to Mister Rogers; our emotional needs haven't changed. If anything, we need what he offers even more!

The next day, I find the Crayola crayon factory episode because it's the one I remembered most, and I put it on for my class. *Please, God, let this work*, I pray silently.

****

Many of our kids have been told that they are the problem. Helping them to understand that what's going on in their bodies is a normal response to abnormal circumstances, giving them the tools to calm their bodies down, to keep themselves safe, to connect to nurturing relationship—I've seen it to be life-changing and lifesaving.
—Dr. Nadine Burke Harris

The *Neighborhood* had been working for *everyone* but him! When he uttered the words to me at my desk—"Mr. Rogers is for babies!"—it was a challenge I initially failed. Dismissing the moment, as it completely floored me, I told him to go sit down. I was feeling a tremendous guilt over my reaction and feared I was failing miserably.

After finishing her notes, my counselor smiles and nods. I need her to give me some ideas, but she's not saying much. Exasperated, I choose to repeat my problem.

"How can he not like Mister Rogers?" I ask, starting to cry.

"He doesn't have to like Mister Rogers. But Mister Rogers liked kids like him."

I pause, wiping my eyes and blowing my nose. Throwing my head back against the chair, I groan. "Why is this so hard!"

"Because you're trying to heal his brain."

I leave the office feeling defeated, unsure what to do next. But I know I'm not going to stop showing the *Neighborhood*. The other children love it and use it in their play. I need it, too, and it's keeping me calm and focused.

One of the greatest tragedies of *insecure attachment* is the "lost voice" of a child. To stay safe, we stop speaking our minds and having opinions. And inside we're a mess of anxieties, insecurities, and fears. Adults haven't imparted the tools to give us the autonomy and confidence to voice what we think or fear when overwhelmed with big emotions.

So I decide to give Blue Eyes a voice. During centers, I call to him, "I need you to come over here, please."

"But I didn't do anything!" he defends.

"You're not in trouble. Just come here so I can talk to you for a minute."

Rolling his eyes and acting exasperated, he flops down on the small stool and looks away. It's his classic stance for our conversations.

"Do you remember yesterday when you told me what you thought about Mister Rogers?"

"Yes," he mumbles, watching the child building with Legos beside him.

"I need you to know that it's okay if you don't like Mister Rogers."

He turns his head quickly to me, surprised. "It is?"

"Yep. Because Mister Rogers made that show because he loved kids like you."

He sits there stunned as the clean-up bell goes off. Children hurry to sit at their seats for snacks and ready themselves for the *Neighborhood*. Rising, he goes to his seat without incident, and I can't help but smile. *Ha! I stumped him.*

As the episode begins to play, I take my seat in the chair in front of the screen, and children begin to sit around me, leaving the "hot seat" at my knees open. This is what always amazes me about young children. They understand as they grow where the love needs to land. It was apparent that Blue Eyes was sitting at the table talking to me, and there hadn't been a big blow-up on his part. No one says a word; they quietly watch Mister Rogers talking about towels and swimming.

Blue Eyes walks over and sits at my knees as the trolley moves toward Make-Believe. "They still have to solve the king's problem from yesterday!" he says, breaking the silence.

My student Mia looks at me and starts to laugh, covering her mouth. Raising my eyebrows slightly and smiling out of relief, I run my hands over his hair.

So, he *did* believe. He just needed to know that I would still love him if he didn't.

The contents of Fred Rogers' wallet, 1992. Lynn Johnson Collection

Chapter 2:

You Are a Story

"The Truth Will Make Me Free"

'm going to let you in on a secret. You're a game changer. Yes, you! If you choose to show up for your life intentionally, wholeheartedly, lives will change. It won't be easy, as nothing worth having is easily achieved. It's about learning to stay in your own lane, not looking at others around you, and recognizing that you've got what it takes to foster genuine connection. "There's an old Italian proverb: 'Chi anda piano, anda sano, anda lontan.' That means: The person who goes quietly goes with health and goes far. Hurrying up and using a lot of shortcuts doesn't get us very far at all."[32] Living an intentional life takes time and hard work. How can you be more intentional? By engaging your whole story.

You are a story. Yes, you read that right. You don't have a story, you *are* a story. Being intentional is taking an active stance in the story you are living. As children, we only had a passive stance, subject to the attachment, attunement, and intention we did or didn't receive from our caregivers. Traumas occurred, because tragedy propels a story forward. As teachers, we are aware of the massive impact of childhood adversity (see ACEs in chapter 5) and collective traumas suffered by marginalized communities through racism, sexism, and deplorable ignorance. But many of us are unaware of the damage devel-

---

32 Rogers, *You Are Special.*

opmental traumas create in our ability to cope with our world. "Developmental trauma occurs if you experienced multiple, chronic or ongoing trauma, most often in an interpersonal [relational] nature in your caregiving system."[33] When I entered counseling, I was diagnosed with complex post-traumatic stress disorder (C-PTSD) from a life story of repeated developmental/relational traumas. If you're on the developmental trauma continuum, your stories of abuse, neglect, and adverse experiences need an empathetic witness to fully heal.

****

A woman was suffering in her thirties from the years of sexual abuse at the hands of her uncle. After three failed marriages and estranged relationships with her children, she reached out to a counseling service that engaged stories of harm from a psychological and spiritual stance. The counselor began the session by asking the woman to close her eyes and ask God what he wanted to tell her.

Doing so, the woman sat in silence waiting and listening. The counselor encouraged her that the spiritual truth would come to her if she had the courage to ask. After a few minutes, the woman began to weep.

"Would you like to share anything?" the counselor gently asked. "Did you see or hear God?"

"I saw him. But he came to me looking like Mister Rogers" she replied.

Why Mister Rogers? Mister Rogers evokes safety for us. A calm, reassuring presence and a calm, empathetic witness for the little girl inside her who had been robbed of innocence and safety. Secure attachment feels like spending time with Mister Rogers. Fred Rogers came along with me to countless counseling appointments as I visualized telling him my stories and learned that I had the strength to go back and rescue myself as a wise adult.

Soon, you will understand that same presence is needed for the children in your care. Gradually, I learned what he would say and do; I learned the postures

---

33 Bessel A. van der Kolk, "Developmental Trauma Disorder: Toward a Rational Diagnosis for Children with Complex Trauma Histories," *Psychiatric Annals* 35, no. 5 (2005): 401–408, https://doi.org/10.3928/00485713-20050501-06.

of love children crave. I didn't want to be Fred Rogers but what he embodied: strong, steady presence.

When I asked photographer Lynn Johnson (the genius behind pictures of Fred Rogers included in this book) what she would do if she could spend one more hour with Rogers, she replied, "I would be quiet and just sit in his presence."

We evoke peace when we know more peace. Fred Rogers had made peace with his story. Below is an example of the first story I worked on when I began to engage my story.

****

I killed my puppy when I was five. It was my first encounter with shame and guilt. One could argue that a young child would not understand the ramifications of such a loss, but I remember the anguish in my heart following me for decades.

Jingles, a sheltie, was born prematurely and died at birth, but his breeder gave him mouth-to-mouth resuscitation and brought him back to life. He was a little miracle, sweet and tiny. I have no memories of him except for those from the day he died—and the large photo my mother had made for me later. I had taken him to the backyard of my elderly neighbor's house, but she had bushes that felt like a maze, and I would often pretend I was lost in a magical forest. It was quiet there, and if my parents were yelling at each other, it was an escape.

While holding Jingles, I thought I would toss him onto the grass. I believed he would land on his feet like a cat. He hit the cement with a loud smack. Still and numb, I scooped him up and walked to my house. My mom stood at the sink washing dishes as I entered the kitchen.

"Mommy," I said.

She turned toward me and screamed, seeing him limp in my arms. "Noooooo!"

She grabbed her keys, and we jumped into the car, with him on my lap. I could see blood coming out of his nose. He was dying, and it was my fault.

There is still a part of me that is afraid to think that I was acting as though he was in trouble before I tossed him, which somehow makes it worse. As she rushed him inside the vet clinic, I was made to wait outside. Alone. My heart smothered by the reality of what I had done. Through a slit of a window, my mother stood holding Jingles' collar, watching them work on him, tears streaming down her face. Our neighbor, Lloyd, had already warned her that he thought I was too young to be walking a puppy around by myself, but she had ignored him. Now she regretted it. I don't remember when I was told he was dead, and as my counselor guided me back through the memory, I was stuck in the unprocessed trauma, a five-year-old, alone outside.

Through her guidance, I entered the story in my mind as an adult and began to attune (pay attention) to myself at five. The kindergarten teacher instantly showed up.

What would you do for the child you love in that situation?

When I approached her as an adult, I told her who I was and that I was there to help her. "What does she need to tell you, Wystie?" my counselor asked.

With my eyes closed, I envisioned her tear-soaked face, her anguish. I knelt down and ran my hands along her arms. Wrapping her arms tightly around herself, she couldn't look me in the eye.

"Hi, Baby Girl. I'm you all grown up, and I've come to help you," I said.

"I killed my puppy!" She burst into tears and fell into my arms. Why was she out here all alone? That was not okay! (You'll have many moments where you will learn to say those same words: It was not okay.)

Be who you needed growing up.

I imagined taking her face in my hands and telling her, "It was not okay for you to be left here. I want to take you somewhere safe. Will you come with me?" She nodded.

I pictured a beach with a log where we could sit and snuggle, she and I in sync and safe. I pulled her onto my lap and could smell her hair, and she still sniffled and cried quietly. Being sure she was secure, I rocked her softly back and forth and allowed the waves to be a lullaby of comfort. I want her to hear my heartbeat. To know that she will survive this horrific moment because I did. It was over. Your trauma is over, but your body needs to know. If we had to navigate traumas on our own, it is locked inside us, influencing our ability to trust, offer love, and manage stress.

Later on, my little girl became a protector of herself and others, hypervigilant, codependent, and experiencing extreme emotions that rarely matched a situation.

I needed a key adult who would sit with me and tell me that I was not a bad person because I made a choice. Grief changed me. It happened. Jingles' death created deep shame in my soul that I had to hide from the world. Who kills a puppy and is still a good person? Are some mistakes unforgivable? These were the questions of a five-year-old child. As I rocked her, I whispered these truths to her:

"This won't hurt forever."

"I'm so sorry this happened. I know you didn't mean to hurt your puppy."

"You are my brave girl, and we can sit here as long as you need."

"You're not alone. I will always be with you. We will heal this together."

What moments were you left to handle alone? Perhaps your parents or caregivers did have a conversation with you, but you needed more: to continue the dialogue or be held a bit longer.

If it happened, it mattered. All of it.

Grab Inspiration Where You Can

Mister Rogers would be the first person to tell you he wasn't perfect. In fact, his widow, Joanne, in her foreword to *The World According to Mister Rogers*, begins with a quote by Bessie Anderson Stanley:

> He has achieved success who has lived well, laughed often, and loved much; who has enjoyed the trust of pure women, the respect of intelligent men, and the love of little children; who has filled his niche and accomplished his task; who has left the world better than he found it whether by an improved poppy, a perfect poem or a rescued soul; who has never lacked appreciation of Earth's beauty or failed to express it; who has always looked for the best in others and given them the best he had; whose life was an inspiration; whose memory a benediction.

Joanne explained,

> There were always quotes like that tucked away in Fred's wallet, next to his neatly folded bills, or in the pages of his daily planner.

Perhaps he liked having words of wisdom close to him as if he wanted—or needed—to be constantly reminded of what was important in life. The outside world may have thought his qualities of wisdom and strength came naturally to him, but those close to him knew that he was constantly striving to be the best that he could be. He was as human as the rest of us.[34]

I take tremendous comfort in knowing that Fred Rogers was a collector of wisdom. I've filled countless journals with inspirations like the one above. My desk is littered with sticky notes of insights, declarations about my purpose, and reminders of how to be a better teacher, mother, wife, friend, and human being.

Because let's face it: Some days we aren't inspired. We're grumpy, overwhelmed, weary, discouraged, and unsure of the next step to take. We forget who we are; we forget our worth, giftings, and resilience. Surround yourself with reminders. Affirm yourself out loud if needed. Apply those same affirmations to others, seeing them through the eyes of compassion. What would they have been like as a child? What type of an adult is the child in your care becoming without a compass?

Like Fred Rogers, I have the same desire to leave the world a better place than I found it. **There's no one you couldn't love if you knew their entire story**.

You Are Important

If you could only sense how important you are to the lives of those you meet, how important you can be to the people you may never even dream of. There is something of yourself that you leave at every meeting with another person.
—Fred Rogers

My grandpa was sober almost fifty years from alcohol. When he died, people began to tell stories about the words he'd spoken in the dark moments of their lives. His favorite saying was "Take care of yourself because you are important."

---

34 Rogers, *You Are Special*.

One woman shared that his words saved her life. She had decided during an AA meeting that she'd had enough. After years of domestic violence and battling her demons, she wanted to die. Grandpa was a fixture at the meetings, and she found him endearing, always offering her warm, candy-like saltwater taffy or Nips caramel candies from his pocket. Having dubbed him the "Candyman," people relied on his wisdom and strong backbone. She had already decided it was going to be her last AA meeting before she'd end it all. But right before she walked away, Grandpa uttered the phrase I'd heard my entire life: "Take care of yourself because you are important." This time it mattered more than he would ever know, leaving a legacy of worth and significance.

People are hungry for love and honesty. Love works for every beating heart, regardless of race, religion, or creed. It's a universal language of significance and "enough-ness." Radical acceptance is transformational love.

Being intentional is about showing up for our lives, doing what we love in front of children, and engaging with the present moment without distraction. Life is messy yet beautiful. You determine the energy, love, and impact found in your classroom. What you're doing matters every single minute! In this fast-paced world, it's easy to forget our impact on others. Never underestimate the power you hold in your hands. You are their teacher—someone who will be forever etched upon their hearts, good or bad.

During a conversation with me in 2020, former *Mister Rogers' Neighborhood* director Paul Lally recalled when TV star Lauren Tewes, best known for her work on the show *The Love Boat*, claimed the *Neighborhood* helped her kick her cocaine habit. One morning when she was home alone, sad and frightened, the *Neighborhood* came on television. During Rogers' signature opening, "It's a Beautiful Day in the Neighborhood," she felt a reassurance like never before. She *was* loved, significant, and valuable. There was at least one person (Mister Rogers) who wanted to be her friend. This profoundly changed her way of looking at herself and others.

Lally shared that Fred Rogers was amazed at the power of telling people they matter, regardless of the circumstances. "Do you remember that day [of the taping]?" Rogers had reminded Lally. "All I wanted to do was go swimming." But he never lost sight of what he believed about God, of his awareness that "the Holy Spirit translates our best efforts into what needs to be communicated to that person in his or her place of need."[35] Regardless of his feelings, Rogers showed up and did what he intended to do, always adding a prayer as he walked into the studio each morning: "Dear God, let some word that is heard be yours." His goal was never to impose his beliefs on his viewers, only to create an atmosphere where viewers felt safe and loved. Speaking the same words he had uttered hundreds of times had saved Tewes' life.

In his personal papers, I read how the iconic ending of the show came to be. A regular episode of *Mister Rogers' Neighborhood* ran roughly twenty-eight minutes long with an introduction, episode content, ending credits, and sponsorship. Often a stickler for details and delivery, Fred Rogers was keenly aware of the time clock ticking at the end of each episode. There are countless photographs of him intensely observing each playback for effectiveness. Rogers' least favorite to film was the on-camera work inside the house because he knew how important it was to get it right. He was much more at home behind the scenes, wearing glasses (he hated the contacts he wore on camera), with a puppet in one hand, while looking into a monitor, interacting with others like Betty Aberlin or Chuck Aber.

One day, he had extra time before exiting through the door, and without much thought, he looked into the camera and said the words once spoken to him by his own beloved grandfather "Ding-Dong" McFeely: "You make each day a special day, just by being you. There's only one person in the whole world like you, and that's you. And people can like you exactly as you are."

After Rogers exited the set, the director yelled, "Cut!" and the crew stood stunned and visibly moved. Rogers indicated that he knew it would be the lasting mark on what he said on the program.

****

By living and working with children, I've learned about the child I was, the person who is always striving to grow within me.
—Fred Rogers

---

35   Susan Duke, *Heartlifters for the Young at Heart: Surprising Stories, Stirring Messages, and Refreshing Scriptures that Make the Heart Soar* (West Monroe, LA: Howard Publishing, 2001).

Every time I think I have something figured out, Blue Eyes throws me for a loop. One day he responds to me, looks me in the eyes (for a minute), and wants to help around the classroom. The next day, he's angry at the whole world, including me. His body constantly reminds him of deficits while I feel locked in a prison of my best intentions. He acts like such a jerk, yet I love him. Some days it's an intentional choice. I believe that love will get through the cracks. Every child needs at least one person who's crazy about them.

Blue Eyes is skilled at hitting all my triggers, and I often find myself thinking negatively:

This will never work.

It's fruitless.

He's too damaged and not responding.

You're just going to be a blip in his education.

Children enter our classrooms with invisible wounds that our intentions must bandage. "Every child deserves a champion: an adult who will never give up on them, who understands the power of connection and insists they become the best they can possibly be."[36] Let's be honest, though: Children from "hard places"[37] create a tremendous pull toward the negative. Yet no child is beyond hope when we focus on what their "pain-based behaviors"[38] are seeking—that is, connection.

Children need to feel safe, known, and heard in their bodies. If you only look for ways to curb frustrating and intolerable behaviors, you'll miss the child within who's screaming for love. Along the way, connection becomes unsafe for their tiny brains and bodies. Let's help children heal before they become adults. Emotional regulation will change the world if we raise children to understand how to feel safe in their own bodies. I'm convinced this is the only way out of the mess we're currently in as educators, parents, and caregivers. Whether it's acknowledged or not, we're all craving validation, voice, love, and acceptance.

---

36 Rita Pierson, "The 50 Most Inspirational Quotes for Teachers," Curated Quotes, March 6, 2015, http://www.curatedquotes.com/quotes-for-teachers/.

37 Karyn B. Purvis, David R. Cross, and Wendy Lyons Sunshine, *The Connected Child: Bring Hope and Healing to Your Adoptive Family* (New York: McGraw-Hill, 2007).

38 Lori L. Desautels and Michael McKnight, *Eyes Are Never Quiet: Listening Beneath the Behaviors of Our Most Troubled Students* (Deadwood, OR: Wyatt-MacKenzie Publishing, 2019).

But I can hear you saying, "I'm only one person! I can't do it all!" I understand. There must be balance, grace, and understanding of our own limits. There will be countless times of victory and profound moments of failure. Being willing and able to sit amid the discomfort and chaos, resting in your purpose, is a true sign you are eager to learn and grow.

How we respond to the intense needs of children will depend on our *attachment styles* and what activates our nervous systems. But do remain curious about your reactions and responses. Be curious and wonder about all the ways you became you. Then consider: How can you use what you did/didn't receive to understand the children in your care? It's not reasonable to say that you can leave everything you feel at the door. Instead, bring it all in and use it for good.

This is a complex idea, but Rogers simplified it. Whenever I find myself bogged down with the complexities of neuroscience, adversity, attachment styles, and solutions, the gentle and simple work of Fred Rogers beckons me home. "Deep and simple is far more essential than shallow and complex," he says. Always think back to what *you* needed. Who loved you well? What did that feel like?

You Were Loved into Being

Take a minute and identify a person, one person, who loved you into being. Give yourself the gift of an entire minute.

Who came to your mind? Did this person have an influence on you becoming a teacher or caregiver?

Fred Rogers did this activity in several speeches he gave. He understood that we are a mixture of all the people, both good and bad, who have come and gone from our lives. Attention must be paid to those who spoke life into the uniqueness hidden within us as children. In a 1993 radio interview, Rogers said, "Isn't that what life is? That we all step into the stream at one point, and we all step out at another? And hopefully, during that time, people along the way have a little bit of us incorporated into what they are."[39]

****

---

39 Paul Zelevansky, "Into the Stream," November 21, 2013, YouTube video, https://www. youtube.com/watch?v=TDFmiWHKauM.

Frankly, I think that after we die, we have this wide
understanding of what's real. And we'll probably say,
"Ah, so that's what it was all about."
—Fred Rogers

"Smiley George" was the first black man I ever met. Growing up in a predominately white, blue-collar town, he stood out with his bright white teeth and thick
glasses. He embodied the motto "Attitudes are caught, not taught," another one of
Fred Rogers' favorites that he learned observing children and families.

George Matthews was a staple of my childhood. Living close to my grandparents, he would accompany my grandmother on her frequent bus rides to her
job downtown. Based on kindness and understanding, their simple friendship
spanned decades. Six months after moving to Spokane in 1980, his beloved
wife died, and then his mother, leaving him reeling. It was in the aftermath that
George met my grandmother. He was vulnerable and shared with her that his biggest challenge was that he could not cook. My grandmother offered him ideas and
recipes, and thus a lasting friendship was born. He supervised the mailroom at the
local newspaper, the *Spokesman-Review*, and "never met a stranger" while doing it.
Taking the time to really see people was George's gift to the world.

His generous gift to my grandma was to be a lookout for me if she was not on
the same bus. I grew up next to two main arterials, busy and visible. If I was outside the house on my big wheel, he would wave to me and report to Grandma that
I was doing just fine. Standing only four feet ten, she couldn't see over the steering
wheel of a car and opted to never get her driver's license. (Perhaps that's why she
had eight children—to ensure she would always have a ride.) My grandma was,
like George, a staple of the bus system and the downtown crowd, since she spent
many years as a custodial worker in a large department store called the Crescent.
(Today, remembering my sweet grandmother continually cleaning up other people's messes, I will grab discarded towels off the floor in a public restroom and
wipe down the counter lightly before leaving. I pride myself on leaving it cleaner
than I found it.)

When I was finally allowed to venture downtown with friends in middle
school, I would often bump into Smiley George, who would embrace me with

a big hug and send me on my way, calling out to me, "Wysteria, you stay out of trouble now."

I always found George Matthews to be beautiful. He, along with Grandma, inspired me to remember people. Not just their names but what mattered to them: children, jobs, hobbies, and little bits and pieces. Seeing George walking past my grandparents' house, I would run out to meet him, and his embrace and laughter swallowed me every time. I saw him as an extension of the safety I felt in my grandmother's care and love. It is no wonder why they got along so well. He saw the world the way she did—full of beauty and good things.

While going through my grandmother's papers after her death, I found George Matthews' obituary. I gasped in delight, finally able to read all the things that were lost on me as a little girl. Before moving to Spokane, he and his wife made their home in Cleveland, Ohio, where he ran a shelter for indigent and homeless men, as well as helped run a home for neglected and abused children. Of course he did. That made complete sense.

"He really cared about you," said a fellow employee at the newspaper. "He had a memory and used it to make people feel good. He never forgot to ask about [people's] lives. He adored people, and they loved him right back. . . . He'd never say trite things like 'Have a nice day.'. . . He'd comment on your life, compliment you somehow. He was so optimistic about everything, and it was contagious. George Matthews was an ambassador of friendship for all of downtown Spokane."

"My dad loved his job, and he loved the people he met and worked with," his son, Reginald Matthews, said. "He really loved [Spokane]. He'd say it was his piece of heaven before he gets there."[40]

Who loved you into being?

****

Trust Your Inner Truth

Where are the places we're pretending to have it all together? Being honest about where we are is hard, brave work. You're safe within these pages. Highlight what

---

40 Bonnie Harris, "Former S-R Mail Center Supervisor Dies," *Spokesman Review*, September 14, 1994.

you love, and make connections to yourself. Take time to journal and reflect on your story and what you uniquely bring to loving children. Fred Rogers said, "The best way to know the truth [is] to begin by trusting what your inner truth [is], [and] trying to share it."[41]

You Have No Rivals

You are unique and valuable, and you matter in the lives of those you teach. There's something you bring to the lives of children that no one else can. What is essential is invisible to the human eye. It must be felt within the heart. It's about resonance, and understanding our unique stories paves the way for our deepest connections. The way you teach and love communicates to the world what you value about yourself—and others. We needn't try to be like everyone else. We're not meant to be. All we need to be is honest. Who you are on the inside is what helps you make and do everything in life.

We want to be great at teaching children. But as I shared earlier, our desire to reach them can become all-encompassing at the expense of our health, our relationships, our time, and the present moment. The only thing we're guaranteed in life is the present, yet teaching has us bouncing back and forth between where a child has been and where they are heading. Not to say that those aren't important to evaluate, but I know in my own life I've become fixated to the point of not looking and listening to what gifts are in the "now."

What is comparison? "Comparison is the crush of conformity from one side and competition from the other—it's trying to simultaneously fit in and stand out. Comparison says, 'Be like everyone else but better.'"[42] The two ideas go hand in hand: comparison regarding the child and also how my teaching of him looks to the outside world. Remember, the outside world isn't inside the chrysalis. Because of this, we can fall into two categories. *Upward social comparison* is when we compare ourselves to someone who is (perceived to be performing) better than we are. *Downward social comparison* is when we compare ourselves to someone who is (perceived to be performing) worse than we are. When we participate in

---

41   Ellen Galinsky, "Fred Rogers: Seeker of Truth," *Early Learning Nation*, November 19, 2019, https://earlylearningnation.com/2019/11/fred-rogers-seeker-of-truth/.

42   Brown, *Atlas of the Heart*.

either comparison, there will be positive and negative effects, but the greatest loss is that we've taken our eyes off the child. Teaching isn't about us but about connecting to the hearts of children.

> Like many other values our children get from us, comparison is more likely to be caught than taught.
> **—Fred Rogers**

As Theodore Roosevelt is credited with saying, comparison is the thief of joy.[43] It crushes connection and creativity. Joy is found not in looking at a child in comparison to who he was, is, or will be, but in considering this question: Who is he right now? Don't focus on where he is on a data sheet or in relation to his peers (super hard, I know, when administrations and districts want that data) but on where he is in relation to himself. It's like comparing a caterpillar to a butterfly—two separate things entirely—without recognizing the intricate and beautiful metamorphosis of changes hidden from the outside within the chrysalis. Our classrooms are the chrysalis, and you and I are privileged to see what very few others will witness in each child's lifetime. We witness the birth of new ideas, mindsets, security, insight, strengths, leadership, and growth. But don't blink! You'll miss it.

In an interview with Charlie Rose in 1994, Rogers said, "The things that are center stage are rarely the things that are most important."[44] What is center stage for you? It's easy to become competitive and worry about how our teaching looks to others within the education community. We want to be told we're doing a good job, receive praise and accolades (crystal apples, stars, and followers on blogs and social media), but loving children often comes at our expense.

Fred Rogers said: "It's not about honors or prizes and the fancy outsides of life which ultimately nourish our souls. It's knowing that we can be trusted that we never have to fear the truth, that the bedrock of our being is good stuff.

---

43 Blair Parke, "Who Said 'Comparison Is the Thief of Joy' and How Is It Represented in the Bible?," Bible Study Tools, April 2, 2019, https://www.biblestudytools.com/bible-study/topical-studies/who-said-comparison-is-the-thief-of-joy.html.

44 Charlie Rose, "Mr. Rogers Interview," Charlie Rose, September 20, 1994, https://charlierose.com/videos/5544.

That's what makes growing humanity the most potentially glorious enterprise on earth."

How will we know the depth of love if we never take risks or have varying opinions about what's best for specific children? Although he was considered kind and open to others, Fred Rogers' steel backbone was unwavering in what he believed was right. To him, children came first, over the intentions of adults and their narrow systems. His plea still rings true: "Please think of the *children* first. If you ever have anything to do with their entertainment, their food, their toys, their custody, their childcare, their health care, their education—listen to the children, learn about them, learn from them. *Think of the children first.*"[45]

I've sat in countless meetings with colleagues who had previously voiced their discontent over things that related to their students, but when given the opportunity to say what they feel, they don't. Why do you remain silent? Are you putting children first, or are you worried about standing outside the group and the popular opinions of others? Ask yourself. Those of us with insecure attachment will see speaking up as running the risk of rejection/abandonment of our peers and administrators or being perceived as a failure. Both scenarios are ways we are abandoning ourselves and conforming, rather than loving with "gritty, dangerous, wild-eyed, justice-seeking love."[46] It's scary. But when we stay comfortable and conform, children lose.

> I don't believe any educational gimmicks can be very helpful
> in teaching children who are burdened with overwhelming
> anxieties. For them, learning readiness really means the
> reestablishment of trust.
> **—Fred Rogers**

Fred Rogers often rephrased his song "Many Ways to Say I Love You" to fit what he was talking about at that moment. As you read the lyrics below, consider where you need to say "I love you" to yourself and your students to emotionally show up each day. It's going to be a vulnerable choice, I promise.

---

45   Rogers, *You Are Special.*
46   Brown, *Atlas of the Heart.*

There are many ways to say I love you
There are many ways to say I care about you.
Many ways, many ways, many ways to say
I love you.

There's the singing way to say I love you
There's the singing something someone really likes to hear,
The singing way, the singing way, the singing way to say
I love you.

Cleaning up a room can say I love you.
Hanging up a coat before you're asked to
Drawing special pictures for the holidays and
Making plays.

You'll find many ways to say I love you.
You'll find many ways to understand what love is.
Many ways, many ways, many ways to say
I love you.

Singing, cleaning,
Drawing, being
Understanding,
Love you.[47]

I would also add: There's the teaching way to say I love you. There's also the consistent, vulnerable, curious, wondering, hopeful, role-modeling, regulated, calm, quiet, enthusiastic, honest, healing our inner wounded parts, setting boundaries, saying no, getting enough sleep, eating well, unhurried, engaging, attuned, intentional, not having all the answers, noncompetitive, forgiving, humble, and kind way to say I love you.

---

47 Fred M. Rogers, "Many Ways to Say I Love You," The Mister Rogers Neighborhood Archive, 1970, http://www.neighborhoodarchive.com/music/songs/many_ways.html.

What would you add?

There's the _____way to say I love you.

Whatever you need to give yourself permission to do and to be for children, do it now.

Fred Rogers talks to a group of students in a Chicago elementary classroom. 1994.
Lynn Johnson Collection.

Chapter 3:

The *Neighborhood* and Us

"Won't You Be My Neighbor?"

It is not the critic who counts; not the man who points out how the strong man stumbles, or where the doer of deeds could have done them better. The credit belongs to the man who is actually in the arena, whose face is marred by dust and sweat and blood; who strives valiantly; who errs, who comes short again and again, because there is no effort without error and shortcoming; but who does actually strive to do the deeds; who knows great enthusiasms, the great devotions; who spends himself in a worthy cause; who at the best knows in the end the triumph of high achievement, and who at the worst, if he fails, at least fails while daring greatly, so that his place shall never be with those cold and timid souls who neither know victory nor defeat.

—Teddy Roosevelt

Since his death in 2003, Fred Rogers has become an icon, often researched after school shootings and other tragedies; he symbolizes goodness, honesty, and comfort for millions of Americans. If you read the comments under a photo of Mister Rogers on social media, you often see things like "I miss him," and "We need Mister Rogers more today than ever." In the lyrics of her song "Dear Mr. Rogers," songwriter Alison Freebairn-Smith writes,

Dear Mr. Rogers, where are you?
I hope it's a beautiful place
With all that you did for all of us kids
I hope you're inside the pearly gates

Dear Mr. Rogers, I miss you
Just like a kind-hearted friend
The love that you gave me is part of what saved me
Though I didn't know it back then

And now that you're gone, your spirit lives on
In the music and lessons I still savor
Wherever you are, here in my heart
You'll always be my neighbor

Dear Mr. Rogers, I'm sorry
It isn't just you that I grieve
The love you proclaimed has fallen to shame
Here in the land of make believe

Dear Mr. Rogers, I need you
Your words always put me at ease
Nothing makes sense
In these current events
I need you to explain it to me

Dear Mr. Rogers, thank you
My feelings for you have never wavered
Wherever you are
Please know in my heart
You'll always be my neighbor.[48]

---

48 Alison Freebairn-Smith, "Dear Mr. Rogers," MP3, Alisongs/BMI, 2018.

Why do we crave Mister Rogers, much like young children want their mothers after falling? We are bruised people, fighting over skin colors, political positions, and whether a person has value after committing a crime. Indeed, we are a mess, and our children demonstrate the emotional disconnect in classrooms across America. Something must change because our children are at stake! We're passing on our traumas and maladaptive coping skills to our children and then are surprised when they can't learn. We live in an age of noise, superficial connections, and disinterest in accountability. It's time to use our stories, insecurities, and limitations so we can be the "Mister Rogers" our students need in our classrooms.

But I'm going to be honest with you. Engaging your whole story is going to slap you in the face with vulnerability. The kind of vulnerability you felt as a child. Exposed and naked. Real and raw.

"No thanks," I hear you saying to me.

"Vulnerability is the emotion that we experience during times of uncertainty, risk and emotional exposure."[49] You picked up this book for a reason. Don't ignore whatever stirs within you as you read.

Collective Arenas of Loss

When I first began to draft this book on fostering secure attachments in the classroom, I had no way of knowing that we'd be entering a global pandemic. We've experienced a collective trauma on a global scale firsthand and lived to tell about it, both now and as the years go by. Families were forced to hunker down, be in one place, and spend time together. This entire book could be filled with the stories of what we all gained and lost during the two-plus years of uncertainty. I keep a sign of all I lost on the windows of my classroom.

Once bright, cherry red, the construction paper mosaic apples made with wax paper and colored tissue hung to catch the afternoon sun. But now they represent what I lost in March of 2020 as we watched the growing numbers of COVID-19 cases skyrocket three hours west in Seattle, Washington. We'd watched *Mister Rogers' Neighborhood* and went to our specials class for the day when the news arrived from the district level that we would be going into quarantine for at least

---

49   Brené Brown, *Dare to Lead* (New York: Random House, 2018).

six weeks. I was tasked with the difficult news of communicating this to my sweet kindergarteners as they returned to the room for their purposeful playtime.

****

One of their favorite activities is the Maker's Space where my students create puppet stages, musical instruments out of toilet paper rolls, and other inventions that would make Fred Rogers proud. The puppet stage has daily reenactments of the *Neighborhood* stories, including the characters from fairy tales mixed in, with the help of finger friends from IKEA. Other children sculpt out of playdough, our future engineers and scientists honing their problem-solving and negotiation skills. The fish tank bubbles in its blue tranquility at the end of the cozy corner, where several children choose to snuggle into my homemade quilts and pillows while looking at class-made books and teacher-read favorites. Dinosaurs trample block-made cities, Hot Wheels shoot down makeshift ramps, and when the timer rings, thirty minutes of play can be cleaned up in record time, as each learner awaits to share their "big feelings" to close the day.

Their buzz of creative play, excitement, and laughter is as much a comfort to me as spending time with an old friend. It's our Neighborhood, our home.

Now I'm about to take away that security and hand them uncertainty. I spend the forty-five minutes of my prep period thinking, praying, and preparing to close our space for six weeks.

Calling my husband, I arrange for him to pick up our beloved classroom pets, Henrietta and Queen Sara Saturday, the rats who stand at the side of their cage, little paws clinging closer as they watch the children playing in the sensory bin. Henrietta is known to climb to the top of the cage during morning calendar and chew loudly to get our attention, until the children say, "Good morning, Hen," and Sara provides countless engineering projects due to her ability to escape her cages—three so far. "Maybe she just wants to be in kindergarten like us," the children concluded, and the concept wasn't far from the truth. Henrietta prefers lounging in the hammock during purposeful play, but Sara will climb all over and run through their cage as if the energy of the children's play was contagious. The "girls" are part of our Neighborhood as a reminder that all living things matter, have basic needs, and require love.

I begin. I remind my precious students that they are fiercely loved and that COVID is an adult problem. They all have adults in their lives who would do anything and everything in their power to keep them safe. Unfortunately, that means that we'd be away from school for at least six weeks. Two of my girls burst into tears, while a few boys cheer, thinking they'd be outside riding their bikes, like it was spring break come early.

"This is serious, so it's important that you listen to the people who love you. The sooner people get better, the quicker we can come back to school." As I demonstrate on the calendar how many weeks we'll be apart, the crying becomes contagious.

"Are we still going to play?" Chase asks, not affected by the sadness around him.

"Of course. Should we start purposeful play for today?" I ask. But the sadness is thick. Chase's enthusiasm deflates as he looks around at his classmates who sit either crying or numb from the news. I pause, observing their faces, and decide to change course.

"Maybe we need Mister Rogers again to help us feel better."

"Two times in one day?" Casen asks.

"Two times in one day. Who wants to just snuggle and watch Mister Rogers together?"

They all raise their hands, and I cue the next episode. As the soothing introduction starts, I take a seat on the floor, gathering them close to my body. I wrap my arms around Maddy and Rainey as Mister Rogers opens the door with enthusiasm. I can do nothing to make it better except remain close, enter sadness with them, and accept heartache.

I soothe with my words as they press closer to my heartbeat. "We will be together again. I promise you." Three reach their hands to rest on my legs, and another runs her fingers in my hair. How could I have ever known that would be the last day we'd sit together huddled in our Neighborhood, surrounded by love? Nothing would ever be normal again.

****

In an age of superficial connections, noise, and disinterest in accountability, it's time to own our stories, insecurities, and limitations. After more than two decades as an educator, I have observed the following losses in my students and families, regardless of socioeconomic status, race, religion, or sex:

- loss of focus: technology is creating a distraction
- lack of trust and security with adult figures
- loss of self-control: inability to regulate emotions, resulting in extreme property damage, physical aggression, expulsions, and classroom evacuations due to behaviors
- loss of a family or family structure: children being shuffled between households, leaving feelings of insignificance
- loss of imagination: acting out only video games
- loss of margin: over-scheduled children in multiple sports and extracurricular activities
- loss of self: low self-esteem, self-harm, aggressively acting out what they witnessed at home or with older siblings/day-care situations
- loss of the simple: an addiction to devices and material possessions, consumerism
- loss of authenticity: relying on social media likes and comments, rather than accountability
- loss of silent reflection, self-care, and established boundaries
- loss of collaboration without defensiveness and blaming
- loss of intentional play to work out big feelings and understand the world
- lack of parental ownership to behaviors in the school setting and the impact of the home environments
- loss of truth: hiding hard topics and situations from children, lacking a moral compass
- loss of community, deep friendships, respect, and reverence
- loss of conversations and asking questions with wonder and curiosity
- loss of appreciation, practice, sportsmanship, integrity, hard work, and discipline
- loss of eye contact and physical touch
- loss of pacing, slowing down, and observing
- loss of integrating traumas: no longer creating cultures of care or neighborhoods helping others without acknowledgment

- loss of valuing growth: not allowing children first experiences that may cause struggle or discomfort
- loss of whimsy, spontaneity, and humor

What do we do with such intense losses, all of which have noticeably worsened since the pandemic? **We heal ourselves first—because children matter, and we've devoted our lives to their welfare.** Karyn Purvis, author of *The Connected Child*, notes that "any unresolved memory or trauma that makes you emotionally absent or distracted by the past is bound to have negative repercussions for the [children] in your care."[50]

> The very most profound thing we can offer our [students]
> is our own healing.
> **—Anne Lamott**

Remembering Your Childhood Is the Key

> Somewhere early on, I got the idea inside me that childhood was valuable, that children were worthy to be seen and heard, and who they were had a lot to do with what our world will become. So, I was always interested in children. I have the feeling that anyone who serves children like we do, be we pediatricians or nurses, or early childhood educators, if we're to do well, probably have somewhere inside of us that conviction that the early years of life are of great value, . . . that the way we adults make our choices, the way we look at others, that the way we think about our world and ourselves has so much to do with who we were as children.
> **—Fred Rogers**

---

50 Purvis, Cross, and Sunshine, *The Connected Child*.

Childhood matters to me. It mattered to Fred Rogers. It's a journey filled with hills and valleys. I deeply believe that as a teacher, I have the responsibility to help my children fall in love with learning. Childhood in my care should be joyful, magical, and protected at all costs.

Every encounter with a child is an opportunity to create a secure base for their future resilience to an ever-changing world. One of the key ingredients to ensure success when connecting with a young child is *remembering*.

Fred Rogers said, "Love is at the root of everything. All learning. All relationships. Love or the lack of it." How we are loved or unloved affects every relationship and interaction, especially in our classrooms. **Your feelings, triggers, emotions, reactions, and healing are your responsibility.** This was a big pill for me to swallow. But as I began the painful process of "reworking" my childhood, I began to differentiate between old and new wounds and the feelings they activated. I learned to observe my emotions without judgment and remain curious.

No one leaves childhood without scars. Although hidden to the naked eye, developmental traumas—broken connections—become the foundation of our daily interactions. We hold our stories close to our chest for fear others will discover that we don't have it all together, yet they ooze out in our daily encounters if left unacknowledged and unhealed. Without being able to recognize when old wounds are triggered, we automatically will assume it's the result of the actions of a child we're teaching, instead of looking deeper. Likewise, when we understand our boundaries, we won't be distracted by our own experiences and can effectively contain and support the emotional experiences of children.

Our brains and nervous systems learned what was emotionally acceptable and not acceptable long ago. Change equaled loss, challenging the roles we play in our family or resulting in developmental trauma. Going back and working on how secure we are and how we learned about nurturing and love feels like death to our nervous systems.

Then why do it? It's simple: We're bleeding out onto children.

Our reactions and insecure attachments are blocking genuine connections with students. The "doctors" can't treat the patients if they're sick themselves. Our school buildings have become hospitals, where children bring all their pain, misunderstandings, and histories every day. Yet we ignore the basics and expect that children will learn without secure foundations. Pretending isn't getting us any-where. Mister Rogers was right all along. Connection must come before learning.

****

Every child who enters my classroom is a story. Stories are meant to be read, shared, pondered, articulated, voiced, and blessed. Because we're wired to be social crea-tures, it's understandable why stories draw us in and mold us into who we are. Secure attachments develop when we feel unconditionally loved, seen, and accepted for who we are. It's the essence of a neighborhood, what Fred Rogers attempted to create on his program—a group of people who "get" you. Who love you. Who see and celebrate you. It's the reason we loved him. We felt he got us, knew us, and accepted all of us. Children often believed he'd know everything about them when they met him in public. He'd have to remind them that he was a "television" friend, that it wasn't the same as really knowing a person. But our attachment to him was built through his gentle gaze and slow pacing, his consistent routines and rituals, his reminders of self-worth and dedication to telling the truth simply, his storytell-ing through puppetry and radical acceptance of silence and peace.

Out of all the songs he wrote for the *Neighborhood*, it was "The Truth Will Make Me Free" that took Rogers the longest to write, as it details in simple hon-esty his process of wrestling with feelings he was told to hold inside as a child. He thought about it for years. Rogers was not permitted to cry or express his emotions in his childhood home, which strengthened his avoidant attachment. What do we know about stuffing our emotions and secrets while keeping them hidden from the world? They make us sick. Rogers enjoyed and treasured his conversations with adults, like his grandfather "Ding-Dong" McFeely, but wasn't permitted simple childhood pleasures such as playing outside with other children, getting into mischief, or interrupting parlor parties. It wasn't easy for him to express his emotions or tell the truth about what isolation, ostracization, and loneliness had done to him as a child. After all, he was born into a privileged existence with all that money could buy or offer, living in a family who was virtually untouched by the Great Depression. He wanted for nothing, except to be understood and seen for what he could genuinely give as his truest, honest self.

"You rarely have time for everything you want in this life, so you need to make choices. And hopefully, your choices can come from a deep sense of who you are."[51] Giving your honest self to your students requires you to fearlessly evaluate who you are, why you exist, and how you will make sense of all that got you here. "There is a close relationship between truth and trust," Rogers said, a concept he explores in the song "The Truth Will Make Me Free":

> What if I were very, very sad
> And all I did was smile?
> I wonder after a while
> What would become of my sadness?
>
> What if I were very, very angry
> And all I did was sit
> And never think about it?
> What might become of my anger?
>
> Where would they go
> And what would they do
> If I couldn't let them out?
> Maybe I'd fall, maybe get sick
> or doubt.
>
> But what if I could know the truth
> And say just how I feel?
> I think I'd learn a lot that's real
> about freedom.
>
> I'm learning to sing a sad song when I'm sad.
> I'm learning to say I'm angry when I'm very mad.
> I'm learning to shout.

---

51 Maxwell King, *The Good Neighbor: The Life and Work of Fred Rogers* (New York: Abrams Press, 2019).

I'm getting it out!
I'm happy, learning
Exactly how I feel inside of me.
I'm learning to know the truth
I'm learning to tell the truth.
Discovering truth will make me free.[52]

No matter how fantastic or horrible your parents were at raising you, your inner adult world will inevitably be darkened by a significant emotional need your parents failed to provide. We are humans, and none of us are perfect. **Understanding our brokenness and limitations is the beginning of having a secure foundation. Imperfections unite us with others with the possibility of a deeper connection if we choose it.**

Instead of pushing those feelings away like I used to, I welcome them in, ask them questions, and let them teach me more. When we wonder, we are learning. My questions often point me in the right direction to meet a specific emotional need, identify a misunderstanding, or circumvent a deep wound for a student—all from listening to how my emotions are communicating to me.

Healing our broken attachments leads to unimaginable depths in relating to children. What used to be my greatest pain has transformed into a way of being with small children—authentic like Mister Rogers.

Why Did You Become a Teacher?

It's late October, the fall of my third-grade year. I'm nine years old and assigned to the portable class of Ms. D., a woman who makes me feel uncomfortable, anxious, and miserable. She's nothing like my beautiful, kind, and affectionate second-grade teacher.

Seven months prior, I'd hit my head in a car accident, resulting in a brain injury that severely impacted my computation and fine motor skills. My second-grade teacher had panicked upon hearing of the wreck and was devoted to my recovery. Still, I found myself in the Learning Assistance Program (LAP), and

---

52   Fred Rogers and Luke Flowers, "The Truth Will Make Me Free," *A Beautiful Day in the Neighborhood: The Poetry of Mister Rogers* (Philadelphia, PA: Quirk Books, 2019).

the shame of being "less than" covered me like a blanket. Where I had once felt valuable and equal to my peers, I now wore a new label: "learning disabled." We didn't call it a traumatic brain injury in the 1980s. I was "slow," "learning disabled," "dumb," "suffering from a mental block," and "just needed to try harder." No matter what I did or how hard I tried, I couldn't overcome the deficit. Red marks littered every assignment that I learned to shove to the back of my desk.

Ms. D. holds nothing back when she interacts with me. Her disdain seeps through her sickly, fraudulent smile, followed by her dramatic eye rolls whenever I ask a question. She's loud and bullies selected children, me included, boisterously laughing at the jokes she makes at our expense. When children misbehave, she states that she will throw us "in the trash can," a nasty reference to the Garbage Pail Kids trading cards recently released to mock the popular Cabbage Patch Kids.

To add insult to injury, we're only a few doors down the hall from my beloved second-grade classroom, although my former teacher has moved to another school. As we enter the building from recess, I occasionally glance in that direction but feel the sting of loss squeezing my chest. I instinctively know if I embrace the ache, tears will come, giving Ms. D. more ammunition. I'm confused by her cruelty and unsure why she's singled me out for her insults and "humor." Every day, I pray that our principal, Mr. Wilson, will enter the room and catch her treating me like this. He loves me, remembers my name, and enjoys listening to my stories and singing. Where is he?

****

For the school's talent shows, I sang in front of the packed gymnasium of Jefferson Elementary. One year, I held a metallic star for "When You Wish Upon a Star" that caused the microphone to squeak and buzz, and the next year, I twirled a ribbon on a stick to accompany my dramatic interpretation of the song "True Colors" by Cyndi Lauper. (I know you're super disappointed you missed these. Believe me, they were epic.)

What made these experiences precious to me was how Mr. Wilson noticed and appreciated me. He would sit in the center of the gym during rehearsals, with complete chaos swirling around him, beside a large pea-green tape player (circa

1984), turn off his hearing aids, and read his Louis L'Amour novels. I didn't have to ask if he loved me; I knew it. He would wink at me after I sang, call me by name, and laugh when I tackled him with a hug in the lunch line. Whenever I had a banana in my lunch, it became a phone, and if there was a ponytail, it was tugged in affection. I loved him. There was no doubt that I was safe in his care. When he announced his retirement in my fifth-grade year, the loss was palpable and cut like a knife. To this day, I have a framed picture of him on my desk to remind me that I carry on what he started in me—that is, being intentional every day with every child.

****

I'm sitting at my third-grade desk constructing a skeleton for Halloween, listening to the other children enjoying our teacher's company and finding myself envious of their connection. I always feel on the outside of everywhere and everyone. We're supposed to attach the joints with gold brads so his arms swing back and forth. I'm so sick of all her little craft projects, and I have zero interest in doing my best work for her. It's never good enough anyway.

Rage in my belly churns as I crumple the skeleton parts into a ball. I've no desire to play her games or make cute things, as though I actually enjoy her class. Chewed pencils litter the ground as they fall out of my desk, but I continue shoving the wadded-up pieces as far to the back as they'll go. She must have seen me doing this. Or maybe one of her chosen favorites ratted me out. She's furious with me now, and like the Eye of Sauron, she zeros in on me, a target of her disdain.

Today, the words have been erased from my memory but not the feelings and sensations. Humiliation. Shame. Loss.

Sitting at my school desk, I feel my stomach tighten as the heat burns my face. I begin to choke back tears, repeating in my head, *I will not cry. I will not cry.* I know that if I cry, she'll have more to make fun of and will humiliate me. Her insults come quicker now, and the kids in the front row start laughing at her jokes.

Suddenly, a sob bursts from my throat, and I wail, "I hate you!" All the sound in the room stops, tears run down my cheeks, and my heart beats in my ears.

Silence.

She's stunned by my outburst and rage. Every child turns my way in wide-eyed shock; they're about to witness my execution.

"You're not supposed to treat me like this!" I cry.

The bell rings for recess, and the class jumps to flee. No doubt they want nothing to do with the atomic bomb I've just detonated.

"Not you, missy," she barks to me. "You put your head down."

Storming over to her desk, she sits down, refusing to look my way the entire recess. She's a cruel and heartless woman. Why doesn't anybody come to rescue me from her? Every time another grown-up enters the room, she becomes sickly sweet. She's a fraud, and I know she doesn't like me. I also know something else: She's a horrible teacher, and I deserve better. I deserve better and told her so. Now I'm being punished for knowing.

****

It wasn't until I put pen to paper and wrote out this encounter with Ms. D. that I realized the deepest truth—*that* was the moment I became a teacher. I stood up for my rights as a child and called out her injustice, abuse, and cruelty. Instinctively, I knew I deserved better, but how? That moment was one of the countless times I would have to stand up for a child's emotional well-being, starting with me. I'd had difficulty pinpointing why I chose to teach, and while writing it out, I finally knew! The answer was locked inside a story that I hadn't ever named, pondered, articulated, and blessed.

Look inside yourself. See what stories or moments don't go away. They may hold the key to unlocking your biggest *why* yet. Why did you become a teacher?

Part Two:
It All Comes Back to Attachment

Fred Rogers interacts with circle of children at Mesa Elementary School. 1994. Lynn Johnson Collection.

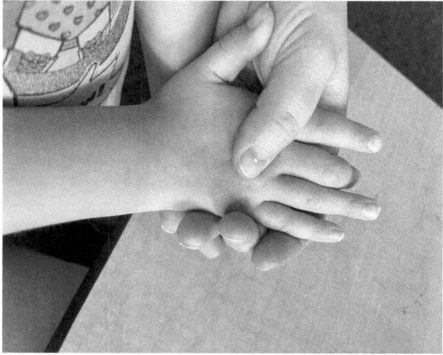
Author holding student's hand. June 2022.

Chapter 4

Attachment Styles of Children

"You Are Special"

> As babies, we're completely dependent on what other people do
> to and for us. Most of what we are learning then about ourselves
> and our world comes through other people, and part of what we
> have to learn as we go is how to adapt to these people while
> still remaining the individuals we are.
>
> **—Fred Rogers**

Curt Thompson, author of *Anatomy of the Soul*, said, "When each one of us comes into this world, we enter it looking for someone looking for us."[53] We are social beings who crave safety, soothing, and security while being seen by our caregivers.[54] *Attachment* is the emotional bond between an infant and their caregiver, established by the infant's primary needs being met, resulting in trust and security. A child's relationship with their primary caregiver shapes their brains more than any other relationship. Established in the first few years of life, attachment becomes a child's reference point—an internal working model—of

---

53   Curt Thompson, *Anatomy of the Soul: Surprising Connections Between Neuroscience and Spiritual Practices That Can Transform Your Life and Relationships* (Carol Stream, IL: SaltRiver, 2010).
54   Daniel J. Siegel and Tina Payne Bryson, *The Power of Showing Up: How Parental Presence Shapes Who Our Kids Become and How Their Brains Get Wired* (New York: Ballantine Books, 2021).

how other future relationships and events will play out. Where we place our attention, neurons in the brain are activated and wire to that "experience," creating a neurological connection: "Neurons that fire together wire together."[55] Millions of neural networks in the brain act like highways to lead us to "safety" and understanding of prior and new experiences.

When parents consistently pay attention to their infants' needs, their brains come to expect that the world is a place that can be understood and meaningfully interacted with, even in times of trouble and pain. "Showing up [for our children] creates neural pathways that lead to selfhood, grit, strength, and resilience."[56] The overall goal is to have a child whose brain is integrated, so a child can "employ the more sophisticated functions of her brain even when confronted by difficult situations and respond to [her] world from a position of security, demonstrating more emotional balance, more resilience, more insight, and more empathy. . . . The child will not only be happier, but also much more socially adept, . . . get along with others, collaboratively solve problems, consider consequences, think about other people's feelings, and on and on."[57]

I can't imagine anyone who wouldn't want more securely attached children in the world. Fred Rogers said: "Children who have learned to be comfortably dependent can become comfortably independent but also comfortable with having people depend on them. They can lean, stand, and be leaned upon because they know what a good feeling it is to be needed."[58]

An infant is born utterly helpless and dependent on their caregiver to meet all their needs and help regulate their nervous system. An attachment bond is created by repeated care transactions and attunement between mother and infant. Her ability to predict and empathize with what her baby needs is attunement. Infants need to be fed, bathed, burped, played with, cared for, cuddled, and rocked, and they use signal cries to meet their needs.

An attuned mother hears her infant's cry and comes quickly to give soothing and care. She learns to predict the needs before they occur or remains

---

55   Siegel and Bryson, *The Power of Showing Up.*
56   Siegel and Bryson, *The Power of Showing Up.*
57   Siegel and Bryson, *The Power of Showing Up.*
58   Rogers, *You Are Special.*

curious, looking for solutions while demonstrating empathetic love and concern—attunement.

Her stable nervous system teaches her young infant that it can rely on her to co-regulate, to help settle down its inward distress and help the infant be at peace. Each time the infant's needs are met, it's as though the caregiver is making a deposit into an attachment bank. The infant finds rest in the attachment (the connection) cycle: hunger, soothe, rest. They're learning to trust their mother, themselves, and the world. This attachment teaches their body that distress doesn't stay forever and they're never alone. Their internal working model of the world and others: *I have a need. I cry, and Mom comes to help me. I am safe and loved. The world is a good place, and people are trustworthy.*

Securely attached babies will grow up feeling comfortable using their attachment figure as a secure base to regulate affect and arousal and promote the expression of feelings and communication while exploring their new world. Their caregivers can stabilize their worlds to create safety, no matter what. Securely attached children know they are valuable and loved.

A Brief History of Discovering Attachment Styles

The roots of a child's ability to cope and thrive, regardless of circumstance, lie in that child's having had at least a small, safe place (an apartment? a room? a lap?) in which, in the companionship of a loving person, that child could discover that he or she was lovable and capable of loving in return. If a child finds this during the first years of life, he or she can grow up to be a competent, healthy person.

—Fred Rogers

In 1969, a test known as the Infant Strange Situation, conducted by the researcher Mary Ainsworth, collected evidence on attachment styles by studying infants and their mothers. Throughout the infants' first year of life, observers would visit their homes and catalog what the mothers were doing and each child's reactions. Was the mother responsive, sensitive, and consistent with her baby's signal cries and bids for connection? Were her responses prompt? Was the caregiver receiving the cue and making sense of the child's inner world to predict (attune/pay attention to) the needs and "respond in a predictable, timely, sensitive, and effective manner?"[59]

Next, Ainsworth had the mothers and infants come to an unfamiliar room for observation. In the room were toys for the child to play with. The researchers would allow the mother to play and interact with her baby then leave the child alone or with a stranger for a few minutes to see how the child would respond when reunited. Ainsworth discovered, based on their responses to the experiment, that infants have either secure or insecure attachments. Her work revolutionized the field of attachment and how child development is strongly connected to our first heartbeat—mother.

Ainsworth identified that all infants fell into three categories: secure attachment, insecure avoidant attachment, or ambivalent (anxious) attachment. Each attachment style demonstrated different characteristics and behaviors based on how the caregivers did or didn't respond to the infants' needs with attunement. This research was the foundation of Fred Rogers' training in child development in the early 1970s and continued to influence his work on television for decades.

Connection and Secure Attachments

Ainsworth observed that secure infants displayed the following specific characteristics:

- showed distress being separated from the mother, crying or whimpering
- greeted her when she returned, seeking proximity
- settled down quickly, as the mother offered aid and comfort
- showed willingness to play with the toys once the mother had returned

Secure attachment was observed in two-thirds of infants, with the other third being insecurely attached infants.[60]

---

59 Siegel and Bryson, *The Power of Showing Up*.
60 Siegel and Bryson, *The Power of Showing Up*.

What Factors Contribute to Secure Attachment?

Protection

The child knows and trusts the care and wisdom of their parent/caregiver. They feel protected and well taken care of, a "felt safety." If there is a need, fear, or worry, they can take it to their wise adult and remain safe.

Presence and Support

Parents are compassionate to their child's needs, understand their uniqueness, and "get them." Children are known, seen, and heard. They have a sense that their parent/caregivers are dependable and support them in becoming their best. There is no doubt that they will have their back in any situation.

Autonomy and Independence

Acting as a secure base, parents allow a child to explore, make mistakes, and learn from their world. Parents give the child the freedom, with guidance, to become their own person, fostering gradual independence. They recognize that a child grows from each experience without hovering over or stifling their growth.

Relaxation

Children feel at ease with parents to be themselves, play, wonder, and try new things. They "delight in each other's company." The child feels valued as an active contributor to the family unit.

Trust

"A sense that the world is predominately a good place—a conviction that even in the dark times, healing, understanding, and goodness will prevail." This mindset "empowers and allows authentic forgiveness."[61]

---

61 Heller, *The Power of Attachment.*

Resilience

Children see the world through a more optimistic lens. When adversity comes, securely attached children recognize that they can learn, grow, and survive.[62]

Characteristics of Secure Attachment in Children

- open to new experiences
- enjoy solving problems by trying out ideas
- make friends easily
- work well alone and with others
- offer forgiveness
- empathize with others' feelings and experiences
- make connections to self and life
- share and include others
- work hard
- are willing to be silly and playful
- articulate feelings and sensations
- recall detailed accounts of stories and events
- understand that grown-ups love them and come back
- have compassion for heartache and sadness
- are responsible for property
- follow expectations with prompting
- ask for help
- act resiliently after a mistake
- calm quickly when soothed
- trust authority figures
- gladly share what they know
- offer kindness and affection to others

---

62 Heller, *The Power of Attachment.*

Broken Connection and Insecure Attachments

An insecurely attached child may view the world as a dangerous place in which other people are to be treated with great caution and see himself as ineffective and unworthy of love. These assumptions are relatively stable and enduring: those built up in the early years of life are particularly persistent and unlikely to be modified by subsequent experience.
—Jeremy Holmes

Avoidant Attachment

Avoidant attachment is an insecure style that was identified in 1969 by Mary Ainsworth's Infant Strange Situation observations with mothers and infants. When the mother left the room, the baby was *not* distressed by her absence. And while in her presence, he would often ignore her, play with toys, have little to no facial affect, and actively avoid eye contact. Avoidant children give off an air of self-reliance, often masking the distress felt within their bodies. An avoidantly attached infant already has an internal working model of *I'm on my own. People won't meet my needs. It's better to not ask than to ask and be dismissed. I'll just avoid depending on anyone.*

Researchers observed that the avoidant infant's caregivers were indifferent, detached, and insensitive to the child's needs: dismissive. They would meet their basic needs, possibly give them a toy, but there was no outward emotional connection or investment. At times, the exchanges could be viewed as transactional. Studies have shown that this type of behavior leaves a child feeling rejected as if their inner world isn't necessary or a priority: *What's the use of crying? Because they won't come right away, and when they do, they don't do what I want or need.*

The infant begins to develop an avoidant attachment style when their caregiver and their emotional reality don't match. Infants in the Strange Situation experiment continued to play with the toys, whether alone, with their mother, or with a stranger. What one may consider a well-adjusted, calm baby is actually one full of indifference and anxiety. "Even when the children are experiencing internal psychological distress, they learn the skill of minimizing their externally expressed need for attachment."[63] Their affect and faces remain blank and disengaged while anxiety churns within their bodies.

Imagine that you are a baby in your crib with a wet diaper. Naturally, you begin to cry so your mother will come and meet your needs. You cannot change it yourself and are entirely reliant on her to help you. She walks to your bedroom door and peers in. Your tiny body floods with warm relief. *There she is*, your small heart whispers. *I need my diaper changed, Mama.*

Without warning, she turns around, ignoring your needs, and leaves.

Panic, fear, and anger surge through you. *Why isn't she meeting my needs? She's the only one I can count on!*

If this interaction becomes a pattern, the baby will develop avoidant attachment. The rage or unmet need sinks into your tiny body. It quickly teaches you that she will not consistently meet your basic needs. She is not providing *enough* comfort, care, and attunement to you. When you do interact, your tiny body recognizes she is just "going through the motions," quick to deposit you back in a container (crib, bassinet, bouncy seat, etc.). You slowly stop crying out in distress and learn to soothe yourself. Who else is going to help you? *You're on your own, baby. Don't get attached, and never let them see you're upset. You cannot depend on anyone. You're independent and strong—avoid closeness and emotional connection at all costs! Attachment is painful and to hope requires too much risk!*

An avoidantly attached infant shuts down its desire and longing for attachment. "Avoidant children often become disconnected from their emotions and will fail to develop a robust sense of their hopes, dreams, desires, and longings. It is simply too painful to hold on to their longings, so they detach altogether."[64]

What Factors Contribute to Avoidant Attachment?

Isolation

The child is often left alone with little face-to-face interaction with adults.

---

63   Heller, *The Power of Attachment.*
64   Heller, *The Power of Attachment.*

Lack of Presence

Caregivers might be physically present but not emotionally present, and they are removed, so the child feels disconnected or as if "nobody is home."

Task-Based Presence

Parents are physically present only to teach them something. "I'm here for you, but only if you're practical and functional."

Absence of Touch

Children are left with "skin hunger" because they haven't been touched enough. They need appropriate and compassionate physical contact.

Emotional Neglect

Caregivers aren't sensitive to the emotional needs of the child. Care is not timely, high-quality, or adequate. Their dominant experience is consistent non responsiveness.

Expressive Dissonance

Parents might use facial expressions that don't match their emotional states (smiling when angry). Kids will often have trouble understanding, interpreting, or sending appropriate social cues later in life.

Disrupted Engagement

This may occur when a child or parent is ill, so secure attachment isn't established. The adult is unable to engage the attachment of their child.

Rejection

This takes place if the child suffers from rejection, whether covert or overt.[65]

Characteristics of Avoidant Attachment in Children

- independent and often too self-reliant for their age
- value activities over relationships

---

65   Heller, *The Power of Attachment.*

- connect more with animals or objects
- lack empathy
- are highly competitive
- lack confidence in their own abilities (fear of failure)
- are relatively isolated as they lack emotional engagement
- focus on self over others
- are task-driven
- are rule followers
- find emotions difficult and hard to label
- have difficulty maintaining eye contact
- don't ask for help
- won't explore new environments
- try to blend in by acting indifferent to new situations
- will create distance to feel safe when overwhelmed
- get defensive and place blame in conflict
- tend to live in the land of the literal and logical
- appear unattached to parents, caregivers, and strangers (don't pick favorites)
- practice perfectionism
- want everything to be predictable and manageable
- in stress, may show sudden and inexplicable tantrums, which are over quickly
- often deny or don't communicate[66] distress
- are uncomfortable with physical intimacy and affection

Strategies for Moving an Avoidant Child Toward Secure Attachment

- Take care of their emotional hurts, no matter how "minor" they seem to be.
- Look for opportunities to encourage, nurture, and interact with them regularly.
- Label sensations and feelings for them.

---

66 Kim S. Golding, *Observing Children with Attachment Difficulties in School: A Tool for Identifying and Supporting Emotional and Social Difficulties in Children Aged 5–11* (Philadelphia, PA: Jessica Kingsley Publishers, 2013).

- Normalize emotions, sensations, and crying as a reaction to sadness.
- Give them a voice without judgment: "How do you feel about _____?"
- Speak about the feelings you are experiencing.
- Practice eye contact: "Show me your eyes."
- Read books about feelings and emotional regulation.
- Use puppets to have children practice voicing their opinions and feelings.
- Emphasize when you see emotional growth.
- Teach the child what words they can use to ask for help, and come to their aid immediately, as you are creating new neurological pathways through positive experiences.
- Identify a key adult for them to engage each day, if not you.
- Give them access to pictures of expressions and word lists to identify feelings.
- Use sentence frames: "I feel _____ because _____." Or "I felt _____ when _____."
- Practice having them speak in a big, confident voice.
- Be consistent with correction, guidance, regulation, and input.
- Create a list of nurturing, self-soothing ideas when they're overwhelmed with anxiety.
- Use verbal affirmations, as they are imperative: "I may not be there yet, but I'll get there!"

Avoidant children are achievement-driven and value performance over relationships. They will "need help to focus on and express their feelings."[67] They blend into the background of your classrooms and are quick to respond to your requests to please you. Look and listen carefully to your students. Avoidant and secure can look similar, but what's underneath is a complex duality of the "unwanted child."[68] These children want to be close, but fear and uncertainty are aroused when their attachment system is activated. A teacher tends to rejoice

---

67 Golding, *Observing Children with Attachment Difficulties.*
68 Heather Geddes, *Attachment in the Classroom: The Links Between Children's Early Experience, Emotional Well-Being, and Performance in School* (London: Worth, 2017).

over children who "actively seek to meet their own needs in Kindergarten."[69] They don't have difficulty using the bathroom, snapping their pants, zipping their coats, or tying their shoes. As securely attached children do many of the same activities, insecure attachment does not draw attention. Avoidant children do their best work and easily receive awards for *most respectful* or *most responsible* in a behavioral program. But "don't be fooled by their helpfulness or pseudo-independence. It may be an anxiety-driven attempt to keep us 'sweet' so that we don't get too close, or alternatively, get angry with them and hurt them. As these children have experienced things being out of control, they make themselves feel safer now by doing whatever they can to have some sense of control. . . . These children are at risk of developing compulsive tendencies, although in milder forms, the behaviors enable children with an avoidant attachment style to be highly functional in school."[70]

Because children with avoidant attachment are often awarded for their achievements, you will see their attachment systems flare with unexpected surprises, perceived slights, or something as simple as not performing a task perfectly the first time.

****

David is crazy about Brianna. They attend the same church, and their mothers are part of various clubs, where they often interact outside of school. It's natural for children to pair up with familiar faces in the classroom, and these two are no different. I will occasionally see him rub her back or say something kind to her while she's creating at the art center. When we write about people we love, he'll add her name to the list.

David comes to school ready to learn. His mother, a certified teacher, spent the time teaching him his letters and numbers, so he is a self-reliant little boy. He's tall, quiet, and kind; he rarely speaks and is always on task.

---

69   Louise Michelle Bombèr, *Inside I'm Hurting: Practical Strategies for Supporting Children with Attachment Difficulties in Schools* (London: Worth, 2007).

70   Bombèr, *Inside I'm Hurting*.

Shortly before Thanksgiving, a colleague who has David's older brother comes to find me in the hallway. "Do you have Simon's little brother in your class? His dad moved out this weekend." My heart sinks. *Ugh.* Divorce is always challenging, but it's devastating and frightening to a kindergartener.

The news puts me on high alert. Knowing David displays avoidant attachment, I realize it could come out in different ways: behavior, dramatic play, physicality, writing, or emotional distress over something minor.

I begin to observe him and wait for the right time. Children will always signal the correct time if we listen and remain available.

"Anything you want to talk to me about?" I ask him, ruffling his blond hair during free play. He's focused on the playdough as he constructs a rocket.

"I'm making a rocket," he says, smiling up at me.

It's not the right time. Two days later, though, it is, when Brianna comes inside from recess in tears. David wouldn't play with her outside, as he usually did, and had been cruel. When I call him over to the table where she and I are seated, he quickly sits down and diverts his eyes.

"I was sad to hear that you said Brianna had an 'ugly face' at recess."

He bores a hole in the table with his gaze.

"You love your friend Brianna. Can you see that she's sad right now?"

He looks at her and nods.

"I know you didn't mean those angry words, David. I don't think she's who you're angry with." I choose to lean into the pauses, watching his body, his breathing. Even with his head bent low, I notice his ears have turned red, and he sucks in his breath with short, labored chops. "David, are you angry with your daddy?"

His tears come as a sweet release. Big, racking sobs heave his tiny body. *Tears are so healing.*

Brianna places her hand on his arm and rests her head against him. "I'm sorry you're sad, David."

Her compassion makes him cry harder. David wraps his arms around her in a hug and cries his heart out. Sometimes, all we need is a good cry and a bit of understanding.

Fred Rogers believed in genuine connection with children: "If the child trusts you, very often, what happens to be on his or her mind will just spill out."[71] It's true. I've had countless moments where children barely make it inside the door before they're disclosing abuse, sharing joy, revealing traumatic events they've witnessed, and detailing their fears. As they see the face of "sweet relief," the dam simply bursts. Their nervous system signals safety, and the floodgates open. "The way you are right now, the way down deep inside you . . . it's you I like."

David was convinced that he was supposed to navigate the big feelings all by himself. Avoidantly attached children see adults as rejecting or dismissive. He'd been living with a mother who did all she could to hide her chaos. He wasn't allowed to discuss his feelings with anyone because it might expose the lies about her marriage. As the details emerged, I learned the home situation was filled with screaming, depression, and infidelity. His mother had needed a compliant little helper, as she was profoundly depressed and had been focused on her crumbling marriage for years.

Research tells us that avoidant attachment is developed when an infant has caregivers who aren't emotionally present and responsive. Parents may discourage or ignore outwards signs of emotions and distress, such as crying, and actively separate from them due to their inability to cope. They often have unrealistic expectations of their children emotionally, academically, and developmentally. When children have needs, they are often met with harsh, abrasive, and neglectful responses, causing the children to retreat into themselves. Emotions are not okay or welcome, and they're shamed if they allow feelings to make any appearance. Although the overwhelming feelings cause a disconnect for the caregiver, the child takes on the shame and receives some clear messages:

I'm bad, not welcome, or enough.

Be good—don't make a scene or let others know you have a need.

Avoidantly attached children are easily missed in a classroom setting or family system. Our attention is naturally pulled to overt behaviors in a classroom setting or when two or more children are present. The squeakiest wheel gets the most oil, so we need to look and listen more carefully.

---

71   Amy Hollingsworth, "How My Unexpected Friendship with Mister Rogers Got Me Through 2 Breakdowns," HuffPost, June 22, 2018, https://www.huffpost.com/entry/mister-rogers-friendship_n_5aec5e77e4b0ab5c3d64bfdf.

Ambivalent (Anxious) Attachment

I believe there's no time in life when stability is more important than in its early infancy. That's because there's no other time when the world is so new, so unfamiliar, so seemingly in constant change and no other time when we have so little experience to bring to understanding the world. . . . The early, deep sense of constancy of care may be our most important resource in coping with the perpetual changes in the world around us and in our lives. As children experience the sometimes-unsettling transitions from day to night, summer to winter, they need to know that even in the darkness and cold, there will be care until light and warmth return.

—Fred Rogers

Ambivalent (anxious) attachment was also observed in the Strange Situation. Researchers noted that ambivalent infants cried inconsolably when their mothers left, but also when they returned. The mother's presence provided little to no relief from the anxiety of being left or rejected. Ambivalent infants often ignored the toys, as they were overwhelmed with anxiety and desperate for reassurance and connection. Many became clingy and then displayed anger, punishing the mother with other distressing behaviors for leaving.

The research indicates that the infants' responses are "typically an outcome of a mis-attunement between the child's needs and the parent figure's attention, illustrated by the child's inability to be soothed [regulated] or return to safety upon the mother's return."[72] Often an ambivalent attachment is created because the parent has unaddressed childhood trauma that interferes with regulating their own child. Ambivalent attachment happens when parents are inconsistently available, perceptive, and responsive. Parents tend to intrude on the child's world with their own emotional distractions and states.

Imagine you are once again a baby in your crib with a wet diaper. You hear Mom outside your room and begin to cry so she'll come to meet your need. It

---

72   Nicole LePera, *How to Do the Work: Recognize Your Patterns, Heal from Your Past, and Create Your Self* (New York: Harper Wave, 2021).

worked this morning, and she had been happy to see you. But while you were napping, she received a call about one of her siblings, who was in crisis. Now she hears your cry but continues talking loudly on the phone, ignoring you. You hear her voice, and it creates excitement and anger simultaneously in you. *Why isn't she coming to get me?* You roll onto your side and scream louder, and she peeks into the room. You're elated. *There she is! Mama!* She looks at you, holding the phone to her ear, and pulls the handle on the door, leaving. *What? No! Mama, I have a need! Mama, come back! I'm confused. This worked last time. Why is it not working now?*

Ambivalent attachment is an insecure attachment created when a parent is "hot and cold" in meeting their infant's needs. As you could see in the above example, the mother had previously met the child's needs, attuning to her infant, but the child was neglected when her own emotional state became turbulent and unstable. If this becomes a pattern, happens frequently, or becomes habitual, then an ambivalent attachment develops.

Such ambivalent attachment also damages our ability to master the concepts of object permanence and object consistency. The cognitive skills are developed after eighteen months of age and are founded in a child's ability to know that an object is still present when it's out of sight. That's why young children enjoy peekaboo (a game Fred Rogers regularly plays on the *Neighborhood*). The face "reappears," teaching the baby that we never really left, affirming their trust in our return. This is why children with ambivalent attachment panic when their parents leave, because "they might as well have dematerialized."[73] Object constancy relates to the idea that although they have exited the room or left the child in the care of others, they will indeed return, as they do consistently. In my classroom, we have taken to repeating Fred Rogers' words: "Grown-ups come back because they *want* to." I emphasize that I will keep them safe and loved until I hand them back to their mommy, and I offer hugs, back rubs, supportive regulation, and empathetic concern.

Diane Poole Heller, PhD, argues that the "ability to detect object permanence and object constancy enables [children] to develop a sense of continuity with their primary attachment figures over time."[74] If the caregivers are inconsistent and unpredictable, it creates high anxiety levels in the child as they wonder, *Are*

---

73 Heller, *The Power of Attachment.*
74 Heller, *The Power of Attachment.*

they going to come back? Will they forget about me? Am I all alone? Who will meet my needs? Will there always be someone who will take care of me?

Plagued with doubts and fears, ambivalent children find it challenging to relax, to have peace that they won't have to meet their own needs. This creates an inner turmoil and anxiety in the baby or young child that heightens their hyper-vigilant state and takes away a consistent model for emotional regulation. When a mother is not regulated, the baby will feel it and know it. We can only be as regu-lated as our environment. A child growing up with ambivalent attachment begins to attune to the parent's emotional states instead of the parent attuning to theirs.

As the ambivalent child grows, the parent will often see them as a "surro-gate spouse" or confidant, so they cannot flee from their parent's emotional roller coaster. Children who grow up as hypervigilant learn how to predict and manip-ulate a parent's emotional states to receive any connection they can.

What Factors Contribute to Ambivalent Attachment?

Insufficient Co-regulation
Without receiving predictable care, their *affect modulation*—that is, their ability to navigate their emotional terrain—wasn't met with their parent's presence or consistent receptivity.

Interrupted Regulation
This occurs when a child is trying to relax and calm themselves during a moment of high-quality attention and love by the parent, but the parent suddenly disrupts the experience without any warning.

Overstimulation
When children are learning to regulate themselves, they typically require lots of space to find their own rhythm and to develop healthy boundaries. Because mothers have their own agendas and needs, they will often ignore, fail, or intrude on their children, worrying that they aren't loved by the child, and thus they overstimulate the child.[75]

---

75 Heller, *The Power of Attachment.*

Characteristics of Ambivalent Attachment in Children

- hypervigilant about the emotions of others and teacher
- preoccupied with "what's next" or when teacher may be leaving them with a specialist
- follow the teacher physically or with their body in their chair around the room (proximity seeking)
- difficulty staying on task
- need reassurance of love
- crave affection, attention, and touch
- speak impulsively (logic later)
- have difficulty with solitary play
- overly chatty and social, resulting in discipline
- possess a large vocabulary
- exaggerate, are hypersensitive and jealous
- may have difficulty sharing friends and teacher/parent
- suffer from departure stress
- overly affectionate with strangers
- observant of details and compliment often
- have difficulty controlling their emotions and self-soothing
- may cry easily or become overstimulated
- overly preoccupied with friendships and will often be in relational conflicts
- will try to micromanage in the classroom

Strategies for Moving an Ambivalently Attached Child Toward Secure Attachment

- Welcome their big emotions and allow them a safe place to express how they feel without judgment; they've often been told or received the messages they are "too much," "too needy," or "too emotional/dramatic."
- Remind them that you are a wise adult and can take care of things—release them from the burden of being older than they are.
- Reassure them that you aren't going anywhere so they can relax; and if you need to leave, tell them when you will return.

- Let them know they can't lose your love, regardless of how they behave or achieve.
- Give them your undivided attention; put your phone away.
- Use eye contact and touch; lean in or squat down while they are telling you something important.
- Compliment their strengths and point out ways you see them "growing" emotionally, physically, and academically.
- Use them as a leader and peer helper for children who are less confident.
- Give them time when they are upset to calm down and feel safe.
- Teach them strategies to use when they are scared and anxious.
- Use mindfulness and grounding activities.
- Use nonverbal attunement: winks, smiles, and gestures.
- Empathize with their big feelings first, before moving to logical responses.
- Hold them when they're crying or dysregulated.
- Give them strategies to manage their emotions when they are overwhelmed (fight/flight).

****

We all long to be cared for, and that longing lies
at the root of our ability to be caregivers.
—Fred Rogers

Caleb's family relocated from California. As he was introduced to me, he kept his eyes on the floor as if they would dig a hole right back to where he came from. This is nothing new for me. Most children will barely speak for the first few days as they observe their surroundings and wait for their own unspoken equivalent of reassurance. Silence is the norm. His older middle-school-age sister, Cadence, was equally quiet and nervous at the first meeting but smiled when I complimented her.

In California, their mother had stayed home with her children, but now she needed to work to pay for the moving expenses, and her children walked into an empty house each day. Over the next month, Caleb demonstrates an eagerness for pleasing me. He values neat work and is never found off task. I can count on him to be a responsible partner for other children who need a role model, and he befriends another boy, who is cut from the same cloth. I'm relieved to see the two running around the playground together, as it's a sign that Caleb is thriving in his new environment in kindergarten.

One Tuesday afternoon, during writing time, two of my precocious boys, Aaron and Ian, are sitting at a table playing with their pencils like swords—not meeting my expectations for responsibility or safety. I instruct them to clip down on the behavior chart.

We have a rainbow behavior clip chart in my classroom. Get to the top, and you earn a prize. Get to the bottom and there are consequences. These two boys are one color away from "Let's have a talk with your teacher."

Caleb sits behind them, on task, unaware that they're closing in on an extensive conversation. As the two boys begrudgingly return to their work, Caleb's sweet voice begins to call out: "Aaron."

I look up at Aaron. He's not one for self-control, so I know I will have to coach him through the moment.

"Aaron," Caleb repeats, unaware of the colossal plight he's creating for his five-year-old buddy.

I shake my head no, and Aaron wills himself to not turn around. The anguish is evident in the way he crinkles up his nose and sucks in his breath. On the edge of a rainbow, one must make an excellent choice. What will he choose?

"Aaron! Turn around!" The agitation is apparent in Caleb's voice. It's clear Caleb does not understand the gravity of the situation and needs reassurance that he's not losing a friendship with his friend.

As in most social coaching, you must be flexible and discern what will help the dysregulated child feel seen, heard, and loved quickly. He needs reassurance and connection from both Aaron and me.

"Aaron, please walk over and place your hand on Caleb's shoulder," I instruct. Aaron shuffles over to Caleb, who already looks upset and confused.

Kindergarten is like an ER. What is the situation? How do I do no harm? What is broken?

"Aaron, tell Caleb why you can't talk with him right now."

"I'm almost on red."

Much to my surprise, Caleb bursts into tears.

"Caleb, come sit with me." Now the entire class looks my way. "Keep writing," I instruct them and pat the table in front of me to indicate Caleb can sit on the table and face me. He quickly scoots up and, when his eyes meet mine, begins to cry harder.

"Sweetheart, he isn't ignoring you because he wants to. You know that Aaron is your friend," I begin.

His tiny body shakes as he sucks in breath after breath. Clenching his teeth, he balls his fists, angry and barely able to get out his words. "*They* always ignore me. *They* look past me. *They* never see me."

At that moment, I instantly know why he's upset. In California, his mother was home, present and consistent. Now he walked home to an empty house with his sister, where they were alone for hours. Everything had changed. Most likely, his parents were exhausted and preoccupied when they returned. How often had I done the same thing with my own children, just trying to survive the day? I had missed moments to truly connect. Distraction is a thief.

"Caleb, look at my face." His dark brown eyes, glistening with fear, connect with mine. "I see you," I tell him. "Every day you come to school, I promise, I will see you. I will always see you." As if the air has been let out of a balloon, he flops forward onto my chest and wraps his arms around my neck tightly.

As I dismiss my students at the end of the day, Caleb gives me a high five and turns to leave. I place my hand on his shoulder and bend down to meet his eyes.

"I see you," I whisper to him.

His face lights up with happiness, and he replies, "I see you too."

Our ritual continues for the next four years. On the last day of the school year, he returns to the gate and says, "We're moving to Texas." I'm disappointed because I hoped we would keep up the routine until he left elementary school.

"Do you know what's the greatest thing about love?" I ask him.

"What?" he replies into my chest as he hugs me tightly.

"It follows us wherever we go. My love will be all around you, even in Texas."

****

Disorganized Attachment

Disorganized attachment, added in the 1990s by Mary Main, a protégé of Ainsworth, was identified when an infant during the Strange Situation had "trouble deciding how to respond when the mother returns to the room, and as a result, demonstrated disorganized, disoriented, or chaotic behavior. Disorganized attachment results when children find their parents *severely* unattuned when the parents are frightening and or/when the parents themselves are frightened."[76]

A disorganized infant grows accustomed to inconsistency, neglect, and fear. These deficits override the child's need for an attachment system, placing more importance on survival—at all costs. Their attachment figure was supposed to offer comfort, soothing, and co-regulation, but instead they are a place of terror or are terrorized. Adversity such as domestic violence causes the mother to live in a state of hypervigilance, which leaves her unable to regulate another person. The child's nervous system, also unable to regulate, learns to not be at rest, to mistrust their own body sensations/cues, and adjusts the behavior to stay alive. Disorganized attachment is true to its name, slamming ambivalence and avoidance together without any predictability. The only thing that's predictable is the unpredictability in a child with disorganized attachment.

Disorganized children are often the hardest to relate to because their outward behaviors are the armor they use to shield their terror, mistrust, and stress. I hope that we will learn to look at all behavior as a way they communicate to us what they need—connection. Children displaying a lot of controlling, manipulative, and aggressive behaviors, or overly compliant and withdrawn behavior, are signaling that they feel anxious, distressed, and insecure.[77]

Going back to the example of the baby wearing the wet diaper in the crib, their mother may try to meet their needs, if she's not defending her life or dealing with addiction and other adverse situations. The child may be passed around to anyone who can look after them or might stay in a day-care situation most days, where his needs aren't the priority. What does he hear? People yelling, cussing, crying, glass shattering, doors slamming, loud music? Noise is most likely constant and unrelenting. There is no, or very little, time for quiet soothing. Nothing

---

76 Siegel and Bryson, *The Power of Showing Up.*
77 Golding, *Observing Children with Attachment Difficulties.*

in their world is predictable, constant, calming, safe, or explained. They're left alone inside their baby body to soak it up like a sponge, a sponge that will eventually become heavy with longing, fill with rage, and cry out with extreme behaviors or dissociative tendencies. This is my kindergartener Blue Eyes.

What Factors Contribute to Disorganized Attachment?

Family Turmoil

Many of our children with four or more ACEs also have disorganized attachment. Home life is unstable and toxic due to divorce, depression, domestic violence, incarceration, addictions, and poverty.

Emotional Irregularity

A hallmark of disorganized attachment is the extreme shift in emotional states, where they are elated one minute and filled with rage the next. It is unpredictable and often frightening. Many times, the parents will act one way to another adult or stranger while verbally abusing the child a few minutes later.

Confusing or Mixed Messages in Communication

Paradoxical injunctions, double binds, and mixed signals (simultaneous "come here" and "go away" messages) are fundamentally confusing to children. When parents create unsolvable problems that set kids up to fail, it may affect the children later on. They may experience shame, fear of failure, a decrease in their creativity and ability to be a problem solver. Inevitably, they lose their sense of self, power, and voice.[78]

Characteristics of Disorganized Attachment in Children

- controlling within peer relationships, leading to a lack of friendships
- demonstrate a diminished range of emotions
- may provoke, bully, or challenge others to maintain feelings of being in control
- may have poor stress tolerance, which detracts from learning

---

78 Heller, *The Power of Attachment*.

- may appear compliant but resist attempts to be helped or comforted
- although often hyperaroused, some cope with excessive feelings of stress by dissociating—appearing "switched off"
- may be unable to accept being taught and/or are threatened by others knowing more than them, as this triggers overwhelming feelings of humiliation
- hypervigilant to what is going on around them, making it difficult to concentrate or attend to a task
- experience strong feelings that can be overwhelming
- may portray a pseudo-mature caregiving role
- likely to be underachievers and possibly at a very immature stage of learning
- tend to be anxious and inattentive
- may demonstrate highly compulsive or obsessive behaviors, which allow them to hold on to a rigid control
- may demonstrate more obsessive preoccupations with being noticed through a combination of aggressive and coy behaviors
- struggle in relatively unsupervised settings, such as the playground or transitioning/moving between lessons
- frequently afraid but tend to mask anxiety through more aggressive and powerful behaviors
- anxiety may be expressed as controlling, omnipotent, and knowing everything already
- may be either quiet and withdrawn or loud and aggressive
- their immaturity and rigid controlling style of relating to other children can lead to social isolation[79]

Strategies for Moving a Disorganized Attached Child Toward Secure Attachment

- Develop a dependable routine, which calms their anxiety about what will happen next.
- Provide highly safe environments.

---

79 Golding, *Observing Children with Attachment Difficulties.*

- Weave low-key, quiet routines into each day.
- Use empathetic questioning and listening that is calm and nonconfrontational.
- Offer safe physical touch often.
- Use the child's name often with an affectionate tone of voice.
- Give the child a safe place to go if they are overwhelmed, anxious, or afraid.
- Help the child feel emotionally "held" and "contained" when they're distressed.
- Use kind facial expressions.
- Give one- or two-step directions, as many steps are too much.
- Recognize that a disorganized child may be developmentally much younger than their actual age.
- Recognize what triggers the child to act out physically and emotionally and create a plan.
- Provide adequate nutrition and hydration.
- Remain flexible and offer choices and compromises.
- Allow the child time to calm down when dysregulated; don't talk too much.
- Offer concrete, rhythmic activities; they often soothe disorganized children.
- Use weighted blankets if they need to cuddle.
- Identify a key adult the child can visit if a break is needed.
- Emphasize eye contact.
- Use discipline that's fair, immediate, and explained—emphasize that they can't lose your love.
- Recognize that they may need your help facilitating conflict resolution, using kind words, and labeling feelings and sensations.
- Be aware that secondary trauma is real; ask for help when needed, participate in self-care, and try not to take their behavior personally.
- Understand where they may activate any trauma you may need to address.
- Celebrate small victories.

Unless relationally altered with intentional methods, childhood attachment styles remain consistent into adulthood. Researchers have followed infants from various studies and have observed that, although our coping techniques become more strategic and sophisticated, our attachment styles don't change. We simply get better at hiding our authentic selves.

****

You cannot lead a child to a place of healing
if you do not know the way yourself.
—Karyn Purvis

She's a wisp of a thing—thin hair cut into a bob, pink and purple outfit that hangs on her gaunt body, brown eyes that have seen too much for her short five years. She's a "foster to adopt," one of her dads explains to me, but it's going to be a difficult road, as she is Native American and the tribe wants her returned as soon as her mother is clean and sober.

The couple, Dave and Kurt, has already adopted Sarah, currently a fourth grader and thriving, but Tiffany has been giving them a crash course in disorganized attachment. There's been so much rage! Although she's a mere sixty pounds, she's managed to pull four doors off their hinges and punch holes in her bedroom wall.

"You should see her when she's mad," Sarah pipes in. "She gets crazy!"

"We're doing the best we know how to do, but there are nightmares and tantrums," Dave explains, as I watch Tiffany coloring a picture, lost in thought. "Some days she'll eat and be cooperative, and the next minute she's acting like we're out to hurt her, refusing to let us touch her or hug her."

His eyes fill with tears, and I reach my hand out to squeeze his arm.

"We recognize that it may be difficult," Kurt assures me, "but you can call us anytime you need. I work from home and can be over here in five minutes."

I laugh. "Don't worry, I'll take good care of her. I'm in your corner now."

The next few months, Tiffany begins to adapt to our classroom environment without many reminders. Our days become predictable as she's eager to play with her new best friend, Sophie Lynn, with whom I partnered her from day one. Sophie Lynn has a quiet, kind presence. Secure in who she is, she bolsters Tiffany's confidence and celebrates when she succeeds. (She's an "old soul" and a gift as far as this teacher is concerned.) Tiffany's quick adjustment has more to do with their friendship than my teaching, guaranteed. The two become inseparable, and Tiffany begins to thrive. It's a reminder of what a little love can do. Each day, Kurt waits with his arms outstretched, scooping her up like a feather, and life is good.

Not that there aren't mishaps here and there. Some mornings, the door opens, and Tiffany is pushed in gently, arms crossed, holding her shoes, her hair still sticking up from her sleep. "It's been a bad morning," Dave remarks.

And I say, "I've got her."

She crawls up into my lap while the class dances to their sight word videos. I rock her back and forth until I feel her relax. Then I whisper down to her, "Pigtails or braids?" This is how we roll. Whatever she needs, we're there to pick up the pieces. Slowly, her small world becomes people attuning to her needs and proving that the world can be a safe place through each interaction.

But around December, there's a dramatic shift in Tiffany. She begins to distance herself from Sophie Lynn. It starts in small ways—her not wanting Sophie Lynn to sit with her during book box time or partner up during center time—and comes to a head one recess. Sophie Lynn enters the room in a puddle of tears, and Tiffany refuses to speak to me, sitting down at the table in a stoic and dissociated state. While the other students go on to music class, I keep the girls behind so we can talk.

I have the girls sit on either side of me. Tiffany's pain is transparent as she hugs her knees, avoiding eye contact with either of us. This is where attunement comes in, and discernment. Attuning to a child is imperative as you read what they're telling you and what they aren't. Children want you to know the truth but are often unable to articulate it. Tiffany already considers both Sophie Lynn and me safe, but her anger is more profound and comes from a place of fear.

"Sophie Lynn, why don't you tell Tiffany why you're sad and crying," I urge softly.

"Why are you mad at me?" she cries as large tears roll down her cheeks. Attunement is about entering uncomfortable places with a child and fighting the urge to "make it better" right away.

I scoop Sophie Lynn to my side, so they're eye to eye. Tiffany grunts and buries her head into my side, not willing to talk. A slight panic threatens to rise up inside me. What if having them talk about it wasn't a good idea? Why, after all the progress, are we back here at the point of anger and distrust?

"How about I ask you some questions, and you can tell me if I'm right?" I ask. "Can you tell me yes or no at least?" She nods her head against my chest.

"Do you love your friend Sophie Lynn?"

Tiffany nods yes.

"Did she do something to make you mad?"

She shakes her head no.

Sophie Lynn looks up at me, puzzled. Then it hits me like a brick wall. She's been in several foster homes for short periods, and it's been over four months since she's arrived.

She's getting ready to leave, I think.

Severing ties to any attachments is far less painful than being torn away. It's a form of self-preservation.

"I've a feeling this might have something to do with your heart, huh?" I say into her hair as I wrap my arm around her. Sophie Lynn's hand rests softly on my leg, and I squeeze it, but her eyes stay glued to Tiffany. "Maybe you could tell Sophie Lynn that your heart is sad inside and that you're afraid."

"My heart is sad," she says, surprising me.

"I'm sorry," Sophie Lynn says.

"Are you afraid you'll have to leave soon and say goodbye?" I question.

"I always have to go away. Nobody wants me."

"Oh, honey, that's not true. We do. Both Sophie Lynn and I love you. So do your two daddies and Sarah. We aren't going anywhere." I hug her close, and Sophie Lynn scoots over to wrap both her arms around her friend's body. Here we were on my kindergarten classroom floor, a pile of people being honest and vulnerable. "I love you very much," I tell her. "I'm proud of you for telling us about how you're feeling."

"I love you too," Sophie Lynn says, and starts to cry again. Her empathy is such a gift. After giving each other another hug, I walk them to music class while they hold hands. Helping a child feel emotionally contained is about remaining curious, open, and willing to receive whatever they need to tell you. Disorganized attached children have changed me every time I witness their growth as they voice their fears, make lasting friendships, and kick shame in the face.

Fred Rogers speaks and greets children in 1994. Notice how he's holding the child's hand and making eye contact, as well as the body positioning. Lynn Johnson Collection.

Chapter 5:

We Are Foster Parents

"I'm Taking Care of You"

> The most important people in a child's life are
> that child's parents and teachers. That means parents
> and teachers are the most important people in the world.
> **—Fred Rogers**

Teachers are "foster parents" every new school year. We receive into our care children with developmental traumas—without control of their home environments. And sometimes without any previous paperwork. What interventions worked for their emotional outbursts? Why do they have difficulty regulating oversharing materials? Have they seen a counselor for their chronic skin picking? Why are they nervous about keeping the classroom door open? Children come to us as puzzles we are asked to decipher. We must also teach them how to read, write, compute, and regulate, all the while knowing that they will enter a new "foster" situation (classroom) to start all over again in a few short months. Perhaps we need to rethink the system, as it is traumatic for many students, especially those with attachment wounds.

Disorganized children and ACEs go together. Children from hard places need to heal relationally. In fact, one caring relationship is enough to foster resilience and hope, changing the trajectory of their lives. One caring relationship. Instead of focusing on the immense amount of data surrounding various trauma-informed practices, childhood behavioral models, and countless medical diagnoses afforded to educators, I decided to concentrate on repairing attachment in *all* my students. I would put all my effort into establishing safety, trust, connection, and support, regardless of where they fell on the attachment spectrum. Whether their attachment was just enough, too little, too unpredictable, or too terrifying, I had them covered.

Disorganized children pose a challenge and effort, but the gains far outweigh the headaches when we intentionally "choose them." Yes, you read that right. You *choose* them, although they might not choose you for a long while. Disorganized children feel unsafe inside their bodies, so our priority needs to be establishing "felt safety" first. Although all three insecure attachment styles create compromised nervous systems and stress reactions, a disorganized child has lost their ability to cope in most situations.

Adverse Childhood Experiences

The original ACE study, conducted at Kaiser Permanente from 1995 to 1997, is one of the largest investigations of the connection between childhood abuse, neglect, and household challenges and later-life health and well-being. Participants were asked to complete a questionnaire reporting traumatic experiences during childhood, and the responses were analyzed jointly with the participants' medical histories.[80] The results were staggering!

Researchers found an overwhelming correlation between developmental childhood trauma and poor health outcomes in adult life. Left unaddressed, ACEs will affect our relationships and influence the way we interact with the world. Sound familiar? ACEs are severe childhood traumas that are ongoing, exposing a child to chronic, prolonged toxic stress. The ten types of adverse childhood experiences can be broken into three different categories:[81]

---

80 "ACES & Toxic Stress," Center for Youth Wellness, 2017, https://centerforyouthwellness. org/ace-toxic-stress/.

81 Jody Carrington, *Kids These Days: A Game Plan for (Re)Connecting with Those We Teach, Lead, and Love* (Victoria, BC: FriesenPress, 2019).

Category of Abuse:

1. Physical abuse
2. Emotional abuse
3. Sexual abuse

Category of Neglect:

4. Physical neglect
5. Emotional neglect

Category of Household Dysfunction:

6. Growing up with someone in your home who suffers from mental illness
7. Growing up with someone in your home who suffers from substance abuse
8. Having an incarcerated relative
9. Witnessing the mother being treated violently
10. Divorced parents

According to studies reported by the Centers for Disease Control and Prevention (CDC) in 2019, ACEs are one of the major health issues in the twenty-first century, with statistics showing the following: one in six adults experiences four or more types of ACEs before eighteen years of age; five out of ten leading causes of death are associated with ACEs; 61 percent of adults have had at least one ACE and 16 percent have had four or more types of ACEs. Additionally, females and several racial/ethnic minority groups are at greater risk for experiencing four or more ACEs.[82] Many people do not realize that exposure to ACEs is associated with an increased risk for health problems across the lifespan.[83] In fact, ACEs can increase the risk of multiple issues, including the following:

---

82 "1-2-3 Care Toolkit," Spokane Regional Health District, 2021, https://srhd.org/1-2-3-care-toolkit.

83 "CDC Vital Signs: Adverse Childhood Experiences (ACEs): Preventing Early Trauma to Improve Adult Health," Centers for Disease Control and Prevention, November 5, 2019, https://www.cdc.gov/vitalsigns/aces/pdf/vs-1105-aces-H.pdf.

- adolescent pregnancy
- alcoholism
- chronic obstructive pulmonary disease (COPD)
- depression
- early initiation of sexual activity
- early initiation of smoking
- fetal death
- health-related quality of life
- illicit drug use
- ischemic heart disease (IHD)
- liver disease
- multiple sexual partners
- risk of intimate partner violence
- sexually transmitted diseases (STDs)
- smoking
- suicide attempts
- unintended pregnancies

We live in a world that has lost its way regarding caregiving.[84] Did you notice what was missing in the ACEs list? Relationship, regulation, attunement, and intention.

No one leaves their childhood without some difficulties and heartaches. Still, a child with developmental traumas has brain damage, and repairing these basic needs is essential to their emotional survival in our current world. It is up to parents, caregivers, and teachers to restore order, calm fears, and establish a secure base for children to "come home" to themselves to begin the process of repairing the damage.

What Is Toxic Stress?

All stress is not equal and can be divided into three distinct categories.

---

84 Purvis, Cross, and Sunshine, *The Connected Child.*

Positive stress response is a normal and essential part of healthy development, characterized by brief increases in heart rate and mild elevations in hormone levels. Some situations that might trigger a positive stress response are the first day with a new caregiver or receiving an injected immunization.

Tolerable stress response activates the body's alert systems to a greater degree as a result of more severe, longer-lasting difficulties, such as the loss of a loved one, a natural disaster, or a frightening injury. If the activation is time-limited and buffered by relationships with adults who help the child adapt, the brain and other organs recover from what might otherwise be damaging effects.

Toxic stress response can occur when a child experiences strong, frequent, and/or prolonged adversity—such as physical or emotional abuse, chronic neglect, caregiver substance abuse or mental illness, exposure to violence, and/or the accumulated burdens of family economic hardship.[85]

Toxic stress increases a child's heart rate, blood pressure, breathing, and muscle tension. Their thinking brain is knocked offline, and their stress responses (fight/flight or freeze/fawn/fold) for keeping safe become the priority. These same stress responses are activated by interpersonal relationships when children have insecure attachments. Without adequate adult support, this kind of prolonged activation of the stress response systems can disrupt the development of brain architecture and other organ systems and increase the risk for stress-related disease and cognitive impairment well into the adult years.[86]

Because our brains are not meant to function in a prolonged state of stress, the activation can produce long-term damage, such as loss of brain cells, damage to brain cell connections and neural pathways, enlargement and shrinkage of certain parts of the brain, and hyperactivity of certain parts of the brain. Early childhood, particularly ages zero to five, is an important window of opportunity for brain development. Toxic stress can result in changes to crucial parts of the brain.[87]

---

85 Purvis, Cross, and Sunshine, *The Connected Child.*
86 Purvis, Cross, and Sunshine, *The Connected Child.*
87 Purvis, Cross, and Sunshine, *The Connected Child.*

What's Your ACEs Score?

For each "yes" answer, add one point. The total number at the end is your cumulative number of ACEs.

Before your eighteenth birthday:

1. Did a parent or other adult in the household often or very often swear at you, insult you, put you down, humiliate you, or act in a way that made you afraid you might be physically hurt?
2. Did a parent or other adult in the household often or very often push, grab, slap, or throw something at you or ever hit you so hard that you had marks or were injured?
3. Did an adult or person at least five years older than you ever touch or fondle you, have you touch their body in a sexual way, or attempt or actually have oral, anal, or vaginal intercourse with you?
4. Did you often or very often feel that no one in your family loved you or thought you were important or special, or that your family didn't look out for each other, feel close to each other, or support each other?
5. Did you often or very often feel that you didn't have enough to eat, had to wear dirty clothes, and had no one to protect you, or that your parents were too drunk or high to take care of you or take you to the doctor if you needed it?
6. Were your parents ever separated or divorced?
7. Was your mother or stepmother often or very often pushed, grabbed, slapped, or had something thrown at her? Was she sometimes, often, or very often kicked, bitten, hit with a fist, or hit with something hard? Was she ever repeatedly hit for at least a few minutes or threatened with a gun or knife?
8. Did you live with anyone who was a problem drinker or alcoholic, or who used street drugs?
9. Was a household member depressed or mentally ill, or did a household member attempt suicide?
10. Did a household member go to prison?

Your ACEs Score: _____

Attachment Style Quiz by Diane Poole Heller, PhD

Instructions: When completing this questionnaire, please focus on one significant relationship—ideally a current or past partner, as the focus here is on adult relationships. This does not necessarily need to be a romantic relationship but must be the individual with whom you feel the most connection. Who is your primary "go to" person if you're sick, in trouble, want to celebrate, call with news, and so forth? This questionnaire is designed to be an interactive learning tool. Please highlight, circle, or comment on any statements that are particularly relevant to you or that you'd like to revisit for exploration at a later time. When responding, consider how strongly you identify with each statement. Using the scale below, respond in the space provided.

Please understand that this is not meant to be a diagnostic tool, but it's a good starting point to begin your personal exploration into your attachment styles.[88]

---

88   Diane Poole Heller, "Know Your Adult Attachment Style Mini-Questionnaire," Somatic Attachment Trainings and DARe Workshops, 2014. Used with permission.

Secure

		Disagree **0**	Sometimes Agree **1**	Mostly Agree **2**	Strongly Agree **3**
1	I feel relaxed with my partner most of the time.				
2	I find it easy to flow between being close and connected with my partner to being on my own.				
3	If my partner and I hit a glitch, it is relatively easy for me to apologize, brainstorm a win-win solution, or repair the misattunement or disharmony.				
4	People are essentially good at heart.				
5	It is a priority to keep agreements with my partner.				
6	I attempt to discover and meet the needs of my partner whenever possible and I feel comfortable expressing my own needs.				
7	I actively protect my partner from others and from harm and attempt to maintain safety in our relationship.				
8	I look at my partner with kindness and caring and look forward to our time together.				
9	I am comfortable being affectionate with my partner.				
10	I can keep secrets, protect my partner's privacy, and respect boundaries.				
	Section Total:				

Avoidant/Dismissive

		Disagree 0	Sometimes Agree 1	Mostly Agree 2	Strongly Agree 3
1	When my partner arrives home or approaches me, I feel inexplicably stressed—especially when he or she wants to connect.				
2	I find myself minimizing the importance of close relationships in my life.				
3	I insist on self-reliance; I have difficulty reaching out when I need help, and I do many of life's tasks or my hobbies alone.				
4	I sometimes feel superior in not needing others and wish others were more self-sufficient.				
5	I feel like my partner is always there but would often prefer to have my own space unless I invite the connection.				
6	Sometimes I prefer casual sex instead of a committed relationship.				
7	I usually prefer relationships with things or animals instead of people.				
8	I often find eye contact uncomfortable and particularly difficult to maintain.				
9	It is easier for me to think things through than to express myself emotionally.				
10	When I lose a relationship, at first I might experience separation elation and then become depressed.				
	Section Total:				

Anxious/Ambivalent

		Disagree 0	Sometimes Agree 1	Mostly Agree 2	Strongly Agree 3
1	I am always yearning for something or someone that I feel I cannot have and rarely feeling satisfied.				
2	Sometimes, I over-function, over-adapt, over-accommodate others, or over-apologize for things I didn't do, in an attempt to stabilize connection.				
3	Over-focusing on others, I tend to lose myself in relationships.				
4	It is difficult for me to say NO or to set realistic boundaries.				
5	I chronically second-guess myself and sometimes wish I had said something differently.				
6	When I give more than I get, I often resent this and harbor a grudge. It is often difficult to receive love from my partner when they express it.				
7	It is difficult for me to be alone. If alone, I feel stressed, abandoned, hurt, and/or angry.				
8	At the same time as I feel a deep wish to be close to my partner, I also have a paralyzing fear of losing the relationship.				
9	I want to be alone with my partner but feel angry at my partner at the same time. After anxiously awaiting my partner's arrival, I end up picking fights.				
10	I often tend to "merge" or lose myself in my partner and feel what they feel, or want what they want.				
	Section Total:				

Disorganized/Disoriented

		Disagree 0	Sometimes Agree 1	Mostly Agree 2	Strongly Agree 3
1	When I reach a certain level of intimacy with my partner, I sometimes experience inexplicable fear.				
2	When presented with problems, I often feel stumped, and they are irresolvable.				
3	I have an exaggerated startle response when others approach me unexpectedly.				
4	My partner often comments or complains that I am controlling.				
5	I often expect the worst to happen in a relationship.				
6	Protection often feels out of reach. I struggle to feel safe with my partner.				
7	I have a hard time remembering and discussing the feelings related to my past attachment situations. I disconnect, dissociate, or get confused.				
8	Stuck in approach-avoidance patterns with my partner, I want closeness but I am also afraid of the one I desire to be close with.				
9	My instinctive, active self-protective responses are often unavailable when possible danger is present—leaving me feeling immobilized, disconnected, or "gone."				
10	Because I am easily confused or disoriented, especially when stressed, it is important for my partner to keep arrangements simple and clear.				
	Section Total:				

Scoring

For each section, add up your responses and record your total number. The section with the highest number will likely correspond to your unique attachment style. You may discover a dominant style or a mix of styles.

This questionnaire is not meant to be a label or diagnosis. It is only intended to indicate tendencies and prompt more useful, precise personal exploration.

After generating your score, I'd suggest flipping back to the indicated style and rereading it with fresh eyes, thinking about yourself as a child.

People can be a mixture, but there tends to be one more dominant style.

Fred Rogers with young boy in bird coop at Green Chimneys. 1994. Lynn Johnson Collection.

Chapter 6:

When Trauma Enters the Story

"Sometimes I Don't Understand"

Be patient toward all that is unresolved in your heart.
—Fred Rogers

Trauma is perhaps the most avoided, ignored, belittled, denied, misunderstood, and untreated cause of human suffering.[89] It comes in like a flash of lightning, overwhelming our sensations and threatening to destroy our trust and safety. Trauma and I have had to make peace through countless counseling sessions. We have walked beside one another as I wrestled with what it needed to tell me. It led me back to attachment and intention and begged me to ask hard questions:

- What is trauma?
- What types of traumas are avoided, ignored, belittled, denied, misunderstood, and left untreated?
- How does trauma affect our brains, emotions, trust, and emotional safety?

---

89   Rachel Yehuda et al., "Transgenerational Effects of Posttraumatic Stress Disorder in Babies of Mothers Exposed to the World Trade Center Attacks During Pregnancy," *The Journal of Clinical Endocrinology & Metabolism* 90, no. 7 (2005): 4115–4118, https://doi.org/10.1210/jc.2005-0550.

- What can I do to heal unresolved trauma in myself and children?
- Could attachment repair be the answer to children suffering from ACEs?

If we have unprocessed stories of trauma and heartache, they will prevent us from fully meeting the needs of the children we love. It is up to us to take a fearless inventory of the skills we have and don't have, because children depend on us to help them weather storms. Taking honest stock of our stories will give us insight into our limitations and strengths. Fred Rogers said, "Some of my richest experiences have come out of the most painful times . . . those that were the hardest to believe would ever turn into anything positive."[90]

Pain, harm, and heartache break our trust in goodness. Children need someone to come alongside to guide them through the heartaches. Adults are facilitators of integration and containers for difficult moments. Children need adults, and adults need tools. We can't give what we don't have. Adults could very well lead children into more profound developmental pain and suffering without wholesome resources. "When we can lovingly turn toward our pain, expressed in various ways by our bodies, we often begin to find we have choices we couldn't see before."[91] What difficult experiences formed you? Who came alongside you offering comfort, understanding, or explanation? Fred Rogers called those people ones who "loved us into being." It only takes one, my friends. Just one. Let it be you. Let it be me.

Trauma is an experience that stuns us like a bolt from the blue; it overwhelms us, leaving us altered and disconnected from our bodies. Any or all of our coping mechanisms may be undermined, and we feel utterly helpless and hopeless. *Trauma is the antithesis of empowerment.*

Vulnerability to trauma differs from person to person depending on a variety of factors, especially age and trauma history. The younger the child, the more likely they are to be overwhelmed by common occurrences that might not affect an older child or adult.[92] Fred Rogers sincerely believed that helping children

---

90 Rogers, *You Are Special.*
91 Aundi M. Kolber, *Try Softer: A Fresh Approach to Move Us Out of Anxiety, Stress, and Survival Mode—and into a Life of Connection and Joy* (Carol Stream, IL: Tyndale Momentum, 2020).
92 Peter Levine and Maggie Kline, *Trauma Through a Child's Eyes: Awakening the Ordinary Miracle of Healing: Infancy Through Adolescence* (Berkeley, CA: North Atlantic Books, 2007).

understand "first experiences" was the best way to give care and love. When we have a cohesive narrative of our own story and experiences, we can predict the moments that need more engagement and attention. What mattered to us but was dismissed or left unanswered in our own hearts? **As we draw from the richness of our own childhood experiences, we can correct that which was broken for ourselves while passing on what we want children to really learn about the world.** You may have needed someone to take the time to speak about the loss of your grandmother, but they were consumed by their own pain and logistics. Now you can take the time, sit beside a student, and ask, invite, and hold space (containment) for whatever they need to voice about their losses. Your job is to be open and fully available. See how that works? *It's intentional until it's habitual.* Vulnerability is the capacity to enter the darkest rooms of our souls to stumble over the gold hiding in the shadows. Your pain is your power redefined for children.

Rogers urged: "Even if our childhoods were relatively problem-free, growing always presents us with difficulties to be overcome . . . and the memories of these difficulties are so easily awakened as our children encounter similar difficulties in their own time. It may be a little easier if we know ahead of time that some of the intensity we feel as we try to help our children with their hard times is very likely related to what we went through ourselves when we were children."[93]

Broken Connections and Trauma

Children trigger our developmental traumas because we "bring all we ever were and are to any relationship we have today."[94] Trauma interrupts our life story like a flood but universally connects us as a human race.

Dr. Peter Levine, an expert in healing trauma through a naturalistic and neurological approach, notes there are universal symptoms of trauma: "Whether it was an adult or a child that was dealt a blow greater than could be tolerated, distinguishing signs appear soon after the event. They are: 1) hyperarousal, 2) constriction, 3) dissociation, and 4) feelings of numbness and shutdown (or 'freeze'), resulting in a sense of helplessness and hopelessness. These reactions represent

---

93 Rogers, *You Are Special.*
94 Rogers, *You Are Special.*

universal symptoms. Together they characterize the essence of the mind and body's response; they are the telltale trademark of trauma."[95]

As we widen our understanding of what is traumatic to young children, it makes sense to take the time to integrate every experience, paying attention to what they tell us through language and behaviors. Prevention of the ill effects needn't be detective work if we create open dialogues with children. The younger the child, the more we will need to look and listen closely to their behavior, play, and physical complaints, which often reveal the inner turmoil present.[96]

Levine's research tells us that all children, especially infants and the very young, show trauma symptoms differently than adults. This is due to incomplete personality formation, dependency on their caregivers, restricted motor/language skills, and limited capacities to respond or cope. Children are totally dependent on their grown-ups to "read" and meet their needs for safety, support, nurturance, self-regulation, and reassurance.[97] Traumas will surface in their play, interaction with others, and new behaviors, fears, or fixations. Our attachment and nervous systems strongly influence how we respond to trauma, making it unique in the context of people's stories and past circumstances.

"Trauma is not what happens to you, trauma is what happens inside you as a result of what happened to you."[98] It is a "wound, injury, or shock"[99] to our system brought on by an event or a series of events. Emotional misattunement feels the same way when we are ignored, rejected, or abandoned. Trauma inevitably shatters "shalom" when we realize the world is a broken and fractured place.

Trauma is even more devastating for young children, as they have little to draw from to understand the event in context. Where information is missing, they write new narratives to understand and cope. Children often lay the blame for divorce, abuse, or everyday mishaps at their own feet. Trauma steals the ability

---

95   Levine and Kline, *Trauma Through a Child's Eyes*.
96   Levine and Kline, *Trauma Through a Child's Eyes*.
97   Levine and Kline, *Trauma Through a Child's Eyes*.
98   Dwana Young, "Dr. Gabor Maté—Trauma as Disconnection from the Self," NJ Resiliency Coalition, March 15, 2021, https://www.pacesconnection.com/g/NJ-Resiliency-Coalition/blog/dr-gabor-mate-trauma-as-disconnection-from-the-self.
99   "Trauma and Complex Trauma: An Overview," International Society for the Study of Trauma and Dissociation, https://www.isst-d.org/public-resources-home/fact-sheet-i-trauma-and-complex-trauma-an-overview/.

to name, articulate, ponder, and acknowledge the truth of a situation and its place in the story we are living. Their tiny bodies become hypervigilant, scanning the world for potential threats. Without help integrating the experience, a small fragment of the child is "left behind" or embedded into the sensations of the trauma.

Peter Levine said:

> Many "ordinary," everyday mishaps that we take for granted as inevitable facts of life can become traumatic, and the younger the child, the less obviously harmful those occurrences need to be to leave a traumatic impact. A "minor" fall, for example, can become traumatic if a child is not supported in processing it healthily and especially if she is shamed for "over-reacting" or labeled as "too sensitive." An elective medical procedure can also have long-term effects if the child is not adequately supported and prepared, and if his reactions are not empathetically received. . . . The adult's first task is to attend to his or her own emotional state since it's only in the adult's calm, competent, and reassuring presence that children find the space to resolve their tensions. **Who we are being is more important than what we are doing.** More accurately, who we are being when facing a difficult situation will dictate both the form and the impact of what we do.[100]

And what is our role as a child's teacher? Through meaningful open communication, we have the opportunity to circumvent and minimize the lasting effects of trauma. What is required isn't perfection but an unshakeable optimism that it will turn out alright. Good will win as we make a conscious choice to show up repeatedly because we *want* to.

We can't control every circumstance children encounter, but we can set them up with the assurances that they are loved, capable, resilient, and welcome to

---

100 Gabor Maté, foreword to *Trauma Through a Child's Eyes: Awakening the Ordinary Miracle of Healing—Infancy Through Adolescence*, by Peter Levine and Maggie Kline (Berkeley, CA: North Atlantic Books, 2007). Emphasis added.

run back into our love, no matter their age. Fred Rogers said, "It always helps to have people we love beside us when we have to do difficult things in life." Loving children "into being" is a messy process during which we learn to tune in to their natural rhythms, pacing, and leading without lecturing or manipulating the situation for our own benefit.

Traumatic Events

Traumatic events leave their mark on a person, family, community, and society. They stand in stark contrast to the world we knew as safe only the moment before. Most Americans can tell you what they were doing during the 9/11 terrorist attacks, much like they could decades ago when Pearl Harbor was attacked, Kennedy was assassinated, or (on the positive side) man first walked on the moon. Understanding a traumatic event as a collective experience makes it feel less random, deliberate, or evil. Tragedy can be used to move us to action, fight for injustice, make laws to keep us safer, and challenge us to look deeper into the motivations of the human heart. Traumatic events have united humanity for hundreds of centuries. Traumatic events can include

- natural disasters such as earthquakes and floods
- war and conflict or terrorist attacks
- being exposed to death, injury, or violence through work or volunteer roles
- being a victim of a crime (e.g., being raped, assaulted, held up, carjacked, or involved in a shooting)
- being exposed to an unexpected, tragic, or stressful event (e.g., the unexpected or violent death of a loved one; a complicated or violent childbirth; painful or degrading medical procedures)
- interpersonal violence and abuse
- severe lack of care, emotional connection, or neglect, particularly as a baby or young child, including prolonged separation from caregivers[101]

---

101 Maté, foreword to *Trauma Through a Child's Eyes*.

Traumatic events are easy to identify and rarely denied as experiences that need to be felt and dealt with. A child's response to a traumatic event depends on many factors, including whether they have experienced traumatic events in the past and whether they have a supportive family and community to shoulder the impact and burden.

Additionally, there are a number of other factors we as teachers should also look into and consider.

Severity of the Event

How serious was the event? How badly was the child or someone they love physically hurt? Did they or someone they love need to go to the hospital? Were the police involved? Were children separated from their caregivers? Were they interviewed by a principal, police officer, or counselor? Did a friend or family member die?

Proximity to the Event

Was the child actually at the place where the event occurred? Did they see the event happen to someone else, or were they the victim or one of the victims? Did they watch the event on television? Did they hear a loved one talk about what happened?

Caregiver's Reactions

Did the child's family believe that they were telling the truth? Did the caregivers take the child's reactions seriously? How did caregivers respond to the child's needs, and how did they cope with the event themselves?

Family and Community Factors

The culture, race, and ethnicity of children, their families, and their communities can be a protective factor, meaning that children and families have qualities and resources that help buffer against the harmful effects of traumatic experiences and their aftermath. One of these protective factors can be the child's cultural identity. Culture often has a positive impact on how children, their families, and their communities respond, recover, and heal from traumatic experiences. However, experiences of racism and discrimination can increase a child's risk for traumatic stress symptoms.[102]

****

Because young children's brains are still developing, they take in traumatic events through all their senses, and these events then lodge into their nervous system as implicit memory. "Their sense of safety may be shattered by frightening visual stimuli, loud noises, violent movements, and other sensations associated with an unpredictable, frightening event."[103] These frightening images tend to reoccur in the form of nightmares, new fears, and actions/play that reenact the event.[104] When a child cannot use language to connect to their overwhelming sensations, we must take the time and care to observe their behaviors.

> To begin, observe—but on an intuitive level. No checklists, no notes, no histories—just watch him. Watch him watching his world. Go silently behind his eyes to see his world. When you see what he feels, you will have learned all that you need to know. . . . Then begin!
> **—L. Tobin**

During his training in child development, Fred Rogers spent countless hours observing children, looking for patterns, and discussing his findings with his professors and colleagues. We often discount the power of simply observing a child's reactions and behaviors to gather evidence and insight. Careful, unbiased observation is developed through practice and intention. What do we know of the child's behavior before the event? How did they handle stress and fears prior? There is always a psychological component behind every behavior, if we're willing to listen to what it's communicating.

---

102 Sarah Peterson, "About Child Trauma," The National Child Traumatic Stress Network, November 5, 2018, https://www.nctsn.org/what-is-child-trauma/about-child-trauma.
103 "Early Childhood Trauma," Zero to Six Collaborative Group, National Child Traumatic Stress Network, 2010, http://www.safy.org/documents/how-to-help-youth-who-experience-trauma.pdf.
104 "Early Childhood Trauma."

Possible behaviors to note after a traumatic event include the following: a child absorbing the trauma/blaming themselves (low self-esteem/self-concept), low IQ, emotional regulation difficulties, destruction of property, self-harm, fearful avoidance, extreme startle response, clingy/fearful behavior in new situations, difficulty being consoled, difficulty sleeping/nightmares, regression in developmental skills (fine/gross motor), potty-training difficulty/bed-wetting, upset bowels/headaches, sudden speech issues, aggressive and impulsive behaviors, poor appetite, yelling/screaming/tantrums, lack of trust in adults and authority figures, and learning disabilities.[105]

Developmental Trauma

Dr. Gabor Maté, a physician with a special interest in childhood development, trauma, and addiction, said, "Children don't get traumatized because they get hurt. They get traumatized because they're alone with the hurt."[106] Due to childhood emotional neglect and toxic stress, developmental trauma is embedded in our attachment styles, nervous systems, and implicit memories. It rewrites how we view our stories to the detriment of our health and ability to emotionally regulate our bodies in times of stress. From the brain stem, the nervous system dictates the reality of a traumatized child.

Babies, for example, can't regulate themselves, so they send out signal cries to receive what they need, creating the reciprocal attachment dance with their caregivers. But without the vital, consistent contact with a caregiver, an infant will not establish a regulated nervous system of their own. They'll then adapt to an adult with a dysregulated nervous system doing whatever is needed to survive. Later, as an adult with unprocessed trauma, they will have difficulty creating secure attachments with their own infants (and students) and will go about their life frightened and unavailable.

Developmental trauma is inextricably interwoven with our physiology, our experience of safety or lack of safety, and our experiences of connectedness

---

105 "Early Childhood Trauma."
106 Laurie Udesky, "The Wisdom of Trauma: Gabor Maté, Peter Levine in Conversation About How the Body Heals from Trauma," PACEsConnection, June 23, 2021, https://www. pacesconnection.com/g/california-aces-action/blog/the-wisdom-of-trauma-gabor-mate-peter-levine-in-conversation-about-how-the-body-heals-from-trauma.

or isolation within our bodies.[107] Because relationships shape development, a collection of "ordinary" mishaps and misattunements can be as damaging as a catastrophic event over time.[108] Peter Levine states, "Trauma is not the event itself, rather trauma resides in the nervous system." It embeds within our systems, changing our reactions, reasoning, learning and function, identity, gene expression, health, and well-being—in short, every facet of our lives. Environmental stressors (think COVID-19) will also increase a young child's need for emotional regulation and support.

As I'll share with you in chapter 8, children suffering from insecure attachment have difficulty voicing and regulating on their own. *Co-regulation* occurs when "a person with a regulated nervous system helps another to regulate their dysregulated system."[109] A regulated nervous system can be described as calm, present, flexible, mindful, curious, joyful, focused, playful, happy, safe, interested, and creative.

What Happens as We Grow with Unresolved Trauma?

Reenactment

This behavior involves re-creating the childhood dynamic, expecting the same result but hoping for a different one. This strategy is doomed to fail because the need is in the past and cannot be resolved. Also, you will interpret everything as a confirmation that you have been betrayed once before.

Loss of Self-Worth

Trauma survivors can swing between feeling special, with grandiose beliefs about themselves, and feeling dirty and "bad." This self-aggrandizement is an elaborate defense against the unbearable feeling of being an outcast and unworthy of love.

---

107 Kathy L. Kain, Peter A. Levine, and Stephen J. Terrell, *Nurturing Resilience: Helping Clients Move Forward from Developmental Trauma* (Berkeley, CA: North Atlantic Books, 2018).

108 Levine and Kline, *Trauma Through a Child's Eyes.*

109 Aimie Apigian, "How Your Attachment Trauma Affects the 3 States of Your Nervous System," Medium, February 14, 2020, https://medium.com/@draimie/how-your-attachment-trauma-affects-the-3-states-of-your-nervous-system-76a3d57e87b7.

Loss of Sense of Self

One of the roles of a primary caregiver is to help us discover our identity by reflecting who we are back at us. If the abuser was a parent or caregiver, that sense of self is not well developed and can leave us feeling phony or fake.

Loss of Physical Connection to Our Body

Survivors of physical or sexual abuse often have a hard time being in their bodies. This disconnection from the body makes some therapies known to aid trauma recovery, such as yoga (mindfulness), harder for these survivors.

Dissociation

To cope with what is happening to the body during abuse, the child will dissociate (disconnect the consciousness from what is happening). Later, this becomes a coping strategy that is used whenever the survivor is overwhelmed.

Loss of Safety

The world becomes a place where anything bad can happen.

Loss of Danger Cues

How do you know what is dangerous when someone you trust hurts you, and this is then your "normal"?

Loss of Trust

This is especially true if the abuser is a family member or a close family friend.

Shame

Huge, overwhelming, debilitating shame. As a child, even getting an exercise or question wrong at school can trigger shame. The child may grow into an adult who cannot bear to be wrong because it's such a trigger.

Loss of Intimacy

For survivors of sexual abuse, sexual relationships can become either an alliance to avoid or one to be entered into for approval (since the child learns that sex is a way to get the attention they crave), and the person may be labeled as "promiscuous."[110]

Pain-Based Behaviors

Pain-based behaviors are "behaviors that have roots in deep emotional pain."[111] Think of pain-based behaviors as a gift from children. They act as "red flags" where attunement, care, and repair are needed. Developmental trauma responses call out to us in extreme and straightforward ways, if we are listening. Don't get so hyperfocused on the outward behavior that you miss its message of need; it is a cry for relief, hope, and grace. Their wounds beg for you to roll up your sleeves and be the one who chooses to get dirty in the name of love.

In an article about the impact of trauma, Michael McKnight wrote:

> Children and adolescents who carry trauma and adversity [insecure attachments] into the classroom also bring "pain-based behaviors" with them. **These behaviors are misunderstood and oftentimes dismissed as intentional acts of disobedience and defiance.** When we use zero tolerance and punitive measures to correct these pain-based behaviors, we are elevating the child's stress response and creating increased fear, aggression, or dissociative behaviors where the child or adolescent simply shuts down. This can become a negative cycle, and we are missing the mark. . . . These students are starving for relationships and regulation.[112]

Common pain-based behaviors include the following:

- Acting-out violence
- Black and white thinking
- Bullying others/allowing bullying for friendships
- Catastrophizing
- Chronic crying/whining
- Chronic fatigue/hunger
- Chronic tattling/martyrdom

110 Louise Godbold, "The Impact of Trauma: A New Echo Infographic," PACEsConnection, September 13, 2017, https://www.pacesconnection.com/blog/the-impact-of-trauma-a-new-echo-infographic.

111 Desautels and McKnight, *Eyes Are Never Quiet*.

112 Desautels and McKnight, *Eyes Are Never Quiet*. Emphasis added.

- Cognitive delays/interference
- Confrontations
- Cruelty to humans/animals
- Daydreaming
- Destruction of property
- Depersonalization
- Difficulty in attention regulation
- Difficulty with transitions/change
- Disrespectful
- Disorientation in time and space
- Disruptive behavior
- Dissociating when angry or upset
- Distrust in adults
- Drawing pictures/illustrations displaying violence
- Eating things other than food
- Excessive licking of lips or fingers
- Flashbacks
- Freezing in place and refusing to move or comply
- Friendship difficulties
- Heightened sense of justice
- Hiding to not be noticed
- Hypervigilance
- Impatience with an inability to cope
- Impulse control
- Inability to give or share with peers
- Inability to identify and label feelings
- Inappropriate school language
- Incomplete assignments
- Interrupting other children
- Lack of concrete thought
- Lack of empathy
- Limited emotional vocabulary
- Limited object constancy and permanence
- Lack of gestures/identifying needs
- Late/tardy
- Licking lips till they bleed
- Little/no eye contact
- Low-level physical aggression (e.g., pushing, kicking, hitting)
- Making self throw up
- Masturbating or genital touching (any sexualized behaviors)
- Micromanaging peers and teachers (beyond bossiness)
- Mimics adult behavior witnessed (good and bad)
- Mistrust in relationships
- Mumbling/stuttering
- Nail-biting/picking at skin
- Name calling
- Negative self-concept/lack of identity
- Nightmares
- No affect
- No space bubble
- Obsessive/compulsive
- Out of seat

- Over-apologizing
- Overly affectionate with strangers
- Over-reactive to tone or facial expressions
- Over-reactive/under-reactive to pain
- Perfectionism
- Physical hyperactivity
- Picking at skin and body
- Playing with feces
- Profanity to upset or offend
- Proximity seeking (needing to be near teacher at all times)
- Unwilling to begin a task or try something new
- Refusing to take off warm clothes/jackets (hiding abuse marks)
- Screaming
- Sensorimotor development disorder
- Sexually victimizing others
- Selective mutism
- Self-defeating aggression
- Self-harming behaviors
- Shifts in personality/motivation
- Socialization difficulties
- Spacing out
- Stealing food or other materials
- Walking out of the room
- Wetting pants frequently
- Yelling at others

After a child has been traumatized multiple times, the imprint of the trauma becomes lodged in all aspects of their makeup. Repeated, prolonged trauma can interfere with all areas of a child's development across a broad spectrum, including cognitive, language, motor, and socialization skills. When children are participating in pain-based behaviors, their nervous systems are being reminded of their trauma in some way. Children with broken connection find it difficult to function in a school setting, as they have reminders everywhere they look and the smallest sensations can trigger their fight/flight systems. Their reenactments of their traumas make them likely to receive the labels "defiant," "oppositional," "aggressive," "unmotivated/lazy," "antisocial," and "a behavior problem."

"When professionals are unaware of the child's need to adjust to traumatizing environments and expect children should behave in accordance with adult standards of self-determination and autonomous, rational choices, these maladaptive behaviors tend to inspire revulsion and rejection. Ignorance of this fact is likely to result in labeling and stigmatizing children for behaviors that are meant to ensure survival."[113] That is why it's so important to provide frequent reassurance and exposure to safe conditions where they can relearn being a child.

Can I Get a Witness?

"Trauma isn't what happens to us, but what we hold inside in the absence of an empathetic witness."[114] We must learn to observe without bias, fear, and impatience to label behaviors, intentionally going "behind their eyes" to see the world from their perspective. There is a simple word for such a process: Empathy. To empathize is to remember our childhood. Do you remember what it felt like to feel helpless, vulnerable, ostracized, afraid, or unsure?

Fred Rogers said, "There's usually an 'inside' story to every 'outside' behavior. Though we may not be able to know that 'inside story,' there's generally some inner reason for what children do."[115] **Behavior doesn't lie.** It's when we combine empathy, observation, and compassion that the magic happens. Our ability to use intuition to guide our journey into the heart of a child affords more intention and authentic communication. We all long to be loved and to love others. Deep within every person you meet, there is a desire to know they are worthy of love and significance. "Children can't be expected to leave the unhappy and angry parts of themselves at the door before coming in," Rogers said. "We all need to feel that we can bring the whole of ourselves to the people who care about us."[116]

But what about when we're missing the mark, or when the emotions and pain-based behaviors of children overwhelm us? I'm going to give you permission to fail—because you will. In fact, I'll let Mister Rogers say it: "Being perfectly human means having imperfections."[117] Making mistakes is part of learning, but it's not an excuse to not try. Instead of focusing on being the "perfect" teacher, or parent, let's become helpless again.

Yep, you read that right. Let's go back to the beginning and remember being a child. Fred Rogers often said, "The child is in me still and sometimes not so

---

113 Van der Kolk, "Developmental Trauma Disorder."
114 Peter Levine, "Peter A. Levine Quotes," Goodreads, https://www.goodreads.com/author/quotes/142956.Peter_A_Levine.
115 Rogers, *You Are Special.*
116 Rogers, *You Are Special.*
117 Rogers, *You Are Special.*

still." We have an inner child living inside us still. Every encounter with a child has *two* children present. As we go back to the broken, unvoiced, unintegrated, unacknowledged places within ourselves, with a healthy guide such as a therapist, life coach, pastor, or trusted confidant, we free up space within us, making room for the children we desperately want to reach.

Can't tap into that little girl or boy through remembering? There's unprocessed trauma blocking your way. If your inner child has never received the love they need, then it will pose a challenge to be a giver to others. "Being a giver grows out of the experience of having been a receiver—a receiver who has been lovingly given to,"[118] Fred Rogers said.

It's about tapping into the child inside and remembering. Rogers wrote: "Since we were children once, the roots for our empathy are already planted within us. We've known what it was like to feel small and powerless, helpless, and confused. When we can feel something of what our children might be feeling, it will help us begin to figure out what our children need from us."[119]

Brain Integration Is Emotional First Aid

No matter what the situation, if we can help children talk about their concerns and their feelings and really listen to what they tell us, we are letting them know we care deeply about them.
—Fred Rogers

What molds our brains? Experience.

When we undergo an experience, our brain cells or neurons become active, or "fire." The brain has one hundred billion neurons, each with an average of ten thousand connections to other neurons. How particular circuits in the brain are activated determines the nature of our mental activity, ranging from perceiving sights or sounds to more abstract thought and reasoning. When neurons fire together, they grow new connections between them, which over time leads to "rewiring" in

---

118 Fred Rogers, *Many Ways to Say I Love You: Wisdom for Parents and Children from Mister Rogers* (New York: Hachette Books, 2019).
119 Rogers, *Many Ways to Say I Love You.*

our brain, neuroplasticity. Our intentional practice of attachment repair activates the same system to build secure connections resulting in somatic safety.

This is inspiring news! It means that we aren't held captive for the rest of our lives by the way our brain works at this moment. We can actually rewire the brain through immersing a traumatized child in pleasurable, safe moments, giving them permission to "just play," and reassuring them that we will take care of everything else. Many children have been carrying heavy burdens they were never meant to carry. What a sweet relief to lay that sack of stones down at the feet of a wise adult.

Dr. Bruce Perry, a psychiatrist who's furthered the understanding of the impact of neglect, abuse, and trauma on the developing brain, says, "What fires together wires together" to describe the process of this neural network connection. He claims that it will become a default setting, positive or negative, if it happens repeatedly and consistently. Our brains are conditioned to protect us, regardless of the situations we find ourselves in. And Peter Levine states, "If you feel safe and loved, your brain becomes specialized in exploration, play, and cooperation. If you are frightened and unwanted, it specializes in managing feelings of fear and abandonment."[120]

I imagine these connections like the scarred roads along what was once the Oregon Trail. Today, if you venture to the trail, you can still observe the large ruts dug out by thousands of wheels moving toward the west. I can only imagine the importance of trying to keep the wheels in the right place, as it would be dangerous to venture off course; a wheel might snap, or an ox sprain its ankle. It made sense to stay in the grooves and follow the same path.

Neural networks act the same way. They connect in our brain based on experiences. If that network has been created in a younger child, it will take more of your time to help "rewire" their brain, but that's not an excuse for us to not do the work. Think of their freedom, of not being chained to the memories, mindsets, reactions, and traumas of the past.

Levine says, "Those who are traumatized in the fragile period during infancy carry the burden of trauma's imprint as a lifelong struggle that seems to add a murky layer over an ordinary existence."[121] One can wrap their brain around the

---

120 Levine and Kline, *Trauma Through a Child's Eyes.*
121 Levine and Kline, *Trauma Through a Child's Eyes.*

clear trauma cases regarding events like shootings, bombings, robbery, kidnapping, and physical and sexual abuse, but what about other everyday events? They can be just as traumatizing for a young child. It's up to us as caregivers to understand that each child is worthy of our intentional attunement.

Fred Rogers was passionate about children's everyday milestones and possible fears, which encompassed his almost nine hundred episodes of the *Neighborhood*, books, videos, and songs to help a child integrate experiences. Such experiences included haircuts, birth of a sibling, going to school, visiting the hospital, going to the doctor's and dentist's office, riding on an airplane, going to day-care, and using the potty.

So how do we integrate? When we attach an emotion to words.

The right side of our brain is where emotion resides. As children, you and I lived in the right hemisphere of our brains, fueled only by our emotional experiences with the world around us. Meanwhile, language resides on the left side of the brain, which develops slower than the right. Think of it as building bridges from one side of the brain to the other. We must connect the experiences, or they live inside us, waiting to get out, felt, and voiced.

****

Blue Eyes is at my desk. "I had a bad dream last night," he says. The other children file into the room and ready for the day.

I stop what I'm doing at the computer, drop down to a squat, and look him in the eyes. The other children have grown accustomed to my having moments with him, and their silent permission puts my heart at ease. They seldom interrupt or complain when Blue Eyes needs more individual care. As he speaks about his dream, his eyes dart around the room, unable to catch mine. He does this when his mind is going too fast and he is dysregulated. I do my best to create the emotional space he needs, not multitasking, holding my attention on him, and rubbing the tops of his hands with my thumbs.

"The monster had spiky teeth and big eyes. It was outside the window looking at me." His eyes dart to my face for an instant, then quickly away again.

"Wow. That sounds scary. Did you talk with your mom about it?"

"She's busy with the baby," he replies, distracted by the boys at their cubbies.

"What should we do to make you feel better?" He shrugs, dismissing the comment, and walks away without another word.

I remember him that afternoon when he receives our "feelings lion" at circle time. "Would you like to talk about your dream with our friends?" I ask.

He relays his dream to the class, who listen and nod their heads. They have come to value the time they are given to hear each other's "big feelings" and remind one another of simple and deep truths:

Grown-ups come back because they want to.

You may not be there yet, but you'll get there.

People can love you exactly as you are.

Lately, we've started to pretend to throw a scary dream into the middle of the circle and growl at it to "scare it away." Emily suggests it this time, and Blue Eyes throws it in. We growl two times because it's *that* scary. (Stories, heartaches, and scary dreams unite us.)

When the nightmare returns, Blue Eyes draws the monster in his journal with large black strokes, googly eyes, and spiked teeth dripping with blood. Integration takes time for the brain. At this point in his journey, Blue Eyes isn't comfortable with vulnerability or being empathetically tended to.

A secure base, or "constant caregiver," as Fred Rogers calls it, is essential for every child to become resilient and self-sufficient. It's not just that the child feels safe in their presence, but receives shalom, peace. Rogers said, "Have you ever watched a frightened child turn to an adult for comfort? Did you notice that the child, in that situation, isn't looking for a diversion? He doesn't want a new toy or game; what he wants is a relationship. He usually needs reassurance from his [caregiver]. He doesn't need or want pat phrases or fancy jargon to help him during stressful times. We should try to understand what he's feeling and then use our own words or actions to communicate our care and concern."[122]

Life is unpredictable, and children are often left wondering about many things. It's important to understand that if any of the following traumas or triggering events (discussed below) have happened to a student, it doesn't necessarily

---

122 Rogers, *You Are Special.*

mean they will be traumatized. A few minutes spent with a child using emotional first aid can minimize the chance of lasting effects. Trauma first aid can also make a child more resilient to inevitable stress, kind of like "stress inoculation" for life.[123] It takes discernment and attunement.

Common Trauma Categories for Children

Children have very deep feelings, just the way parents [teachers] do. Just the way everybody does. I feel that our striving to understand those feelings, and to better respond to them, is an important task in our world. Children carry feelings for a very long time if they don't have an opportunity to talk with someone about them. And when they are able to trust and share their feelings, they often feel free to be more communicative in a variety of ways.

—Fred Rogers

Accidents and Falls

Every baby will have their occasional falls as they're learning to walk. It's a common occurrence, but falling off chairs or counters, down steps, out of bed, and off playground equipment can be traumatizing. Car accidents, even a minor fender bender, can be frightening and jarring. Whenever a child has a shock, there is an opportunity to have the wind knocked out of them from a fall or collision with a playmate, near drowning, getting tangled up in blankets, or aggressive tickling; their body responds as if they are being suffocated. We must encourage children to cry out their fear, as it is imperative to get them to release the emotional build-up and the stress such an experience can cause. Unfortunately, many parents use "tough love" concepts of telling their children not to cry. Giving children the freedom to express fear through tears is a healthy response.

****

---

123 Levine and Kline, *Trauma Through a Child's Eyes*.

In the winter of 1988, my world was forever changed. One crisp morning, a neighbor, BJ, myself, and my father loaded up to make the drive to school less than a few miles away. It was a large, beat-up truck, rattling along, full of my father's masonry supplies, and the floorboards were caked with the mud and mortar of various jobs. I squeezed in the middle of the seat, excited that BJ was riding to school with us. As we pulled toward a four-way intersection two blocks from our house, another truck approached us from my father's side of the truck. He had just instructed me to put my seatbelt on, as I had not, most likely because I was too excited to have BJ in the truck. I never got it latched. The oncoming truck hit black ice and, with a sound so abrasive and assaulting on a quiet morning, flew into the side of our truck, creating a tailspin.

My father, in a futile attempt to protect me, threw his arm out, but my tiny body slid right underneath it, and I smacked my head on the dashboard. When we came to a stop, my father jumped from the truck and began screaming at the other man. He was shorter than my dad but similar in appearance, his face covered with a black beard, a flannel shirt of red and black tucked into jeans, and work boots. (Maybe I'm just creating a picture now, as I fill in the empty spaces. More than a year later, in a therapist's office, he explained that the truck was small with a canopy, although I was convinced it was larger than ours.) The other man was apologetic, as I sat in the truck, stunned. Our neighbor had already called 911, and then my mother was there sobbing.

She'd heard the accident two blocks away, and now she was there in her pajamas crying, and I was pulled into her chaos. I took my cue from her and started to cry. At some point, my mother realized that BJ was gone. In his shocked state, he had run all the way to school and entered the classroom without any warning to his teacher that he had been in a life-altering car accident.

When my mother called the school, they would not give her any information about him, and she finally yelled, "Can you just tell me that he's there and safe!" Finally learning he was indeed there and seemed to be doing well, she hung up the phone. Unfortunately, they did little to reassure my beloved second-grade teacher, who was only informed I had been involved in a car accident, and she conveyed years later in my teacher training that it had been paralyzing to her.

What ensued were some of the worst years of my young life, as the hit on my head created tremendous difficulty with my fine motor (handwriting) skills and ability to perform mathematical computation, and I was filled with rage. Why did that man have to be there? My father also strained his neck, which resulted in life-debilitating migraine headaches—another obstacle in our already avoidantly attached relationship. Now he was always in pain and unapproachable. There were endless court appointments, and we had to prove that I had suffered a brain injury and that my father's life had truly been altered.

In third grade, I entered the office of a therapist named Dr. Pollack, who had been recommended to my parents. It felt like my little life had just gone to hell, all because of Mr. S. who, in my mind, had deliberately not stopped his truck from running into us. This, coupled with the fact that I loathed my third-grade teacher, created the deepest shame within me. No matter how hard I tried or willed parts of my brain to work, there was no success, or extraordinarily little, in my opinion. Dr. Pollack would test my cognitive skills with weird pictures, and I was left with a sense that I must be a failure because I could never read his expressions, as he filled his yellow legal pads with his thoughts about me. What was the purpose of these visits? Climbing the old stairs in a spooky building, entering an office where the chairs swallowed me—and I would leave even more confused than our last encounter.

And that is how we coexisted, Dr. Pollack and I, in his strange office that smelled of cedar, file folders sitting on top of the cabinets, with me keenly aware of the ticking clock and my growling stomach, hoping we might stop by McDonald's on the way home.

At some point I shared how much I hated Mr. S., and I was asked to draw him and get all my feelings out. Even as a nine-year-old child, I was amazed at the rage and tears that spilled out of me, as I covered his body with scribbles and crossed out his face with a big black *X*. It was cathartic. I handed it to my therapist feeling satisfied by my ability to erase him with my artistry. Dr. Pollack arose from his chair and, to my horror, taped my drawing up on the wall. "When you feel differently about him, we can take it down. You just tell me when you're ready."

There is freedom for a child—when an adult is strong enough to handle their negative emotions. I was angry for all that I lost (and it is still with me in small ways today; mental math can be a challenge), but forgiveness slowly came as

Dr. Pollack was willing to hold space for me and my big feelings. As we worked together on a puzzle one day, I pointed to the picture on the wall and said, "You can take that down now." He rose, walked over to the picture, gently removed it, and placed it into the trash can. Sitting back down on the floor with our puzzle, he looked me in the eyes and said, "Now, where were we?"

Medical and Surgical Procedures

I like to be told, if it's going to hurt . . .
—Fred Rogers

Our "deskside manner" is imperative when dealing with young children and injuries. The sight of blood scares children. If we're aware they're about to undergo a procedure outside of school, we can do our best to prepare them for what might happen, or to synthesize the experience upon their return. "Children need to be prepared and supported before undergoing tests and treatment so that the advances in technology [sonograms, brain scans, MRIs, and other stressful procedures that some would consider routine] can do more good than harm."[124]

These medical procedures may include surgery and operations, dental procedures, life-threatening illnesses and high fevers, prolonged immobilization or limited mobility (casting, splinting, traction, wheelchairs, crutches), poisoning, fetal distress, and birth complications.[125]

****

I have a confession: I used to be the biggest Band-Aid jerk in the world. My philosophy was "If you're not gushing blood, spit on it, and you'll live." Well, maybe not that brutal, but I didn't understand the constant barrage of students claiming that they needed a bandage for a cut I literally could not see, even if I had a magnifying glass.

Behold the paper cut, hang nail, or "red bump" that had to be treated for fear of death, while I was teaching math or counting during calendar time.

124 Levine and Kline, *Trauma Through a Child's Eyes.*
125 Levine and Kline, *Trauma Through a Child's Eyes.*

Why did I find such annoyance in the Band-Aid fixation of kindergarteners? It completely usurped the tongue depressor as my childhood nemesis years ago. The only thing that could be more annoying after taking the time to bandage their invisible wound was to look out over the sea of their faces and observe "said child" now pulling the Band-Aid off! *Serenity now! This is my reality. They just wasted another Band-Aid!* I could tell you this is only one child, but it is at least 98 percent of all the Band-Aids I give out. I must add that there are also the wounds that really do require covering, to prevent infection or flat-out grossing out everyone around them. I've now reached an early-childhood motto: *All band-aids need to be lifted and examined as often as possible.* To all the children I taught before 2018, I am sorry. If you come to see me, I will supply you with a box of Band-Aids.

Simple and deep. Mister Rogers came and healed this concept for me and gave it a name—body integrity.

Body integrity is important to young children, so it was important to Fred Rogers. It's a real fear of young children: If a toy can fall apart, can they? In his children's book *Parts*, author Tedd Arnold comically depicts his body falling apart as if he has stuffing inside, but Fred Rogers would remind us that this is real to a child, and not to be taken lightly.[126]

Children are naturally curious about bandages on themselves and on others. If I have a Band-Aid on my body, I can guarantee that a child will ask about it as soon as they see it. In episode 1621 of the *Neighborhood,* Mister Rogers enters his television house wearing an adhesive bandage on his hand.

> How are you, television neighbor? Did you notice what was on my hand [shows his Band-Aid to the camera]? I hit my hand on a piece of metal and cut my skin. So, I put this adhesive bandage on it. When I was a boy, I would see someone with a bandage, I used to wonder if there was anything under the bandage. Well, when I got hurt and my dad would put on a bandage, on me, he would let me look underneath to see that that part of me was

---

126 Tedd Arnold, *Parts* (New York: Puffin Books, 2000).

still there even though it was covered up with the bandage. Here, I'll show you [lifts one corner of the bandage]. See? My hand is still there, even when the bandage covers up some of it. It's all still there. It's sort of like playing peekaboo, you know, when you cover up your face [uses a pillow to demonstrate], and then uncover it. It looks like I've gone away and come back. I was really here all the time. Yeah, just like my hand is always under this bandage when the bandage is there.[127]

This same theme is woven into his song "Everything Grows Together." Written in 1968, it explains that our bodies are one piece and don't fall apart. The cumulative song is a test for not only running out of but remembering the order of all the body parts:

Everything grows together
Because you're all one piece.
Your toes grow
As your feet grow
As your legs grow
As your fingers grow
As your hands grow
As your arms grow
As your ears grow
As your nose grows
As the rest of you grows
Because you're all one piece.[128]

In his book *Mister Rogers' Parenting Book: Helping to Understand Your Young Child*, released just a year before his death, he writes about going to the doctor:

127 Fred M. Rogers, "Mister Rogers' Neighborhood: Episode 1621," The Mister Rogers Neighborhood Archive, 1990, http://www.neighborhoodarchive.com/mrn/episodes/1621/index.html.
128 Fred M. Rogers, "Everything Grows Together," The Mister Rogers Neighborhood Archive, 1968, http://www.neighborhoodarchive.com/music/songs/everything_grows_together.html.

As children grow physically, they also grow in awareness of their own bodies and their ability to remember pain experiences. At the same time, in those preschool years, they have many fantasies and misconceptions. . . . Some parents have wondered why their children get upset when a medical professional looks into their ears with an otoscope, listens to their hearts with a stethoscope, or takes X-ray pictures. Most likely it's because children often worry that doctors can see or hear what they are thinking and feeling when they look inside them or listen to their hearts or read their X-rays. It's important for children to know that no equipment can tell what they're thinking or feeling. People's thoughts and feelings are their own—to share or not to share—with whomever they wish.[129]

In 1996, children's letters sent to Fred Rogers were published in a collection, *Dear Mister Rogers, Does It Ever Rain in Your Neighborhood?* Here's one particularly pertinent excerpt:

Dear Mister Rogers,
    One day I got hurt and had to go to the hospital. . . . I slipped and cut my foot . . . and it hurt. I got stitches . . . and I had to have my pink blanket, and my teddy, and Daddy stayed with me at the hospital.
    Sara, age 4

And then his reply:

Dear Neighbor,
    It meant a great deal to me that you wanted to write and tell me about the time you were hurt and had to go to the hospital. I am sorry that your foot was hurting, but it is good that there

---

129 Fred Rogers, *The Mister Rogers Parenting Book: Helping to Understand Your Young Child* (Philadelphia, PA: Running Press, 2002).

are people at hospitals who know how to help children when they have a problem like that. And the best part is when you can come home from the hospital.

It was interesting to hear about what helped you when you were in the hospital. You said you had your pink blanket and your teddy there, and that your daddy stayed with you in the hospital. It does help to have special things from home and the people you care about close to you at times like that. You are growing so well—inside and out. I'm proud of you.

Mister Rogers[130]

Today, Band-Aids have a deeper meaning in my classroom. If I run out, the dollar store is always around the corner. As I place the Band-Aid on their "wounds," I remind them, "Do you remember what Mister Rogers told us about Band-Aids? Will you still be you underneath? It's just like peekaboo." It's easy to trust people who tell you the truth, like your teacher and Mister Rogers.

I'm happy to report that the perpetual lifting has decreased significantly, since my attitude adjustment. Children need wise adults to reassure them that everything is going to be okay and that cuts heal. No matter if it's a red bump or a gushing wound, we will help and comfort— although we should never underestimate the power of pink blankets and buying stock in Band-Aid.

Violent Acts/Attacks

It's only the peace of God emanating from all of our hearts
that can ultimately bring lasting peace to our world.
—Fred Rogers

Countless people used their phones to video the second plane hitting the Twin Towers on September 11, 2001. Through their screams of disbelief, we, too, witnessed the deaths of hundreds of Americans in a single moment. Bessel van der

---

130 Fred Rogers, *Dear Mister Rogers, Does It Ever Rain in Your Neighborhood?* (New York: Penguin Books, 1996).

Kolk, MD, in his world-renowned book, *The Body Keeps the Score: Brain, Mind, and Body in the Healing of Trauma*, recounts this powerful story:

> On September 11, 2001, five-year old Noam Saul witnessed the first passenger plane slam in the World Trade Center from the windows of his first-grade classroom at PS 234, less than 1,500 feet away. He and his classmates ran with their teacher to the lobby, where most of them were reunited with parents who had dropped them off at school just moments earlier. Noam, his older brother, and their dad were three of the thousands of people who ran for their lives through the rubble, ash, and smoke of lower Manhattan that morning.
>
> Ten days later I visited his family . . . and he showed me a picture that he had drawn at 9:00 a.m. on September 12th. The drawing depicted what he had seen that day before: an airplane slamming into the tower, a ball of fire, firefighters, and people jumping out of the tower's windows. But at the bottom of the picture, he had drawn something else: a black circle at the foot of the buildings. I had no idea what it was, so I asked him. "A trampoline," he replied. What was a trampoline doing there? Noam explained, "So that the next time when people have to jump, they will be safe." I was stunned: This five-year-old boy, a witness to unspeakable mayhem and disaster just twenty-four hours before he made that drawing, had used his imagination to process what he had seen and begin to go on with his life. . . .
>
> At the time the disaster occurred, he was able to take an active role by running away from it, thus becoming an agent in his own rescue. And once he had reached the safety of home, the alarm bells in his brain and body quieted. This freed his mind to make some sense of what had happened and even to imagine a creative alternative to what he had seen—a lifesaving trampoline.[131]

---

131 Bessel van der Kolk, *The Body Keeps the Score: Brain, Mind, and Body in the Healing of Trauma* (New York: Penguin Books, 2015).

Peter Levine says, "A frequently overlooked subcategory of violent acts is witnessing. Our children are now part of 'Generation M (electronic "M"edia).' Like it or not, they are bombarded with violent images from video games, TV, computers/YouTube, and music."[132]

Fred Rogers said, "I have long believed that the best use of television happens when the program is over, and people integrate what has been presented. TV may be the only appliance that is more useful after it is turned off."[133] Although Fred Rogers made his living working in television, he was quite content to spend his free time reading a good book.

After reading an article in the 1980s about the Atari gaming system, Fred Rogers reflected his concern that it was just another screen to get in the way of human connection. He valued the slower pace of a meaningful conversation and reflection. What would he think of us now, forty years later, bingeing Netflix and scrolling our devices? He could see that it was not the gaming system that would be the problem, but the distraction it would provide from what mattered most—people. Rogers urged, "Nothing will ever take the place of one person actually being with another person. Let's not get so fascinated by what technology can do that we forget what it can't do. It's through relationships that we grow best—and learn best."[134]

****

Violent acts and violent attacks include bullying, animal attacks, family violence, witnessing violence, gang and drug-related violence, exposure to violent pornography, physical/sexual abuse and neglect, war, displacement, threat of terrorist attacks, and kidnapping/child trafficking.

Have we become too accustomed to witnessing violence? When Dylan Klebold and Eric Harris committed their assault on Columbine High School, law

---

132 Levine and Kline, *Trauma Through a Child's Eyes*.

133 Jeana Lietz, "Journey to the Neighborhood: An Analysis of Fred Rogers and His Lessons for Educational Leaders" (dissertation, Loyola University Chicago, 2014), https://ecommons.luc.edu/luc_diss/1097.

134 Junlei Li, Kelly Martin, and Kalani Palmer, "The Simple Human Interactions That Make Learning Possible," Remake Learning, January 6, 2016, https://remakelearning.org/blog/2016/01/06/the-simple-human-interactions-that-make-learning-possible/.

enforcement was looking for answers and believed that along with the boys' music choices, depression, and fixation with firearms, a major contributor was violent video games, such as Doom.

"Fred had strong opinions about violence and chaos in children's [television] programming. . . . Fred also took issue with programs and producers who didn't sensitively consider children's developmental needs. Though his arguments now seem a little naive, there's no doubt he held his beliefs strongly, and they informed everything he did on the *Neighborhood*, where each line or lyric was thoroughly, painstakingly considered."[135]

Living in a world that too often turns to wars, riots, or other forms of violence in order to solve problems, Fred Rogers often told children, "When I was a boy and I would see scary things in the news, my mother would say to me, 'Look for the helpers. You will always find people who are helping.'" If attitudes are indeed caught, not taught, then it will be up to us to instruct our children in the sacredness of life and the beauty in our similarities and differences—to stop ignoring pain and intolerance and to be advocates of peace. We must search within to determine anything that will stand in the way of embracing our neighbor in the way he was created to be loved. Fred Rogers believed that God is our advocate, while there is also an accuser, living and rampant in our world, dividing us in any way he can. Rogers often quotes his beloved theology professor, Dr. William Orr, who said, "There is only one thing evil cannot stand, and that is forgiveness."[136]

Blessed are the peacemakers. Peacemakers are helpers. Violence is always wrong, and any war is a bad idea. If we investigate what makes us human beings, we determine the infinite worth of a life or what love can do inside the human heart. All people are worthy of radical acceptance and love.

This became a hallmark for the way Fred Rogers viewed people, as he stated in a speech at the Fourth Annual National Dropout Prevention Conference, quoted by author Michael Long in his *Peaceful Neighbor*, a deeper look at Rogers' passivism: "[When a person] feels at peace and feels loved and valued, the chances are

---

135 Tuttle, *Exactly as You Are.*
136 Rogers, *You Are Special.*

that that person is not going to blow up an airplane or shoot a fellow student or get hooked on drugs or step into the alley of hopelessness and despair."[137]

Hurting people hurt people. It's a simple and deep truth. As a man deeply committed to a theology of peace, Fred Rogers recognized the necessity of meeting people right at their place of need. It's often the simple things in life, those no one sees, that make the biggest impact.

Perhaps our deepest wound is simply a misunderstanding of what love is and its power in our lives. "Love is at the root of everything—all learning, all parenting, all relationships . . . love, or the lack of it," Rogers claimed. Our life is a journey about giving and receiving love. If we have an abundance of water, we must lead the thirsty to where they get what satisfies their souls. Without malice or judgment of how thirsty they may be. We may witness miracles as we reach into the needs of others.

****

As a young student teacher in the spring of 2000, I was placed in a fifth-/sixth-grade combination class. One of the students, Henry, was a refugee from Bosnia, who had fled to America for a better life with his mother and older brother. They had barely made it out alive, as the ethnically rooted war raged around them. Henry had been crossing a large square innocently with his older brother when they were caught in gunfire. His brother shielded his tiny body with his own, and still had the shrapnel in his leg to prove it. Henry was a kind and thoughtful boy whom I grew to be very fond of. His smile was full of a bit of mischief, and he loved to make me laugh.

I could not help noticing, though, that his pictures lacked color. They were always drawn in black and white. It was not until the end of my teaching experience that a counselor spoke to me about that happening with many of her refugees. It was if their brains were able to function only so far, just enough. As Henry began to add color, it was if to say, "I'm ready to start seeing the world again." When he felt accepted, at peace and surrounded by love, he began to open

---

137 Michael G. Long, *Peaceful Neighbor: Discovering the Countercultural Mister Rogers* (Louisville, KY: Westminster John Knox Press, 2015).

his heart again. I count myself lucky to have witnessed such a simple and deep example of rebirth from violence. Neuropsychologist, neurobiologist, and Nobel laureate Roger Sperry said, "Prior to the advent of the brain, there was no color and no sound in the universe, nor was there any flavor or aroma and probably little sense and no feeling or emotion. Before brains the universe was also free of pain and anxiety."

Loss

Young children don't know that sadness isn't forever. It's frightening for them to feel that their sadness may overwhelm them and never go away. "The very same people who are sad sometimes are the very same people who are glad sometimes" is something all parents need to help children come to understand.
—Fred Rogers

No one escapes childhood without experiencing loss. We are powerless to control it, but as teachers and parents we can create a defensive barrier to its aftermath. We are called to protect the hearts of our children, and how we teach them to cope will empower them later in life, building resilience.

What is loss? What feelings accompany it? What happens within our brains when we experience it? Fred Rogers says, "We need time to grieve the people and things we lose."[138] Loss includes the death of a loved one or pet, divorce, separation, being lost, the loss of possessions (in a natural disaster, theft, or homelessness), moving, the loss of relationships, and the loss of family members' attention due to the arrival of a new baby.

****

After being a teacher for fifteen years, I know I'll have to adjust to my new school, which is located on the east side of the city, near the freeway, surrounded

---

138 Rogers, *You Are Special*.

by industrial facilities. I speak only English and have entered a community that serves 100 percent poverty and speaks Spanish as their first language. Most of my incoming students have not been away from their mothers or caregivers for long periods of time. Entering the classroom is not only brand-new but terrifying for them.

Amelia climbs underneath the table wailing, "I want my mommy!"

Christopher, who has long hair covering his face, escapes on several occasions and is located running toward the parking lot.

And Annalia, carried in kicking and screaming, stands at the tiny window pounding her feet and screaming at the top of her lungs.

A small group of boys begins to take out every toy and puzzle, while I play the triage nurse and assess the situation. About the time I have most of it under control, the door opens and a secretary brings in more kids. I feel like a clown car. The panic floods my senses, and I catch the eye of my para-educator, Brian, who reminds me to breathe. I pick up my phone and text my friend: "I hate this. I want to go back to what I know." Is that not how we always feel when faced with the unknown?

Change is always accompanied with loss. Regardless of how miserable we might have been or how ready we were to move on, somehow it seems easier to return than to push our way through the discomfort of change. Change is loss. Good change or bad change, loss is inevitable and must be felt, acknowledged, and integrated.

"I believe in you," comes my friend's reply.

"No, I'm serious. This is awful. Come rescue me!"

At lunch, I breeze through the teachers' lounge and catch the attention of one of my seasoned colleagues, a no-nonsense barracuda whom you would not want to meet in an alley at night.

"How's it going, *Why-steria*?" She never pronounces my name correctly, which she uses to demonstrate her disdain for me. I shrug and make a face. It stops her in her tracks. "Are you going to cry?" she exclaims.

"No," I reply, while I suck in my breath raggedly, stifling the sob threatening to burst out.

"No crying!" she snaps, and the door shuts behind her. Great pep talk.

When I pull into my garage that evening, my son Ben comes out to greet me. He stops short as he sees me. "Mama, why are the toys and stuff back in the car?" I burst into big, heaving sobs. "Oh, wow, that bad, huh?"

I hug his chest and cry my heart out. I hear my husband, Matthew, emerge but continue to cry. "It was like herding cats," I finally blurt out. "I was so mad, I loaded up all my toys and came home."

My husband groans, as he had labored in taking them all into the building just days earlier.

"You know what sucks?" I whine.

"What?" Ben asks.

"They expect me to come back tomorrow."

And my son starts to laugh.

Death of a Family Member

Sometimes adults feel the immediate restitution is best after there's been a loss. But unless a child is given time to grieve, to cry and play out the significant losses of childhood, the consequences could continue for a lifetime.

—Fred Rogers

Death need not be a frightening concept for our children, if we're willing to embrace whatever feelings happen. Our ability to help them regulate their emotions and to field their questions depends on the intentional choices to be honest, real, and open. As you reflect on your own losses as a child, what questions did you have? What misconceptions? When you reflect on what you may have needed and did or did not receive, it will become your guide to facilitating the conversations with your child.

Luckily, we have Mister Rogers to guide this difficult topic, which he tackled early in his career. He said,

Death is the subject of many misunderstandings, perhaps because adults often have a hard time talking about it simply and directly. Saying that "Grammy went to sleep and never woke up" may seem like a gentle way to break the news of a close relative's death, but it has led to nighttime fears for many children who begin worrying that if they let themselves go to sleep, they may never wake up either. . . . We need to be honest with our children, saying that we don't know when we don't . . . and that we sometimes wonder about death, too.[139]

Expressing emotions in front of children can be helpful too. Children need to know that we can comfort each other in difficult times. Fred Rogers shared this memory when he was discussing death: "I remember, after my grandfather's death, seeing Dad in the hall with tears streaming down his face. I don't think I had ever seen him cry before. I'm glad I did see him. It helped me know that it was okay for men to cry. Many years later, when my father died, I cried; and way down deep I knew he would have said it was all right."[140]

Anger is also a part of grief, and we can let children know that it is a natural part of the process:

I've sometimes said to a child who has had a loved one die, "It can make a person mad to have someone go away and not come back, doesn't it?" I've had children nod in reply as if to say, "Yes, that's what I'm feeling." Then I might say something like, "Well, a lot of people feel mad when someone they love dies." Just identifying and hearing that there's nothing wrong with it seems to be a big help to a child and to make it possible for him or her to talk about it—then or later.[141]

Grief can often become a companion that vies for our attention at inconvenient moments. The more receptive we become by attuning to a child's verbal and nonverbal cues, the more it will empower them to express their grief in a variety of

139 Rogers, *You Are Special.*
140 Rogers, *You Are Special.*
141 Rogers, *You Are Special.*

ways, such as through language, art, dance, play, or writing. For young children, pretending is a healing activity, where they enact what they wish would happen or speak about their important feelings through puppets. And enjoying picture books is a chance to pull children close to our heartbeats and read stories of resilience. When children are allowed to express their feelings, integration is occurring in their brains, and feelings need not be scary or overwhelming when they have your company on the journey.

Death of a Pet

How is loss different when a beloved pet dies? It's not. A death is a permanent separation, and for many children, the death of a pet can be just as sudden and traumatic as the loss of a person.

In episode 1101 of the *Neighborhood*, Mister Rogers goes to feed the fish and realizes that there is a dead fish floating at the bottom of the tank. He is talking about how beautiful fish are when they swim, and then it happens: He notices a dead fish. He tries to revive it but to no avail, so he explains that it is dead and he'll need to bury it. As he does so, he tells this story:

> When I was very young, I had a dog that I loved very much. Her name was Mitzy. And she got to be old, and she died. I was very sad when she died. Because she and I were good pals. And when she died, I cried. My grandmother heard me crying, I remember, and she came, and she just put her arm around me. Because she knew I was sad. She knew how much I loved that dog. And my dad said we'd have to bury Mitzy. And I didn't want to. I didn't want to bury her because I thought I would just pretend that she was still alive. But my dad said that her body was dead, and we'd have to bury her. So, we did. . . . I really missed her when she died.

Mister Rogers always had a way, author Michael Long writes, "of inviting us to see animals as valuable, as deserving of our love and as desirous of our care."[142]

---

142 Long, *Peaceful Neighbor*.

Separation

Young children can't be sure when they'll be back
with the people they love.
—Fred Rogers

When Natalie enters my classroom after full-time online instruction in January, it's the first time she's been physically separated from her mother, a single mom who's devoted to her daughter and navigating working from home and making ends meet. While the other students are busy dancing, I kneel down to speak to Natalie and welcome her to kindergarten. Her black hair is pulled up into a side ponytail with an oversized sequined bow, and she wears a jean jacket, printed leggings, and *Frozen* T-shirt.

Taking her small hands into mine, I squeeze them until her eyes meet mine. "I'm so happy you are here. I'll keep you safe until your mommy comes back at the end of the day. Would you like to learn and play with us?" She nods her head in agreement as I catch her mom's eyes slowly filling with tears. As I have her settled in her place, I take the time to reassure her mom that she's in good hands. (*Every* child is someone's whole world.)

About an hour into instruction, she tucks her chin into her chest and begins to cry, "I want my mommy."

I make sure to go to her quickly, getting below her and whispering, "I know you do, sweetie. Mommy misses you too. But I will take good care of you until you can see her again. I promise you. Do you need a hug?"

She comes into my arms without hesitation.

"Whenever you need a hug today, you just let me know." The cuddles of my kindergarten babies do wonders for my heart. I count it an honor to snuggle them close when their parents aren't with them.

Touch kids. Don't be so afraid to give them what you know they need.

"Would you like to meet my special friend?" I ask her. "He'll help you feel better. We spend time with him every day."

"Yeah, he loves us," Luna, her table buddy, states. "It's Mister Rogers,"

"Okay," Natalie whimpers.

What would I do without my teaching partner, Mister Rogers?

By the end of the day, Natalie hasn't cried again. And she's made it to our last activity. We pass around our feelings lion, as the children pull out their feelings and label them. There is red—mad, angry, frustrated, and annoyed; blue—sad and disappointed; yellow—happy and excited; green—calm and secure (or as we say, "How we feel when we spend time with Mister Rogers").

We take the time to connect feelings and sensations at the end of each day, listening to our friends, acknowledging, and naming easy and hard things. All feelings are mentionable and manageable.

When the feelings lion reaches Natalie, she confidently takes out the yellow circle and states assuredly, "I am happy because today Mrs. Edwards kept me safe and loved me. And now I'll see my mommy!" Grown-ups come back because they want to. Even when we can't see those we love, they are still there, loving us from afar.

Divorce

Divorces don't wreck children's lives, people do.
—Fred Rogers

There was a time when Fred Rogers faced a dilemma. How would he handle the topic of divorce? When Fred Rogers was growing up, divorce wasn't as common as it was becoming in the early 1980s. Approximately 40 percent of all marriages made in the US will end in divorce or separation.[143] Fred Rogers was disheartened by the growing trend in the early '80s and wanted to explore the way that children understood divorce and may misinterpret their fears during a parental separation. "In his conversations with [mentor] Margaret McFarland, she reminded him that every time parents quarrel, children fantasize that they may separate—the children's greatest fear."[144] The loss of a family is the death of a dream.

---

143 Beti Prosheva Gavrilovska, "How Many Marriages End in Divorce—Fascinating Facts and Stats," Review42, July 4, 2022, https://review42.com/resources/how-many-marriages-end-in-divorce/.

144 King, *The Good Neighbor.*

Fred Rogers rose to the challenge, stating, "Whatever is mentionable is manageable." He taught this to children through the eyes of Prince Tuesday's misunderstanding his parents, King Friday and Queen Sara, quarreling. In the episode, Queen Sara is unhappy that King Friday is entertaining the idea of purchasing another plane for himself and leaves in a huff. As Prince Tuesday witnesses the argument, he turns to Lady Aberlin, who represents the safe person, and states, "I don't like it when my mom and dad are mad at each other. Is it my fault that they are fighting?"

Divorce is painful. I've had children thrust into fights, witness abuse, and testify before juries without care or concern. Big feelings need to be integrated by parents and teachers after children witness disagreements, as well as divorce proceedings and outcomes. Children are often left to draw their own conclusions, as parents are preoccupied with their own pain and logistics. The loss of a family structure is traumatic for a young child, and unprocessed trauma changes the structure of their brain.

Trauma writes a new narrative and sets up a child for future success and failure. Therefore, it's up to us as teachers to understand the current situations our students face and be a safe place for their expression, their doubts and fears. Fred Rogers spoke to children about the importance of allowing a grown-up to see inside their world: "Sometimes children wonder if other people know what they are thinking. People don't know what you're thinking if you don't tell them. So, if you're worried about something, it can really help to tell the people you love what you're worried about. Each person is different; like pretzels, they may look the same, but they are individual and distinct. If you want someone else to understand what you are thinking and feeling, you must tell them."[145]

The inner world of a child is a sacred and holy place; we're only ushered in when we are deemed safe and wise. Our counsel must contain the certainty of care and truth, and a reassurance that even tough times help us grow. It must also contain the knowledge that that child is not alone.

In the 1980s, Fred Rogers relied on the fact that a child had one caring adult who could speak to them about tough topics—a statistic that has greatly dimin-

---

145 King, *The Good Neighbor.*

ished in the past forty years. Just as Prince Tuesday is unable to reconcile with his parents until he speaks about his big feelings, our students need an opportunity to voice their confusion and angst relating to disagreements and divorce. We are encouraged, loved, and comforted in the telling of our stories. As journalist George Gerbner explained, Fred Rogers remains an exceptional teacher as "his dreams, his stories, offer ways to control the chaotic life of the streets and neighborhoods in which children live. Children are starving for a story, the kind that builds on hope, the kind that echoes for a lifetime. We need story in our lives, not dreams based on greed. Mister Rogers turns to the viewer and says quietly, 'I believe in you. It is your story that is important. It is your mind and heart that can make things possible—just because of who you are.'"[146]

****

"Lincoln's dad is here to see you. He says he will not be able to meet with you if his mother is there because there is a restraining order involved," the school secretary tells me over the phone. "Are you willing to meet with him for a few minutes?"

The day had already been hectic, as I was setting up my classroom and meeting with parents for their entrance interviews. I sigh as I agree to the weight of the situation landing on me. I have dealt with parents who could not get along before, but when restraining orders are involved, it ramps up the chaos. Somehow, I always feel caught in the middle when people are divorcing, acting as a referee to keep the student in my care emotionally safe.

As I sit at a table in the hallway, I meet Ken, a man broken down by the tragedy and loss of a dream, the dream of raising his three boys with a woman he wanted to grow old with. Mental illness had arrived after her last child, causing explosive physical abuse aimed at him, fights where the police were called, and recently they have begun the divorce process.

As Ken relays his story, Lincoln's older brother takes him and their younger brother outside to the playground. I'm struck by the sweet way the older boy interacts with his brothers. It's not an inconvenience, but an act of genuine kind-

---

146 George Gerbner, "Fred Rogers and the Significance of Story," Current, February 16, 2015, https://current.org/1996/05/fred-rogers-and-the-significance-of-story/.

ness and affection. I remark to Ken that he has "wonderful children," and tears begin to spill down his cheeks.

"I'm so worried about my kids. I don't know what to do."

I reach out and place my hand on his arm. "I understand how hard this must be for you. No one gets married, thinking they will ever be divorced. But I can make you a promise. If Lincoln is in my class, he will feel loved. I've got him."

He lets out his breath loudly as he wipes his face. "Thank you," he manages to say. That was all he needed to hear. A promise to see and understand.

Every child in our classroom is someone's whole world.

I wish I could say that Lincoln did not show the effects of being pulled between his parents, but aggression, impulsivity, and vandalism come as the year progresses. He can calm down, after some time in the calm-down area, and makes amends in most circumstances, but it's an uphill battle.

Luckily, Lincoln understands that school is a safe place for him. He shares his concerns and feelings candidly in our community circle. "Last night I had a dream that I was with my mommy and daddy, and then they threw me in the water, where sharks kept biting me."

Can you imagine feeling the anxiety over saying the right thing when a parent grills you with questions? He's stuck in the middle and trying to not be devoured. His heart's breaking before my eyes.

One February afternoon, Lincoln receives another bad report from a specialist, and I know something has to be done. As they enter the room, I tell my students, "We are doing another community circle, and this time I want Lincoln in the middle." They quickly comply and sit behind Lincoln. He relaxes back onto me as I snuggle him in close.

"Boys and girls, we know that Lincoln is having a tough time with his mommy and daddy divorcing."

They all nod their heads in understanding.

"It seems that the storm on the inside of Lincoln is starting to erupt outside him, and he needs to remember how much we love and support him. I want you to reach out your hand and place it on Lincoln if you can. If you have trouble reaching him, place your hand on a friend who can touch him. We are going to tell him what he needs to hear."

They situate themselves around the circle, placing their hands on Lincoln.

I begin. "Lincoln, we love you. You are brave."

Chase speaks up next. "I love you, Lincoln."

Without a pause, encouragement begins to spill from the mouths of my students:

"You're brave."

"You're special, Lincoln."

"Don't forget you're growing inside."

"Let the good inside put up a fight."

"It's okay to make mistakes. If you need to, make a big one."

"You can do anything."

"You may not be there yet, but you'll get there."

I continue. "You are safe. You are loved. We are right here with you. You don't have to solve any adult problems. We are here to help you during this sad time." I begin to sing the *Neighborhood* song "You Are Special," and the class joins in as I rock Lincoln back and forth: "You are my friend, you are special."

At the end of the song, I say, "The last thing I want you to do is to close your eyes and send Lincoln all the love you can." As I glance around the circle, little noses scrunch and eyes slit as they pray and sent BIG love to their friend. In my arms, a little boy grows heavy and relaxed. We should have been doing math, but Lincoln needs attunement.

Brené Brown says, "Rarely does a response make something better. What makes something better is connection."[147] What hurting children need most is connection and security. Divorce is a grown-up problem, and children need not be stuck in the middle, or used as mediators. It's not their fault that their parents can no longer be together.

****

I've had two selectively mute children in my career, but my first one was a little boy who had enough of his parents using him as the "go-between" communicator, while they engaged in a combative divorce. "What did Daddy say?" and "Did you

---

147 Brown, *Atlas of the Heart.*

see what Mommy was doing?" After several months of being pulled between two competing and fractured people, he stopped speaking. That was his extreme reaction. In his mind at six, he decided that he would no longer be the mouthpiece, and he fell silent. It's important to me that I create as much emotional security as possible for him. As he enters my class, I bend down and look him in the eyes. Big, beautiful brown eyes.

"I want you to know that I will do my best to take care of you. I just need you to use your voice if you feel unsafe. Deal?" He nods his head and smiles while he works on the puzzle I've given him.

During free play, while the other students play with blocks or cars, or in the home center, he sits across from me as we draw a continuous line picture. I start in my corner and make a design, then stop; then he adds a bit more and stops. As we work together, I choose to be quiet, too, entering his world. I want desperately to know how I can help him feel safe. What does he need? I just have to remain attentive and responsive.

After two weeks, we fall into a predictable routine, he and I making elaborate drawings and then adding colors with markers and crayons. I grow to understand that he finds peace in my presence and the ability to sit with his big emotions.

Suddenly one day, mid-drawing, he looks up and says, "Can I go and play with them now?" As if I've been making him sit there with me and not play!

"Sure" I reply, and that's it. No big bells and whistles, just trust. I do not know what moment things changed for him, but showing up, and loving him right where he is, is enough. To earn a child's trust is holy work.

Rogers explains, "Children need adults who realize that losses to children are every bit as painful as losses to adults. . . . There are no perfect parents [teachers], and there are no perfect children. But imperfect parents [teachers] can be loving parents [teachers], and the gifts of their love can be enough to preserve the 'child within' from the despair when times get tough."[148]

While Fred Rogers was taping a television special on divorce, he was moved by a woman in the studio audience who shared: "I will always be grateful to my mom because she encouraged my own loving feelings towards my dad. I knew

---

148 Rogers, *You Are Special.*

mom didn't have those feelings, but she cared enough to let me have them and go on to build my own relationship with him."[149]

Being a child of divorce, I daily tell my students, "There is nothing you can do to lose my love. Nothing." Maybe that's the little girl in me still voicing what I needed. Reassurance that I will always have love, even when dreams die. Mister Rogers reminded his hurting neighbors by saying: "Divorce is sad and painful. During a separation or divorce, children feel as if their family is 'broken.' They might even worry that 'Since my parents stopped loving each other, they may stop loving me.' Divorce changes families in many ways. But it's still possible for children to feel safe, secure, and loved, even when their parents don't live together."[150]

Being Lost

Think back to your childhood. Were you ever lost? What was the story? Who was there? I recall hiding inside clothing racks in a department store and having my mother panic, become irate, and then cry out of relief. As a child, you cannot quite grasp the panic that surges through a parent when they realize their child is missing. Most of us had moments of panic, followed by the inevitable hugs of reunion.

My first original play produced in Chicago was entitled *Broken Thread*, which detailed the aftermath of the abduction of a white child in a large city. Her parents are people of privilege, and we see how they cope in the interim before their absolution.

While researching the piece, I scoured countless cases of missing and exploited children and contacted the Chicago FBI to have an interview with an agent to make sure the work was authentic. The FBI believed in the project and assigned an agent to the play who was willing to take my actors through a mock interview and loan us props. It was only the second time in history that they had partnered with the arts, the other being *Public Enemies* with Johnny Depp. I also met some of the most courageous people, many becoming personal friends, people who had been thrust into the spotlight through evil circumstances when their children were taken and murdered by predators: Marc Klaas, Erin Runnion, and Mark

---

149 Rogers, *Mister Rogers Parenting Book*.
150 Rogers, *Mister Rogers Parenting Book*.

Lunsford, parents who've since become advocates for missing and murdered children. Their stories are uncommon, as only 1 percent of child abductions are perpetrated by unknown persons. It's the people children "kind of" know, or know well, who are hurting our children. They include, for example, coaches, doctors, neighbors, teachers, grandparents, aunts, uncles, cousins, schoolmates, childcare workers, spouses of workers.

Many of you may be experiencing red flags going up as you read this. I suspect you were injured or traumatized by your parents trusting the wrong person with your care and safety. If that is the case, you deserved better. I'm deeply sorry. Your pain is real and needs to be heard.

Here is some wisdom I gleaned from my experience working on *Broken Thread*:

- Heal your own wounds. If you have unresolved trauma regarding past sexual, physical, or emotional abuse, it will be in the driver's seat as you make choices for children. Although you may think you are "protecting them," you could be harming them by your anxiety, ambivalence, or avoidance.
- Define three safe people children can go with in case of an emergency. It should be people they do not automatically live with. Talk with the child about who they feel comfortable with and write the names of these people down. These are the people parents should list for the emergency contacts at school. They need to keep it current.
- Have a code word that these three safe people know and remind the child to not share it with anyone.
- A grown-up does not need to ask a child for help to find a lost dog or to locate a place, for example. The grown-up needs to ask another adult.
- No labels displaying children's names should be visible on their property or person.
- Children should never answer a front door alone.
- Teach children about their space bubble. *The Safe Side* video calls this their "Safe Side Circle." It is smaller at home with people they know and love, and bigger when they are in public. If a person enters their circle in

public, they need to run to get close to their "Safe Side Adult." A good rule: If you cannot see your adult, they cannot see you.

- Practice going outside and having children yell, "You are not my mom! You are not my dad!" Emphasize that it's never okay to say this about their parents, but it should be used when it's necessary to keep them safe.
- If they are to get lost, they need to freeze and look for a woman, especially one who has children. Women are less likely to offend and will help a child.
- Teach your child their full name, phone number, and address. Also teach them your full name. Many small children cannot tell a teacher their first and last name, as well as their parents'. Practice this as you drive in the car. It is empowering for children to know they have the information to reach you.
- Practice! Practice! Practice! Role-play the "what if" game by giving children scenarios, then have them show you what they would do. For example, "What if you couldn't see your safe adults and someone said that they would help you find them?" or "What if a man offered to help you?" or "If you were lost, what would you do?" [151] [152]

Environmental Stressors

Many children live in places where natural disasters are a part of life: hurricanes, flooding, wildfires, and tornadoes. But other environmental stressors and extremes have the potential to create trauma. Environmental stressors include the following:

- exposure to extreme weather and temperatures (babies and young children are not able to self-regulate or move out of harm's way, such as leaving a hot car or a freezing cold room)
- natural disasters (fires, earthquakes, floods, tornadoes, hurricanes, volcanoes, and tsunamis)
- pandemics, diseases, and illnesses

---

151 Katherine Lee, "How to Teach Your Kids What to Do If They Get Lost," Verywell Family, May 2, 2019, https://www.verywellfamily.com/what-to-teach-a-child-to-do-when-lost-620557.

152 "National Center for Education Statistics Home Page," National Center for Education Statistics, 2020, https://nces.ed.gov/.

- sudden loud noises for babies and young children, especially if they're left alone (arguments, violence, fire drills, lockdowns, alarms, construction, parties with lots of people or stimulants, thunder and lightning, and horns)[153]

****

Emily is afraid of the fire drill. Our school building is old and outdated, and when the fire alarm sounds, the wail is high-pitched and startling, whether it's a scheduled thing or not. Accompanied with flashing lights, we must walk in lines out to the adjacent field and line up facing away from the school. This is all fine and easy, when you're not in charge of twenty-four five- and six-year-olds who do not see the logic in walking quickly, instead of whipping each other back and forth, as we hold hands in the line. There is something inside me that goes into high alert, and I'm much more aware of my lack of patience during drills. After all, we're practicing for crisis! But young children do not grasp the importance of such things.

The first drill of the year, Emily is so startled that she instantly falls to the ground in a ball and begins to sob. I scoop her up as we make our way to our meeting spot. Her tiny body shakes in my arms, and the weight of her on my hip, while pulling the line along, makes it difficult to maneuver through the thin doors with other classes. Still, she clings to my neck, and I don't think one could remove her if they tried. I'm her secure base, and she will not budge. Even after we've been in our safe spot for several minutes, I have to coax her with my words and deep breathe with her before she releases her intertwined hands and settles into my lap.

The terror is evident, and it changes everything. She's a bright little girl, full of imagination, normally able to cope, but the loud noise has assaulted her senses. For weeks, she's obsessed with the next drill, explaining to me and to her mom that she's terrified. Each time she brings it up, I reassure her that she's safe, and during writing time we work together as she illustrates her fears.

When our principal announces in an early morning meeting a few months later that we'll be having a drill after lunch, I fetch some Silly Putty from my desk.

---

153 Levine and Kline, *Trauma Through a Child's Eyes*.

Taking out the red egg, I'm reminded of the countless times at the summer pool when my mother would shove the soft putty into my ears, before I had tubes put in. It was to prevent the ear infections that had plagued me much of my first three years of life. As Emily sits at her desk work, I slowly place the putty inside her ears and wink. Talking louder because her ears are plugged, she says, "Oh, I know what this is for." It's become a game.

"It will make it so that this time, you will feel different about fire drills," I tell her.

Neurobiology has a saying: "What fires together wires together." For Emily, the neural networks created a path in her brain relating that fire drills will always be loud and scary. This time, we're creating a new pathway with a positive experience. We first give language to her feeling and the experience and then work to override the experience with a positive one. By the end of the year, the Silly Putty is no longer needed, and she doesn't startle with the drill. It's about giving her the gift of time and telling her, "You are safe. I am here. It's going to be okay."

****

The mass shooting occurred Tuesday, May 24, 2022, when eighteen-year-old Salvador Ramos entered Robb Elementary School in Uvalde, Texas. An AR-15 and a shotgun killed nineteen children and two adults (two teachers trying to protect the pupils). It has become the deadliest school shooting since the Sandy Hook mass shooting in Newtown, Connecticut, almost ten years previously, in which twenty-six people were killed, including twenty children.[154] This is our new reality in education.[155]

> Every teacher you know has thought about it.
> Every teacher you know has a plan for an active shooter.
> Every teacher you know has weighed their point of fight or flight.
> Every teacher you know has walked their room looking for blind
>   spots.

---

154 Isabel Martins, "Texas School Shooting Review: Five Things You Need to Know," *Newsweek*, May 30, 2022, https://www.newsweek.com/texas-school-shooting-five-things-know-1711312.

155 "Sandy Hook Elementary School Shooting," Wikipedia, https://en.wikipedia.org/wiki/Sandy_Hook_Elementary_School_shooting.

Every teacher you know has passed their classroom to see what it would look like from the outside.

Every teacher you know has wondered how fast they can lock a door.

Every teacher you know has had a talk about the "spread out" or "group together" methods.

Every teacher you know has gotten jumpy at least once at the sound of a fire alarm, unplanned announcement, or screech from the quad.

Every teacher you know has wondered if they could be in the way long enough to prevent damage.

Every teacher you know has thought about how hard it would be to keep 25 young people quiet.

Every teacher you know has walked into a different classroom and noticed where the doors and windows are.

Every teacher you know thinks it can happen, so they hope every day it doesn't.

Every. Teacher. You. Know.

And, at some point in their lives, children in a classroom think at least one (if not all) of these things as well.

Every teacher you know has had a conversation with their loved ones about what to do in case of tragic event.

Every teacher you know has thought about how to keep kids safe while getting themselves home safe.

Every teacher you know has cried at the thought of making a choice.

Every. Teacher. You. Know.

Every single one.[156]

****

---

156 Katie Kindelan, "Teacher Shares Classroom Fear in Viral Post after Deadly Texas School Shooting," *Good Morning America*, May 25, 2022, https://www.goodmorningamerica.com/living/story/teacher-shares-fears-deadly-texas-school-shooting-viral-84968953.

The lockdown alert comes across the speakers minutes after I've placed my kindergartners in the lunch line. *Why would they do this right now?* I think, annoyed. But something stirs within me, and I run out of the staff lounge toward my kids. They're still where I left them, looking a bit mystified, several reaching out to hug me in relief. "Look at me. Turn around, move, move, move!" I instruct them to follow me into the lounge, gathering them and shuffling them into the women's restroom. Images of Sandy Hook flood my mind.

"But I'm hungry," Bailey moans.

"Everyone get on the floor. I'm turning off the lights. Sit on your bottoms and be very quiet. Do you remember what we practiced?"

They all nod and I turn off the lights. Several whisper as they wiggle into their spots.

"Tanner, open up your lunch box and eat something quietly, sweetie," I whisper to my student with diabetes. His blood sugar is in a constant roller-coaster state, and the last thing I need is for numbers to drop.

"I'm scared," Amy whines at me. "I don't like the dark."

I reach out in her direction and say, "Move toward my voice."

She shuffles to me and crawls into my lap. Frantic knocks come on the door, and she jumps into my lap, nestling in my chest, while another child wraps around my right arm, and tiny fingers surround my left ankle.

"Wystie, are you in there?" I hear my school nurse calling out to me in a whisper. More frantic knocks. "I need to get in with Tanner!"

I reach for the lock, and she quickly moves beside me, snapping the lock in place.

"He's over there and eating," I reassure her.

"It's not a drill. This is real." Her words hit me like a brick wall. "A man is walking near the school with a gun. The police just told us."

Her hand grabs mine. My mouth goes dry as reality cascades over me. For a split second, I fight the urge to cry and place my face into Bailey's hair. She's still in my lap. I have someone's daughter in my lap. I am surrounded by other people's children.

"You're doing wonderful, boys and girls. Be very, very quiet as they shake the doors."

We sit for thirty minutes in the dark, the unknown hugging the silence. And then the "all clear" comes across a radio off in the distance.

Later, we learn a man cleaning his gun decided to walk to his mailbox and wasn't close to the school. But the moment cements into my nervous system.

During a discussion in his university class surrounding school shootings/gun control, my son Ben raised his hand and said, "My mom is a kindergarten teacher in Washington State. I live with the reality that if there is a shooting, she'll die protecting her kids."

This is the burden of every teacher's spouse, partner, and children. Whatever stance you take in "the debate," we are all vulnerable to broken connections when children don't receive care and inflict harm on others. Instead of looking for "warning signs," let's confront and transform the broken connections in children through intentional repair.

Finding Mister Rogers' Trauma

It all began with a fall from the park's monkey bars. The toddler, Fred Rogers' youngest son, John, had a broken jaw. Unfortunately, he sucked his thumb, which would delay his healing. Doctors suggested he wear a jacket equipped with wooden slats from the shoulder to the wrist at night to prevent access to his thumb. Soon after, John pulled a pot of hot coffee down upon his leg, causing a severe burn. The burn stopped his regular swimming in the ocean all summer on Nantucket Island. Understandably, such extreme injuries were stressful for the young parents. Children don't come with instruction manuals, and John's accidents were severe. The following year, while working in Toronto, Fred and his wife, Joanne, took young John in for a routine operation to repair two hernias present from birth. One was in his abdomen and the other in his groin. What should've been a standard procedure left father and son deeply traumatized for decades.

Trauma results in moments where we feel powerless, unseen, unheard, unloved, terrorized, shamed, ignored, isolated, or abandoned. Fred Rogers felt helpless, ignored, and fearful. He was traumatized. "'They needed a blood test,' said Joanne [Rogers], 'and Fred said [John] was just terrified, and he held him and talked to him soothingly while they did that. So, he was just settled back down with us again when they came and said it was time to go, and they just grabbed him and took him. Screaming and crying.'"[157] Unable to accompany him, Fred and Joanne listened to him screaming down the corridor.

"To this day, I have nightmares about it," Fred said in a 1987 speech.

> And I get so angry when I talk about it that I find it hard to be the least bit charitable. If I'd known then what I know now, those people would have never taken our son from us that way. I would have insisted on being with him until he was asleep. We later learned that it took the surgical team forty-five minutes to get him sedated, and those forty-five minutes changed all our lives. Yes, his hernia was repaired, but his emotions were severely damaged. . . . To think that one morning in a hospital can cripple a two-year-old emotionally.[158]

John continued to have ongoing physical, emotional, behavioral, and developmental difficulties long after the surgery. Eventually, the Rogers sought out psychiatric help. They couldn't understand how he could go into the hospital an average sixteen-month-old child and be returned to them so altered. One doctor said that he believed John was "psychotic," a word that would terrify any parent. John Rogers would spend the next decade in and out of therapist offices, leaving Fred Rogers convinced it all went back to that morning in the hospital.

John himself recalls not his surgery but the accident-prone aftermath. "One thing I remember . . . that was troubling," he said, "was slamming my hand with the car door a few times in a row, and it got to the point where my parents wouldn't allow me to close the car door. There must have been something in my unconscious that affected me."[159]

Fred Rogers told John's story in speeches from a father's perspective only a few times in the early 1970s, later choosing to reference him simply as a "young man I know" to protect his family's privacy. Yet the message remained the same—children's emotional lives must be protected at all costs.

---

157 King, *The Good Neighbor.*
158 Tuttle, *Exactly as You Are.*
159 King, *The Good Neighbor.*

Fred's oldest son, Jim, later recalled that his father felt guilty for years that he wasn't able to help John. That same sort of guilt had shown itself earlier when Rogers's older son was barely a year old, in Florida with family on vacation. As the story was relayed to him later,

> Mom . . . had taken me down by the water's edge and was holding me, and a big wave came in and pulled me out of her arms and out into the surf. Dad frantically ran out and managed somehow to grab hold of my foot and drag me out of the water. He would say to me, "Oh, you swim so well, and I'm surprised that you would even go near the water after what happened to you." And I just remember thinking, "Well, you know, it was scary for you. I don't remember it, so it doesn't really bother me."[160]

In Fred's sons, we observe the different schools of thought regarding childhood traumas. Jim's stance is one of the-past-doesn't-affect-the-present, while Fred and John were acutely aware of the lingering echoes of trauma. Trauma activates our nervous systems and insecure attachments as we experience powerlessness, abandonment, separation, rejection, and fear. It leaves the child alone without an empathetic witness.

> In bearing witness to his son's trauma, in feeling its fallout, he became Mister Rogers—his purpose crystallized—and he learned, in a way that even the best teachers in the most prestigious institutions of learning couldn't teach him, what was at stake in children's lives. He already believed in honoring children, treating them with respect, and taking them seriously. But now he knew firsthand, through the experience of his own child, what could be lost, even in the small, typical, day-to-day experiences of childhood. He was a witness in both senses of the word. He witnessed the trauma, as he watched and listened closely to

---

160 King, *The Good Neighbor.*

what happened, and he also witnessed to the trauma, spreading the word and telling the story. . . . Bearing witness for Mister Rogers was transformative, and going to work to heal what he saw as largely preventable wounds, he became more himself.[161]

Fred Rogers wasn't one to get angry often, but he couldn't tolerate hearing of children suffering at the hands of foolish or thoughtless adults. His associates at Family Communications, Inc., later reported on more than one incident in which he became furious if he thought he observed hospital staff being thoughtless and insensitive with young children. "To think that one morning in a hospital can cripple two years emotionally," said Rogers later in a speech to a family court association. "What I've come to appreciate more and more, the older I get is the long-lasting effects of things that happen to us in childhoods."[162]

✳✳✳✳

At the archives, I stared at the speech, worn down from the years, with Fred Rogers' familiar script on the sides and breathed out, my heart beating faster as I walked down the hallway to ask about what I had just read. It was as if I had overheard a conversation, a secret whisper from the past.

"Oh, yes, that never went away. It stayed with him for the rest of his life," David Newell (who played Mr. McFeely on the *Neighborhood*) remarked when I asked about Fred's trauma over John's experience.

"Would it be okay to share something like this in my book?" I asked.

"Of course! Fred wasn't perfect. He struggled. But he worked hard at every-thing he did."

Somehow, telling the world that Mister Rogers struggled with trauma seemed wrong. We've elevated him to this place of perfection with honor and reverence. But honoring someone is looking at them and loving them for all they are, regard-less of their limitations and faults. As children, we wanted to believe that our parents loved us perfectly and did the best job they could. Many of us would

161 Tuttle, *Exactly as You Are.*
162 King, *The Good Neighbor.*

still claim that as our reality today. We didn't see Mister Rogers' faults, but we witnessed people we loved letting us down, breaking our hearts, and shaming us. People's angry words still linger within us, forgiveness has turned to bitterness, and dark places are still waiting to be felt and voiced. It's what makes us human beings in need of grace, our deeper longing for real love and acceptance. Fred Rogers understood that he was made up of all the moments in his story, not just the ones that sounded lovely in interviews. Tragedy moves our story forward and chisels out our purposes and callings. Would the world embrace a Mister Rogers who didn't have it all together?

As I met those who knew Fred, I could put them into two categories: those who wanted to preserve his legacy of perfection and those who stressed his humanity. Perhaps he has become a symbol of goodness, an ideal we aspire to, a place of nostalgia and timeless optimism. I decided to put it to the test on my social media by creating a post: "Mister Rogers Struggles, Too." It quickly became my most popular post. Interestingly, more men than women opened the post, most being in their mid to late forties. What if understanding that Fred was human is the greatest legacy he left? He was human, and intentional. After all, he was the one who urged us to talk about our real feelings and understand that they are natural and necessary for growing.

Vulnerability about the tragedies we've experienced and how we survived them inspires others and unites us as a human race. Children don't need perfect adults, but real ones. Fred Rogers worked tirelessly to integrate the trauma surrounding his son's hospitalization through programs and literature, but it still showed up in his personal life. He was known to avoid doctors' appointments, even putting off a chronic stomachache for a trip to Scotland with friends, which eventually turned out to be the stomach cancer that claimed his life. Trauma changes us. It sticks and can influence us for better or worse. Healing our own trauma and making peace with the past is the greatest gift we can give to children we love and serve.

On the day we met, David Newell reached into a pile of vintage *Neighborhood* posters and pulled one out. "You should have this."

I looked down and saw the promotion for a Mister Rogers book published in 1977: *Going to the Hospital.* Yes, it made perfect sense.

We are all born with the need to be safe, loved, known, connected, vulnerable, and seen. Trauma is the greatest thief of all. And do you know what heals trauma? Connection.

Diane Poole Heller, PhD, describes trauma as "broken connection: broken connection to our body; broken connection to our sense of self; broken connection to others, especially those we love; broken connection to feeling centered or grounded on the planet; broken connection to God."[163]

The best way to help children become resilient to trauma is through relationship. As we remain close and available, providing compassionate exchange and emotional regulation, we circumvent the deep effects of the moments when trauma takes root. A child's nervous system learns to co-regulate by receiving information directly from ours, and that regulation becomes who they are at a neurological level. The type of regulating environment young children experience will determine their interactions with others and how they see their worlds for the duration of their lives.[164] All they need is you. Just you.

---

163 Heller, *The Power of Attachment.*
164 Heller, *The Power of Attachment.*

Part Three:
Simple and Deep Applications for the Classroom

Lynn Johnson Collection.

Fred Rogers interviews young girl at Mesa Elementary School. 1994. Lynn Johnson Collection.

Chapter 7:

Attunement

"Look and Listen"

When you combine your intuition with a sensitivity to other
people's feelings and moods, you may be close to the origins
of valuable human attributes such as generosity, altruism,
compassion, sympathy, and empathy.
—Fred Rogers

What did you need when you were little? This is the question at the heart of *attunement*. It's about entering the emotional journey of another, and letting it affect us. We recognize a child's emotional state by detecting a need and responding accordingly. It goes beyond empathy while connecting in a more profound way that honors the child in their current state and moment. The gift of our undivided attention sends the messages "I see you. You're safe in my love."

Fred Rogers stated, "As we continue to engage in the work of understanding ourselves and others, we are really engaged in love."[165] Attention fosters hope and bears witness to the story a child is living. "Stories are about how *we*, rather than the world around us, change."[166] It's allowing them to affect us and having the

---

165 Rogers, *You Are Special.*
166 Lisa Cron, *Wired for Story* (Berkeley, CA: Ten Speed Press, 2012).

confidence on their behalf that goodness will come.[167] Believing goodness will come is a bold and radical idea.

If you were a child abandoned to silence, abuse, neglect, or unanswered questions, you might struggle with believing goodness will come. Acknowledge that to yourself, and don't pretend. Next, ponder what you would've needed as a child to have felt heard and seen. What actions would've reassured your heart? Do those for the children in your care. It's a conscious choice to plant your feet and be who you needed when you were younger. Every interaction with a child holds tremendous power. Future pain or positive impact: The decision is yours. Attunement lies at the core of good teaching and loving. Adopt the philosophy, "If it matters to you, it matters to me."

****

We speak with more than our mouths.
We listen with more than our ears.
—Fred Rogers

Amid the buzz of regular play, I hear a child whine in protest, "Br-a-d-ley! Stooooooop!" Never a good sign. I can see Bradley, a normally quiet and kind child, using a larger block to topple each of the towers his friends are building. The chaos is mounting, and his arms are coming close to hitting his playmates in the head.

"Bradley, no!" I call out firmly from across the room.

He drops the block and jets underneath the table outside the block center. Of course, this all happens right as the timer indicates it's cleanup.

"I'm sorry I said your name so loudly. Did I scare you?"

Bradley moves quickly to the other side of the table when I peek my head underneath to speak with him. Suddenly, he begins to bash his head over and over against the metal leg of the table. The children are busy cleaning, unaware of his

---

167 Dan Allender, Cathy Loerzel, and Rachael Clinton Chen, "Story Sage Series" (digital course, Allender Center, n.d.), https://theallendercenter.org/offerings/online-courses/story-sage-series/.

distress. I spring into action, lifting the table up and to the side, exposing him. Surprised, he looks up at me wide-eyed.

"I love you too much to let you do that. I'll come back in a few minutes, and we can talk about what's going on in your heart." He places his head back into his folded arms, pulling his knees up to his chest in a tight cocoon.

After settling the children into their next activity, I return to Bradley, who sits staring at the ground. I touch his hair slowly and run my hand over his back. "Would you like to snuggle?" I ask, sitting cross-legged beside him. He quickly climbs into my lap, burying his head in my chest.

I begin rocking him from side to side. I let him listen to my breathing and the rhythm of my heartbeat. "I love you. You're safe, Bradley. I'm not angry," I say to soothe him. "You can never lose my love."

Bradley feared he had crossed an invisible line where the love of his teacher could be lost. He was ashamed and angry at himself for jeopardizing that relationship. I chose to tell him the truth, with words and actions. It's not until conferences that I'm informed his father had been in a coma due to a motorcycle accident for more than ten days! Bradley had been suffering alone until I scooped him up and witnessed his sadness.

We never know what chapter we've just walked in on for a child. Often, it's you and them against their history and present circumstances.

Our hearts were "created for relationships; moreover, relationships that bring attunement, care, and ultimately rest. But a heart that cannot rest cannot play."[168] Notice that in trying to play, his wounding became apparent. Watch children as they play; it will give you insights.

Be a Container

"Containment is the capacity to create and hold boundaries that provide honor, delight, and insight."[169] We need attunement and containment to work in tandem for deep, authentic connection. Containment honors the child's personhood. They feel valuable and learn that their feelings and emotions aren't less significant or important than an adult's. For children with

168 Allender and Loerzel, *Redeeming Heartache*.
169 Allender, Loerzel, and Chen, "Story Sage Series."

ambivalent attachment this is critical, as they are often enmeshed with one of their caregivers and not afforded autonomy. The avoidantly attached child will shy away from telling the truth about their feelings or have difficulty labeling them, as feelings are not usually welcomed. Disorganized children will bounce back and forth between receiving and rejecting attunement and containment, because vulnerability is unsafe. I've learned to use the phrase "It makes sense _____."

"It makes sense that you're angry about not being invited to the birthday."

"It makes sense that you're sad about your friend moving away."

"It makes sense that you're sleepy if you had a nightmare last night."

"It makes sense that you feel anxious when there's a guest teacher."

Telling the story and voicing their truth brings the deepest illumination and movement out of a dysregulated state. Let them be heard. Empathy—being a container—creates a bridge back from the shores of chaos or rigidity, while fear and uncertainty dissipate in the care of another. Often, we can't make a situation "all better," but just being with someone they know loves them is enough.

Take Off Your Shoes

Fred Rogers was always taking off his shoes. He was known for it. Those worn Sperry Top sneakers were his staple signaling to our young bodies, "I'm here to listen to you. Welcome home." His unhurried and available heart was open to the interruptions of the divine. Availability will cost us something, but it results in more profound connections with the human heart. "The older I get," Rogers claimed, "the more convinced I am that the space between communicating human beings can be hallowed ground."

In his song "Look and Listen," Rogers illustrates that observation is essential for understanding others. It is through observation and reflection that we learn and grow in relationships with others. Notice his emphasis on "looking":

> If you will look carefully,
> Listen carefully,
> You will find a lot of things carefully.
> Look . . . and listen.

It's good to
Look carefully.
Listen carefully.
That's the way you learn a lot of things carefully.
Look . . . look and listen.

Some things you see are confusing.
Some things you hear are strange.
But if you ask someone to explain one or two,
You'll begin to notice a change in you.

If you will
Look carefully.
Listen carefully.

That's a way to keep on growing carefully.
Look, look, look, and listen.[170]

As we look, we gather information. Is what we see normal for this child? What do they usually do or say in a situation? Should we ask them a question or gather more evidence? Fred Rogers has taught me to take the extra time to step back and wait patiently for the answers to come. It isn't through rough poking or intrusiveness, but children will reveal what's hidden in their hearts through our gentle availability. Of course, none of us would want to believe that we are rough or intrusive, but our lack of patience and annoyance at a child's discomfort send messages to their young bodies. We want to shield them from possible harm, confusion, and pain. Our attuned responses are guided by keen observation of the obvious and the hidden.

We all know when we have been attuned to.

It generates feelings of comfort, peace, and "being seen." Such moments make us crave more, as they are a glimpse of the divine, an encounter with love.

---

170 Fred M. Rogers, "Look and Listen," The Mister Rogers Neighborhood Archive, 1970. http://www.neighborhoodarchive.com/music/songs/look_listen.html.

Finally, our hearts can come home and find rest in the solace of another whom we can trust. When they contain our moment, telling us it makes sense, empathizing with our wounding with sincerity and kindness, trauma slowly integrates, and our nervous system regulates.

Attunement requires bold choices, like moving tables and naming the big things that the world doesn't want us to voice—developmental trauma, heartbreak, limitations, apathy, and fear. It will cost you time and energy and make you doubt if it's the right choice. Do it anyway.

Use Eye Contact and Lean In

Fred Rogers' ability to attune to the camera was based on sound advice he received while working at NBC in the 1950s on *The Gabby Hayes Show*, one of the first Western children's programs on television. The vaudeville entertainer George "Gabby" Hayes was someone Fred Rogers viewed as having a gift. Eventually, "he asked the wily Hayes how he managed to connect so well with his audience, and Gabby replied that the only way to manage a television role in which one is asked to speak directly to a disembodied, distant audience is to convince oneself that one is speaking only to one little child. 'Just one little buckaroo,' Hayes told Rogers; just think of talking only directly to 'one little buckaroo.'"[171]

Fred Rogers' complete focus on *a* child is notable in all his work on the *Neighborhood*. In an episode of *Mister Rogers' Neighborhood* in 1985, for example, Joe Negri brings six-year-old Niki Hoeller to the television house, where he plays two classical pieces on Mister Rogers' piano. The boy plays with confidence and ease. And as his fingers dance atop the keys, Rogers' gaze remains steady on Niki's face. He's absorbed in the musical moment and the child's delight in sharing a bit of himself. Attunement—a silent exchange, pleasure, and musical connection. At that moment, Niki Hoeller is the most important person in the world to Fred Rogers. Using a theme he would adopt while interacting with anyone he met, Mister Rogers turns the spotlight on the child, taking pleasure in being an appreciator.

---

171 King, *The Good Neighbor.*

When famous cellist Yo-Yo Ma appeared on the *Neighborhood* for the first time in 1985, Rogers' authenticity made quite the impression. Ma said, "He interviewed me, and he put his face about three inches away from my face and said, 'It's so nice to see you and to be with you.' It scared the living daylights out of me. But I realized this is what children do to adults."[172] Where the world would step back, Rogers leaned in and waited. In education, we call it "wait time," but Rogers did it naturally. He was genuinely interested in someone's response and in no hurry to get to the next thought. A great example of this is when he does a factory visit in the *Neighborhood*. When he's touring an assembly line, he'll often stop to talk to a man or woman working, such as assembling dolls or tricycles, and ask, "Did you like to play with dolls when you were a little girl?" or "I wonder, do you often think about the children who will ride this tricycle you are making?"

We have it backward, especially those of us who like to talk. Listening can feel inactive when our mind is racing with ideas or we're aware of the time. Fred Rogers was annoying to interview for this very reason. He would always turn the interview back on the other person. People would walk away shaking their heads, wondering how they just got interviewed when they were doing a piece on him. Predictably asking direct questions, followed by silence, was his forte, as he genuinely wanted to hear what you had to share. Then, after you'd share, more silence. He wasn't afraid of silence. Interestingly, people would share more! It takes time for people to gather their thoughts, and deeper connection need not be rushed. His eyes didn't dart around the room but rested on the person who deserved his attention. It was always a choice.

Smile with Your Eyes

As I write this, we're entering the second year of a worldwide pandemic. The students I sat down on the kindergarten rug and told, "It will only be six weeks" are now second graders. Never before has eye contact been so vital to connection. When we're wearing masks, the eyes are all we can see.

"How do you smile with your eyes?" I asked my students at the beginning of the year. "Can you smile with your eyes like this?" We've worked hard to use

---

172 *Won't You Be My Neighbor?*, directed by Morgan Neville (New York: Focus Features, 2018), https://www.netflix.com/title/80231412.

our eyes to show our feelings and emotions because our smiles are hidden, and expressions are lost.

When people learn I'm a kindergarten teacher who has taught online learning during the pandemic, they're curious to hear how it was. No, it wasn't fun trying to get houses to be quiet. I was thankful for the mute-all button when parents forgot I could hear their conversations, babies started to cry, and dogs barked. All those things were challenging, as well as the technology. Students had difficulty logging in, and parents were frazzled. We all experienced some form of Zoom fatigue and helplessness.

What I did love was that every morning we were a community. Each of their precious faces appeared inside their boxes, looking back at me, ready for learning and love. I had them for six months before we went online, so I knew everything about them, how I could make them laugh, engage. I used all that I had learned from Fred. Leaned in and looked at their eyes. I sent love and believed it would land. If Fred communicated love through the camera, I could too. I had to learn to "hold" them with my eyes. Holding requires strength and courage. And our eyes tell them things, important things:

I'm so happy to see you and be with you.
Just the sight of you makes me happy.
Do we need to sit and talk?
I'm right here, and I know that it's hard.
I see you and I think you're wonderful.

The Invisible String of Love

Evelyn has missed our first Zoom call, and I'm worried. I arrange for her mom to connect her and wait for her little face to pop onto my screen. The moment her eyes connect with mine, she bursts into tears.

"I know, honey," I soothe her. "It's okay to cry."

Her sunshine blonde hair sticks to her cheeks as she hugs the tablet closer and closer to her face. The ache is profound and palpable. There's no relief in sight, either. So we sit together in our moment. Happy and sad all at once. Life is super messy, but better together.

"I love you, my brave girl. I'm right here and I'll stay here as long as you need me to."

"I'm happy and sad," she says.

I smile, as she's terrific about explaining her feelings.

"Sad because I feel like I will never see you again and happy because I love you."

I wish I could hold her. What would've taken five minutes in the classroom takes at least twenty minutes over the internet. "I need you to look at me, Evelyn," I say. "There's nobody else like you in the whole world, and you will never lose my love. I'm still your teacher, and I'm sad too. We can even be mad about not getting to see each other. That makes sense to me."

She nods in agreement.

"Have you been watching Mister Rogers?"

"Yes." She has her head buried into her chest, covering it with her hands. The ache is so raw and tangible.

"Good, Evelyn. That's so good. Tell me about Mister Rogers. What did he tell you today?"

"We made applesauce, and I saw Chef Brockett," she mumbles.

"Do you remember when we made applesauce, and the classroom smelled delicious? I think you even had seconds."

"I did." She sniffles. "I like watching Mister Rogers because when I do that, I can feel you loving me." *Oh, be still my beating teacher heart.*

We read a book together on her bed, me leaning close to the screen as she moves the screen awkwardly, often only showing me half the text. I knew she would have the hardest time being away from me, as she's often called my "mini-me" at school. Bold, sassy, and opinionated. Full of love and emotions and needing to be affirmed daily. When I was teaching her our classroom expectations in the fall, she'd often ask, "Are you mad at me?" She was terrified to lose my love and favor. It took months to break down those insecurities, and now I can't reach out to her and hug it better.

"We can do this together. Because . . ." I wait for her to add on.

"Because we can do hard things," she answers, using a phrase we learned in class.

"And it's okay to feel whatever you feel. You can call me anytime, sweet girl. I love you very much."

"I love you too," she says, smiling at me.

"I'm going to send you some love through the phone so you can catch it."

Making a heart with my hands, I throw it toward the screen. She drops the phone with a loud "Whoa!" and I hear her fumbling. When she gets back on camera, I say, "Did you just drop me on the floor?"

"Yep! It was a lot of love. It knocked me over!"

"Wait for My Wink!"

How I wish that all children in this world could have at least one person who could embrace them and encourage them. I wish that all children could have somebody who let them know that the outsides of people are insignificant compared with their insides: to show them that no matter what, they'll always have somebody who believes in them.

—Fred Rogers

Blue Eyes has difficulty with eye contact. It unnerves him. Each time we sit together to work through one of his choices—hitting, bullying, or muscling another child—I say, "Show me your eyes." Children who've experienced developmental trauma may see sustained eye contact as a threat. When eyes directed upon them in the past were filled with condemnation, rage, or violence, they only learned to fear. His blue eyes are stunning, but behind them I sense countless times he's witnessed drug abuse and domestic violence.

As an infant, his body absorbed the screams, fights, and shattering of dreams. Stillness and quiet unnerve him. His brain and nervous system feel "at home" with chaos, not the attuned attention of his teacher. In his experience, when another's eyes rested on him, rage would soon follow, shame and disappointment aimed at him as the convenient target. It wasn't his fault his mother had been abused or that his father had used drugs, but his little heart believed the lies. He's waiting for people to betray him and leave. Why would I be any different?

When he's dysregulated, Blue Eyes tugs hard on his fingers, as if pulling them out of their sockets. His eyes gloss over while his arms and legs stiffen, recoiling at the slightest touch. Through his crystal-blue eyes, I became the pupil and he the teacher. It was his chaos that first led me back to the *Neighborhood* and Fred Rogers, as I began to type out one afternoon all that I wished for him and how the world had failed him. How could a little boy be so broken?

As a teacher, what can I repair in only nine months? Every year a child is old, it will take that many months for their brain to adjust to secure attachment. For a kindergartener, that would mean five to six months out of nine in a school year.

Blue Eyes had been left in emotional pain far too often, with a broken heart and shattered trust. While at recess, one afternoon, he joins me near the wall, where I ask him to sit for a few minutes to rethink his word choices. "So, why did I have you come over here?" I ask him, sitting beside him and mirroring his posture. His arms rest on top of his knees, and his back leans against the brick wall.

"I don't know," he mutters, looking out at the boys running on the blacktop.

"You called your friends losers," I remind him.

"Yeah," he says.

"What's a loser?" I question him. He sits quietly, staring off across the playground.

"I need your eyes," I prompt him.

His face turns, and he looks at me for a split second and then above my head.

"Come back to my eyes, please." I keep my tone soft but firm and place my hand on his arm for a slight squeeze. Each time we have a moment together, I believe it will help rewire his brain through the experience of attunement. His eyes land on mine, and I say, "[Blue Eyes], I think *you* feel like a loser, and I need you to tell me why."

Without hesitation, he says, "We were late for recess because of me, and that makes me a loser."

"You are not a loser," I state. "You're five, and you're learning. Yes, we had to wait while you cleaned up your mess, but we had to wait for Cameron this morning, remember?"

"I guess," he mutters and drops his head.

"I need your eyes," I say. "I need you to know something. You are not a loser. I love you, and you are important to me. I love you exactly as you are."

"You sound like Mister Rogers," he says, smiling.

"That's because he was right about kids like you. Now, wait for my wink."

He looks me in the eyes as I pause for a few seconds. Then I wink. He winks back at me and jumps up.

Watching him run off, I take a deep breath and enjoy the freedom of knowing he heard me. He may need to listen to it a thousand times until he believes. It's a routine we discovered together. A pair of kind eyes looking back at him with love. I would often watch him walk and visualize placing a bubble of love around him for protection. Love in front of him to fend off the world's assaults and love at his back to remind him where he'd been.

****

I have always loved the quote "Motherhood is like seeing your heart walk around outside your body," but teaching has become the same for me. As their teacher, their foster guardian, for a short nine months, I must learn all the ways I can reach their hearts. Then I hand them off to another who may or may not understand all the life I've poured into them. What if they aren't a good fit? Will they take the time to listen and care for him, or will he be written a referral and sent away? I shared my frustrations with a long-time colleague of Fred Rogers while visiting the Fred Rogers Institute in 2019. She nodded and asked, "Do you remember the episode with Jeff Erlanger in the wheelchair?"

Fred Rogers talked to Jeff, a young boy who used a wheelchair due to a spinal injury. Sitting at eye level on the stairs, Rogers authentically engaged Jeff in conversation, allowed him to pace their interaction, and demonstrated care and attention. As it wasn't possible to rehearse the segment in advance, Rogers chose to spontaneously sing "It's You I Like" with his young guest, creating what Fred Rogers affectionately called his "most treasured moment."

Years later, when Rogers received his Lifetime Achievement Award, Jeff rolled onto the stage. Fred Rogers bounded onstage like a young man in his twenties to wrap around Jeff with all his love and appreciation. Seeing Jeff was his reward, not the trophy in his hands.

Referencing the *Neighborhood* episode that aired years before, Fred's colleague at the institute said to me, "You may have missed it before, but at the end of the segment, Fred says, 'Goodbye, Jeff. I'll watch you as you go.'"

The message wasn't lost on me, and my eyes filled with tears. Nothing could be more accurate. Every year as our students leave, it's like a small death. We watch them as they go, with all our love at their backs. The next year, as I watched Blue Eyes round the corner with his new teacher, I kept my eyes on his back and said, *I love you, I love you, I love you* in my mind.

Get Below Who You're Talking To

In infancy, a mother mirrors her baby through facial expressions and sounds, holding the child closer to her face to maximize closeness. This *mirroring* signals to a child's brain that they are seen and valued. An attachment bond is being created. Much like Fred Rogers established safety for us through a screen, our bodies invite children in for deeper contact—or not. Children with insecure attachments may find someone mirroring them odd or frightening. Yet mirroring a child is a nurturing and bonding activity that will gradually slow down their fight/flight response. By watching a child's reaction when you try to match, you will learn subtle lessons about their fear and readiness to share closeness.[173] And the behaviors we then model must be what we value and desire.

"Fred could squat faster than anyone else I knew. He'd see a child, and he was like an elevator," said former *Neighborhood* director Paul Lally.[174] He saw children as his equal, valuing their ideas, feelings, and perspectives on the world. What better way to gain their perspective than getting down on their level? Coming to them by sitting, squatting, or kneeling is the quickest way to show them "I'm here and I see you."

If Fred Rogers was interviewing a child, he would lean his body closer and place his face in his hand while he listened. I've spent a large portion of my career close to the floor as my students explain a problem from recess or relay a story from the weekend. If you can't get below them, use your eyes and hands to signify they have all your attention. During work times, I taught students to place a hand

---

173 Purvis, Cross, and Sunshine, *The Connected Child.*
174 Lally, "Fred's Friend."

on my shoulder instead of interrupting. I make an effort to put a hand on top of theirs to signal, "I know you're here."

Use Affectionate Touch

We live in a world that is terrified of touch, especially in education and childcare settings. Our culture has made us afraid of allegations and misunderstandings. As cases of alleged abuse and neglect flood our headlines, we do what we know best—avoid. No touching! But children haven't gotten the memo, and they long to be close to the people they love. I can recall sitting at the feet of my first-grade teacher during a read-aloud and touching her ankles and shoes. Her nylons bunched together, making bumpy ridges above her bony foot. I wasn't worried about her telling me no or scolding me, as my touches were welcome. The hungry hands of young children are busy and curious, full of wonder.

Years ago, I taught a girl who was orphaned in Romania. The orphans there gain half their expected weight and height because they are touch deprived.[175] She was tied to her crib and remained cross-eyed until adopted by her American parents. It wasn't until she received consistent, safe touch that her body began to thrive. Touch has healing properties. "Research shows that children who get frequent and safe, open-hand caresses fare better than children who are not touched often or are touched only with fingertips. . . . Touch is important for everyone's physiological health and is an expression of affection, appreciation, and valuing between two people. Touch builds interpersonal bonds and actually improves brain chemistry."[176]

Touch is a bonding experience, and quantity *does* matter in childhood. "Scientists believe that the most important factor in creating attachment is positive physical contact (e.g., hugging, holding, and rocking). It should be no surprise that holding, gazing, smiling, singing, and laughing all cause specific neurochemical activities in the brain. These neurochemical activities lead to normal organization of brain systems that are responsible for attachment."[177]

---

175 Purvis, Cross, and Sunshine, *The Connected Child*.
176 Purvis, Cross, and Sunshine, *The Connected Child*.
177 Bruce D. Perry, "Bonding and Attachment: Consequences of Emotional Neglect in Childhood," ChildTrauma Academy, 2013, www.childtrauma.org.

My friend Jim Judkas recalls the first time he met Fred Rogers in his Pittsburgh studio in the late 1970s. He was there to do a shoot for *People* magazine and extended his hand in a greeting. Jim recalls how Mister Rogers clasped his hands warmly and said kindly, "Please, call me Fred." Judkas was instantly at ease in his presence. Fred Rogers often held others' hands in pastoral reverence, gently cupping his right hand over theirs, a natural gesture that demonstrated genuine presence and attunement.

During the photo shoot, Jim Judkas witnessed Rogers receive children who were severely handicapped and deformed in an empty room. In an action now captured in an iconic photo, a young boy ran through the doors yelling, "It's Mister Rogers!" Plowing through the crowd of children and around wheelchairs, he haphazardly seized Fred Rogers' face and planted a kiss on his mouth. Nose to nose, Rogers and this young boy laughed together as Judkas captured the encounter. Years later, after the Sandy Hook school shooting, this same photo was teamed up with Rogers' quote "look for the helpers" and shared all over social media, bringing comfort to America.

During *Mister Rogers' Neighborhood* each day, I place a chair in front of the screen so students can cluster around my feet. I've nicknamed the place at my knees the "hot spot." It's where I place the child most in need of attunement that day. It was often Blue Eyes. It provided a solid twenty-eight minutes where I would intentionally touch him, pray for him, and know that he had an adult giving him positive attention. It's the only time I allow children to lay on their tummies or backs and relax. As they snuggle into my sides and legs, I make a point to stroke their hair, rub their back, or give their shoulder a squeeze. Looking out over the rest, I'll catch their eye and wink, smile, or sign "I love you" to them like Maggie Stewart demonstrates on the *Neighborhood*. I read the calmness of their bodies and the soothing it brings as they connect with me, a secure base, and then return their attention back to Mister Rogers. It is a dance of connection, full of intentional moments.

The day Blue Eyes allowed his rigid, anxious body to relax into me, becoming heavy against my legs, I had to hold in my joy over such an exchange. I used my fingertips to gently rub his forehead and hair as we watched the Neighborhood of Make-Believe. He was beginning to trust me. When working with children from difficult places, give yourself permission to stay 1 percent longer in the good moments. Easy moments can be rare and fleeting.

****

During an episode one afternoon, Blue Eyes stands up and begins to walk behind me.

"Where are you going?" I ask, afraid he's up to no good. I'll admit it, I still have my doubts.

"I'm getting a drink of water," he replies.

I take in a deep breath and choose to trust him, returning my attention back to the screen. Suddenly, I sense him behind me. He wraps his right arm and then his left around my neck in a hug.

I freeze, surprised. Then slowly, I reach my hands up to cover his and began to sway, ever so softly, back and forth. The rhythm of my body connects to his as he allows me to rock him. "I love you," I say softly.

"Yeah, I know," he replies matter-of-factly.

And thus begins our new routine. Every day, about fifteen minutes into the episode, he rises, gets his drink of water, and then returns to me to be held on his terms.

****

Touch is imperative for connection and emotional regulation. Our society has made touch dirty, illicit, and wrong. Culturally sensitive and abusive. I understand that there are boundaries, but I have had quite enough of the bad getting all the attention.

We base our opinions of situations on fear, experience, and stereotypes. Our snap judgments ruin reputations and relationships, keeping us wide awake with worry. If you're a man and teaching fifth-grade girls, you will have to exercise extreme caution. Our world loves a good story, and the news is full of teachers, priests, caregivers, friends, families, and celebrities doing horrible things to children. I am an advocate for justice, and if you were abused, I want you to experience freedom and peace. Let's remember that abusers aren't the majority of those working with children. Be vigilant. Be aware, but don't let worry override love and attunement. Has our own wounding caused us to shy away from connecting with others in meaningful ways regarding touch?

Touch heals, helps, and restores. Children have the right to refuse touch, and we should ask them for permission, always exercising discernment. A quick hug, hair ruffle, or shoulder squeeze can solve a problem a thousand words won't. Give a child a choice. Let them lead, but don't avoid touch because of creeps.

Here's another thing I've noticed: *Those who have trouble with touch are often the first ones to point fingers.* My grandpa used to say, "When you're pointing one finger at someone, remember you have three fingers pointing back at you." Do you have trauma around touch that you are forcing on others? Ask yourself why you're concerned with a kindergartner hugging their teacher, taking their teacher's hand, or having their head touched? I know you may play the culture card, possible allegations, and so on. I hear you. But I needed touch as a child. You needed it as a child. And while the insides of children haven't changed, the world around them has. Let us empower children to know the difference and not be afraid that touch is inherently bad. It's all about intentions.

Children with attachment trauma crave affectionate touch. Blue Eyes craved safety and comfort. His nervous system was seeking out the connection he had never received, through meaningful interactions that involved physical and emotional "holding." As we found our daily rhythms of rest, restoration, and routines, Blue Eyes eased into a fractured sense of trust. I often felt as though I were in a corral with a wild horse, watching him running slowly and learning to believe that I would keep him safe with my reliable presence and reactions.

One afternoon, I found myself wanting to record my students singing along with Fred and retrieved my phone, sitting on the opposite of a dividing table to get the best view. Blue Eyes got his usual drink of water and, finding me not in my normal chair, made his way to where I was. Instead of wrapping his arms around my neck for a hug, he climbed into my lap and placed his head against my chest like a baby. I wrapped my arms around him as he leaned back. Slowly, I began to rock him from side to side, as his long legs dangled off my lap. Gone was the angry six-year-old child, as his nervous system regulated to my calm presence. I was quite aware of an exchange with the divine, a moment so pure, so full of the existence of something greater than myself. Instinctively, my mother's heart held my precious, disorganized blue-eyed boy, thankful for such a moment of calm.

"May his body remember this moment, God, although his memory will forget," I prayed silently. These few precious minutes were a confirmation that I was on the right track. Fred Rogers had been right all along. How had everything become so muddled and complex? Do we really need to look into motivations of behavior, or should we just become more open to giving what we all crave?

I was also rocking my own heart, rocking the sadness of making teaching about things that were fleeting—competing over scores, cute classrooms, and celebrating overworking and overspending. I was coming back to the *Neighborhood*. To the place where my heart was at home. To an ease and a deep knowing that this was right.

What have you forfeited for peace? Where have you compromised love for the sake of validation or prestige? Why do we celebrate things that are fleeting or temporary? Loving is sacrificial. Loving is hard. Loving is vulnerable. To love is to empty ourselves of the façade that we are in control and have it all figured out. We all need to be rocked and told it will all be okay, because we aren't alone. I think the lyrics from the musical *Dear Evan Hansen* summarize this best: "Even when the dark is crashing through, and you need a friend to carry you and when you're broken on the ground, you will be found."[178]

Listen to Internal Rhythms

Our bodies are naturally rhythmic. We have predictable physiological and psychological processes that allow receptivity to our environment. Things such as hunger, thirst, needing to use the restroom, waking, sleeping, comfort, and so

---

178 "You Will Be Found," *Dear Evan Hansen*, music and lyrics by Benj Pasek and Justin Paul.

on, all play a role in helping us respond to the world around us. Our hearts beat, our eyes blink, and air moves in and out of our lungs. If our goal is to attune to children, then sensitivity to natural rhythms is paramount. To know someone well is to know and understand their rhythms. What makes them peaceful? When do they feel soothed or at rest? Does the world fall apart when they are tired or afraid, or is there a stubborn resolve that won't quit even when sleep beckons them closer? We all have natural rhythms that make us unique, and alike. Perhaps you feel most alive in the morning as you take a run, watching the sun peek up over the top of your world, while another enjoys the stillness of nighttime when all noise fades away. Taking the time to understand each of your students' natural rhythms will help you key into moments where they are needing support and extra attunement.

Dancing with Children

Attunement is the dance of predicting what a child needs before they need it. A person's capability to "dance well with others" in life directly correlates to the quality of attunement they received in childhood. It's as if we hold them up to our eyes and dance before their feet can touch the floor, giving them a forever assurance that our hands and hearts are steady and trustworthy.

In episode 1574 of *Mister Rogers' Neighborhood*, Fred Rogers brings a rolled-up dance mat for the floor. "I've been doing a lot of thinking about dancing lately," he explains. "And when I was a little boy, I watched my parents dancing, and I wanted so much to learn how to do that. My mother helped me by holding me up and pretending that we were dancing around, but my dad got me a big piece of paper and put foot marks on it and showed me how to follow those marks with my own two feet."[179]

Instead of marking the steps on pieces of large butcher paper, we as teachers predict when and where to lift a child emotionally if they need a break and when to encourage them to experience the thrills of letting go and spinning on their own. Life is like a dance. "People dance at any age because people have feelings at

---

179 Fred M. Rogers, "Episode 1574: Mister Rogers Talks About Dance," The Mister Rogers Neighborhood Archive, 1987, http://www.neighborhoodarchive.com/mrn/episodes/1574/index.html.

every age. Very young people and very old people. All have very deep feelings, and everybody likes to have healthy ways of expressing those feelings,"[180] Rogers says before ending the program.

Are you a reliable dance partner? "Learning to maneuver the hard times is all about having dance partners you can trust. Much in the same way as musical groups and orchestras ensure their instruments are in tune before beginning their performance, [children] rely upon . . . emotional attunement with their teachers and caregivers."[181] "Good emotional 'immunity' comes out of feeling safely held, touched, seen and helped to recover from stress, whilst the stress response is undermined by separation, uncertainty, lack of contact and lack of regulation."[182]

This is why it's imperative to understand our own natural rhythms, reactions, and trigger points. Attunement also involves understanding when *we* are becoming flooded with our own overwhelm and stress and taking emotional breaks to recharge or reset. Look for ways to check in with yourself. I've found it profoundly helpful, for example, to take five to ten minutes during lunch to meditate, pray, dim the lights, and breathe deeply. And during the introduction to *Mister Rogers' Neighborhood*, as I settle into my chair, I've made it a habit to take three deep-cleansing breaths, reminding my body to rest, slow down, and receive all that I need for the next twenty-eight minutes.

Still, at times, and despite my best efforts to attend to my own natural rhythms, I know it's inevitable that dancing won't always be harmonious and smooth. Some children's nervous systems are chaotic and difficult to get "in sync" with. They make unhappy dance partners and almost enjoy stepping on our toes. Sometimes, I wish there were a map to follow or a guidebook. But at its core is

---

180 Fred M. Rogers, "A Visit with Arthur Mitchell," *Mister Rogers' Neighborhood*, episode #1574, March 12, 1987, https://www.misterrogers.org/episodes/a-visit-with-arthur-mitchell/.

181 Maira Holzmann, "What Is Attunement? And Why Is It Important in Healing from Early Childhood Trauma?" Somatic Therapy Partners, August 21, 2020, https://somatictherapypartners.com/what-is-attunement-and-why-is-it-important-in-healing-from-early-childhood-trauma/.

182 Sue Gerhardt, *Why Love Matters: How Affection Shapes a Baby's Brain* (Hove, East Sussex: Routledge, 2015).

sensing, discerning, and adjusting the course to meet whatever the circumstances throw at you.

And always remember that life is unpredictable, so learning to dance with children sometimes flops. Misattunements occur, and mistakes are made. We can beat ourselves up or laugh at our own ability to make everything so serious all the time. Adulting makes us forget the pleasure of not having to know everything, and we put tremendous pressure on ourselves to be perfect in the eyes of children. Fred Rogers understood the importance of allowing children to see that we are imperfect people living honestly. It's far more precious than gold. It generates ease and confidence, celebrating the process over the product.

"I'm still discovering the truth about me," he tells us. Children need us not to have all the right dance moves but to provide our solid presence in their lives for them to fall into. Let us never forget. Rogers' childlike willingness and wonder about growing on the inside is inspiring and a model for us. As we enter a moment with a child, we are there to learn from it and from them too. Oh, that we would remember the beauty of wonder, the excitement of curiosity, and the hopeful expectation of not knowing everything.

Skin Trust is established in small steps. In 1994, during the filming of the PBS special *Fred Rogers' Heroes: Who's Helping America's Children*,[183] where Rogers spent time with four people who were making an impact in their own neighborhoods, he visited Green Chimneys. Nestled in upstate New York and founded by Dr. Sam "Rolo" Ross, the working farm was a place for troubled youth, many from the foster-care system in New York City, to come and find solace learning to take care of animals. The formula was simple: A child is responsible for caring for an animal. Many of the children had never experienced nurturing and attachment, so the bonds they made with doves, owls, sheep, and other animals were profound and real.

Next, the child was teamed up with another child to work in tandem providing animal care. And when the children trusted one another, then, and only then, an adult would begin establishing a bond through counseling and mentorship. Many of the animals on the farm were being rehabilitated due to a

---

183 Fred M. Rogers, "Fred Rogers' Heroes," The Mister Rogers Neighborhood Archive, http://www.neighborhoodarchive.com/video_film/heroes/index.html.

broken wing or ailment. The goal for the animals was to eventually return them back to the wild. Much like the young boys Fred Rogers interviewed while tending to their animals, Green Chimneys exists to prove that there is goodness in the world. Given enough time, all children can heal, but we must follow their lead.

Model writing that included what we had watched
that day on the *Neighborhood*. 2018.

Love note mailed to author
during the pandemic. 2020.

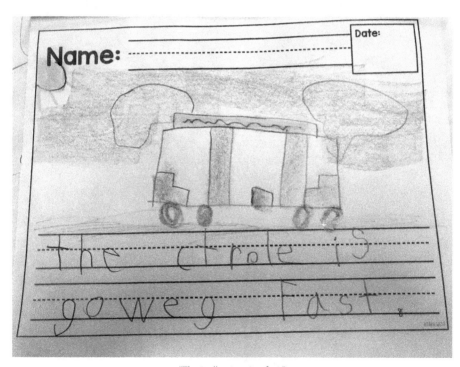

"The trolley is going fast."
An example of student writing inspired by the episode where Trolley
was speeding through the Neighborhood of Make-Believe. 2022.

A handmade doll of Mister Rogers, a gift from a student alongside a purchased stuffy and various books from author's collection. 2019.

Boys playing with magnetic Mister Rogers sets. They became so popular we had to get two. 2018.

Sisters Aavery and Aandersan, after a tough day of distance learning, cuddle up to find some peace and quiet with Mister Rogers. 2021.

We received many "Speedy Deliveries" at school from David Newell (a.k.a. Mr. McFeely, the delivery man on *Mister Rogers' Neighborhood*).

Emma proudly displays her gift from the author.
2020.

Vintage *Neighborhood* puppets acquired by the author
to use with students. 2018.

Calm-down area in our classroom. Materials gifted by a classroom parent from Generation Mindful, a recycled photo of Mister Rogers and posters from Pocket of Preschool a Teachers Pay Teachers Seller. 2022.

Mister Rogers re-created fish tank for the classroom located in the calm-down area. 2018.

Caption: "Look, Mrs. Edwards! I made the Neighborhood of Make-Believe!" (The Museum-Go-Round at the top is my favorite.) 2022.

Chapter 8:

Important Talk

"What Do You Do with the Mad That You Feel?"

I have always called talking about feelings "important talk."
Knowing that our feelings are natural and normal for all of us
can make it easier for us to share them with one another. . . .
It's only natural that we and our children find many things hard
to talk about. But anything human is mentionable, and anything
mentionable can be manageable. The mentioning can be
difficult, and the managing, too, but both can be done
if we're surrounded by love and trust.

—Fred Rogers

I see her sitting in the office, leaning back on the green bench. Her book box beside her, knees curled up to her chest, trying to be invisible to those entering the front doors or children returning from lunch recess. My Evelyn. Once a precious kindergartener who cried to me over a screen, separated from her beloved teacher due to COVID, now a second grader sitting alone.

I slide down beside her and can feel her tense up. Running my hand over her blonde hair, I ask, "What's going on? Why are you sitting here?"

Without looking up, she recognizes my voice, and a muffled reply comes from beneath her arms. "I don't want to tell you. You'll be mad at me. It's poisonous."

I wrap my arm around her and scoot her to me. She smells like the peanut butter sandwich from her lunch and the shampoo I recognize from two years before. Evelyn is my "mini-me." She is loud, opinionated, a natural leader, and fiercely loyal to those she loves. She's the only child of her parents but now the oldest of two blended families, leaving her looking for her place and identity.

It's common for children like Evelyn to exhibit pain-based behaviors as bids for connection, whether in the form of yelling out, stealing, bullying, friendship difficulties, or messiness. Although she's often scolded by other staff members, Evelyn has the timing down to "use the bathroom" at recess when I enter the cafeteria with my kindergarten class. She confidently makes her way to the lunch cards so I can engulf her in an embrace. Should she be doing it every day? No. But she is still mine, and I won't turn her away. Her hugs soothe my own sadness and regret for the months I lost as her kindergarten teacher over two years ago.

"I have to sit here for two whole days, today and Monday. It's bad."

"Well, that sucks," I say.

We sit for a moment in silence as the bustle of the office swirls around us. Although I'm missing my own lunch, I'm not going anywhere. Evelyn is my priority, and that's what you do for people you love.

"You know there's nothing you can tell me that will make it so I don't love you," I say. It's a statement Evelyn had heard countless times from myself and Mister Rogers.

"It's bad. I'm bad. Really bad. Poison." Her shame is thick. What could be so horrible?

"Okay, this is silly," I reply. "I'm not understanding this. Tell me what you did."

She looks up at me, her crystal-blue eyes begging me to change my mind. I hold her gaze, allow the silence, and wait.

With a deep breath, she blurts out, "I put hand sanitizer in Ian's water bottle."

"Why did you do that?"

"I don't know!" she proclaims, exasperated. "I keep doing bad things."

As her nervous system begins to respond to mine, her body relaxes against me. A familiar peace and comfort.

"It was poison! He could've died!" There was the dramatic side, and whatever someone had told her had not only taken root but traumatized her in the process.

The last I heard, no one has died from eating a squirt of sanitizer, but that fact would've been lost on her at that moment.

"He didn't. He's still alive, and now we're sitting here talking together. It was a mistake. Remember when Mister Rogers told us that mistakes are part of growing?"

"This is too bad," she mumbles.

I lift her chin up to get her to look at me. "Even I've done bad things. We just need to own it and say, 'Yep, it was me, and I did it, and I'm sorry.'"

"Yeah," she says.

"Are you feeling sad about something else inside? Maybe mad? Confused about something?"

"I don't know," she says.

Lunch ends, and the classes file in through the front doors. Evelyn buries her head into me as her second-grade class walks in. "They're all going to look at me and see me sitting here. See?"

Old feelings of humiliation rise to the surface inside my body. I can see the corner I was told to stand in during sixth grade and the smugness of my peers as I watched them go to recess while I was left behind, exposed and "bad." My perception was that if I was smarter, I wouldn't make such dumb choices in school. More than humiliating, it confirmed the lies shame whispered inside my heart. *See? You aren't enough, and that's why nobody loves you. People will always reject or leave you.*

"Come on, I'll walk you back," I say, grabbing her book box.

As we walk down the hall together, she takes my hand like when she was five, and a familiar rhythm falls between us, just like when she was in kindergarten.

"Well, Ev, I guess this could have been worse. He could've drunk it."

"HE DID!" she says, exasperated.

Without thinking, I laugh. "Oh, wow!"

"It's not funny! It's poison, and I'm bad!"

Kneeling in front of her, I grab her hands and pull her closer to me. "I'm sorry I laughed. It isn't funny, you're right. I need you to look at my face." Even though I'm not supposed to, I pull down my mask so she can see me.

Her eyes lock on mine.

"You are not bad. You are my beautiful, brave girl, and this dumb mistake doesn't change that for one minute. Do you hear me? Not one single minute. I love you more than anything in the world, and you are not a bad choice!"

She bursts into tears and falls against me. It's the moment she remembers who she is. "To love [a child] is to strive to accept that [child] exactly the way he or she is, right here and now."[184] We need to be reminded of our worth and infinite value, as we are prone to forget. Each of us is loveable exactly as we are.

When left alone with an unvoiced story, we tend to forget we are enough. Our brains integrate the hard things when discussing them with people we love. We all need one person who is our safe harbor. Alone, in front of the bathrooms, Evelyn fell back into her Neighborhood, home, and safe place—me.

When the Canoe Flips

Imagine you're in a canoe with a child you teach. You can see either side of the banks as you're rowing peacefully along. Suddenly, without warning, the canoe capsizes, and you and your student are splashing violently in the water, gasping for air, and grabbing for the canoe to stay afloat. The image may already be making your blood pressure rise a bit, but this is a perfect illustration of what happens to our nervous system when a trigger sets off the alarm bells. Things are fine, then they aren't. *Splash!* We're both in the waters of dysregulation, trying to survive, looking for something or someone to hold on to.

I first read about this analogy in the brilliant work of Dan Siegel, and it's stuck with me ever since. He details it in his book *The Whole-Brain Child* with fellow author Tina Payne Bryson.[185] They call one bank of the river "rigidity" and the other bank "chaos." If you look at how the two common *insecure attachment* styles handle conflict and stress, it makes sense. *Avoidantly attached* children will swim toward the bank of rigidity, looking for order and control, while *ambivalently attached* children will swim for the bank of chaos. And where would the *disorganized attached* child go? He would be swimming to each bank (rigidity and chaos) not finding relief, only to sink below the surface

184 Rogers, *You Are Special*.
185 Daniel Siegel and Tina Payne Bryson, *The Whole-Brain Child* (London: Constable & Robinson, 2012).

unable to cope. Do you teach any children like that? They don't have healthy options to draw from.

Our job, as wise adults, is to help every child in our classroom to safely right the canoe, get back in, and row calmly down the river. How do you do that? Here are some suggestions:

- Heal your own crap.
- Really know your students. Deeply know them and their stories. Let them break your heart.
- Understand what the brain does when it dysregulates, and how you can bring a child back to the safety of the canoe.

Yes, all of these are important. But they're not the *first* thing to do.

What *would* save a child's life?

It's not lecturing them about what they shouldn't have done: "What were you thinking?" It's not telling them to calm down when they're crying or raging: "That's not how we act in this classroom." It's not letting them crawl into a place and not come out all afternoon while the rest of the class participates in learning.

The answer is *empathy*: "That was so scary. Were you afraid when the boat capsized? I was. I was really scared. I'm so glad you're okay. It makes sense if you need a little time to feel like things are okay again [empathy]. I'll be over here if you need me, and I'll come back and check if you'd like to be alone [assurances]. Do you need a hug? Those always make me feel better. It makes sense that you're sad, angry, or afraid. It makes sense [validation of experiences] I'm not going anywhere, because I love you. I'm here, always [assurance of worth]."

Name It! Claim It! Explain It!

Emotional safety is found in the ability to express how you feel and know that a loss of love or support is *not* a possibility. But the security of being emotionally held is easier to give when we've "felt" it ourselves. Therein lies the dilemma. Many of us are *still* children who didn't receive the support we needed to regulate and manage our emotions. If we dismiss our own emotions, we run the possibility of dismissing those of young children, at our own peril as parents and teachers.

The next time you observe a child experiencing an emotion, try the simple *Name it. Claim it. Explain it. Strategy.*[186] It falls in line with Rogers' belief that feelings are mentionable, manageable, and controllable.

Let's first discuss the strategy's three parts. Then I'll cover in more detail the sound reasoning, the why, behind them.

Name it. Help children name the emotion you suspect they are feeling. For older children, you can ask. With younger children, you can help by making statements like:

- "It looks like you feel mad."
- "I'm noticing that your face looks sad. How do you feel inside?" (You may want pictures to have students choose from.) Ask questions.

Fred Rogers cautioned, "There's no 'should' or 'should not' when having feelings. They're part of who we are, and their origins are beyond our control. When we believe that, we may find it easier to make constructive choices about what to do with our feelings."[187] Children need to know that they are not their feeling. But emotions and feelings are temporary responses to a situation or a thought. They won't last forever.

Claim it. Give children a chance to claim the emotion, especially if you labeled it for them. If you ask them, "Are you mad?" and they nod, then have them say it. "Go ahead and say, 'I'm mad.'" I've found that children find this incredibly empowering, as many have never been encouraged to share big feelings. Be sure to reassure them that saying they're angry won't get them into any trouble. Children who are avoidantly attached need this absolute from you. Naming our experiences validates our understanding of the world, creating a cohesive narrative. When my student was able to say to her alcoholic father, "You make me feel unsafe when you drink!" it empowered and validated the experience. Having voice and expressing it was a catalyst for her father entering rehab.

---

186 Janet Gonzalez-Mena and Dianne Widmeyer Eyer, *Infants, Toddlers, and Caregivers: A Curriculum of Respectful, Responsive Care and Education*, 10th ed. (New York: McGraw-Hill, 2015).

187 Fred Rogers and Joanne Rogers, *The World According to Mister Rogers: Important Things to Remember* (New York: Hachette Books, 2014).

Explain it. We want to help children understand what caused their emotion and what solutions they have for working through the problem. All emotions are valid, but not all responses are appropriate or safe. You can use statements such as these:

- "It looks like you're feeling mad because you wanted the T-Rex, and he is playing with it. Are you mad?"
- "When you're mad, what can we do to make you feel better? What are some safe choices?"

Fred Rogers understood that self-control is founded on the ability to recognize a feeling, make a choice, and live through the experience, becoming stronger each time.

Why *Name It*

Feelings are natural and normal. Managing them constructively is where we get muddled. Children are often confused or frightened by big emotions, believing that they are the only ones to feel that way. It's time we normalized all feelings: positive and negative. It's what Mister Rogers did best! Talking about feelings and emotions is not only constructive but also vital to our interactions with everyone we encounter. We need emotions to be validated, not shunned.

Why *Claim It*

Even if our childhoods were relatively problem-free,
growing always presents us with difficulties to be overcome . . .
and the memories of these difficulties are so easily awakened as
our children encounter similar difficulties in their own time.
It may be a little easier if we know ahead of time that some
of the intensity we feel as we try to help our own children
with their hard times is very likely related to what we
went through ourselves when we were children.
—Fred Rogers

Anger showed up on the *Neighborhood* more than any other emotion. Why? Fred Rogers grew up with adults who told him not to cry. He later commented on the subject: "People have said, 'Don't cry' to other people for years and years, and all it has ever meant is, 'I'm too uncomfortable when you show your feelings. Don't cry.' I'd rather have them say, 'Go ahead and cry. I'm here to be with you.'"[188]

Fred Rogers understood how his body felt when he wasn't allowed to express his feelings with words. Music became his refuge. "I was always able to cry or laugh or say I was angry through the tips of my fingers at the piano. I would go to the piano, even . . . when I was five years old, and start to play how I felt. It was very natural for me to become a composer."[189] And later, when he was bullied, he spoke about crying "through my fingers as I made up songs on the piano." He was left alone with the feelings of isolation, the trauma of being bullied, and the careless way those in his life dismissed his pain. "I resented the pain," he said. "I resented those kids for not seeing beyond my fatness or my shyness, and what's more I didn't know that it was right to resent it, to feel bad about it, even to feel very sad about it. I didn't know it was all right to feel any of those things, because the advice I got from the grown-ups was 'just let on you don't care, then nobody will bother you.' Let on you don't care! I felt I had no friends, and I was told to let on that I didn't care."[190]

All feelings need to be felt, named/claimed, validated, processed, and integrated—regardless of the age of the person. The adults in Fred Rogers' life failed him in the biggest way, but they set him up for his later unrelenting resolve to "let children know it was all right to share their feelings—especially negative ones."[191] "When we treat some emotions as negative, we end up going to war against ourselves . . . intensifying difficult feelings," researcher John Freedman urges. "How would it feel to stop judging our own feelings? What if emotions are [simply] neutral messages from us, to us . . . to help us thrive?"[192]

---

188 Rogers and Rogers, *The World According to Mister Rogers*.
189 King, *The Good Neighbor*.
190 King, *The Good Neighbor*.
191 Amy Hollingsworth, *The Simple Faith of Mister Rogers: Spiritual Insights from the World's Most Beloved Neighbor* (Nashville: Thomas Nelson, 2007).
192 Joshua Freedman, "Integrated Emotions: Feelings Are Allies," Six Seconds, March 22, 2021, https://www.6seconds.org/2020/08/17/integrated-emotions/.

Emotions are merely signals to us about what is important and needs our attention. They help give us data about how we perceive opportunities and threats. Yet we vilify them and choose which ones are socially acceptable—without understanding their purpose. Ask yourself: *Why am I feeling_____ at this moment?*

What is your perception of emotions? Why do you have them? Are you listening to what they are communicating to you? "Emotions focus us toward what matters. When we experience big emotions, we are perceiving something important."[193] They identify our core needs and whether they're being met: to be seen, loved, connected, validated, and safe. When Fred Rogers called discussing feelings "important talk," he wasn't wrong. Every emotion must be acknowledged, otherwise it lodges in the body stuck. It is imperative that we take a nonjudgmental stance toward them. Feelings shouldn't be "'blindly obeyed,' but nor should they be ignored."[194] As we become more open to the reality of our feelings, we begin to understand whether our reactions are new or old. What we don't reveal to ourselves can't ever heal.

Why do we suppress emotions? There are many reasons: to cope, to conform, to survive, because we're told to, because we were shunned/shamed, or because a trauma is just too difficult and painful to process.[195] After all, we can't lash out in anger at our boss, cry all day long at our desk, or sleep on the job. We learn this as we conform to societies' standards of what is acceptable. Big emotions often cause discomfort, and we don't like to feel out of control or vulnerable. It feels unsafe in our bodies, so we distract ourselves, dissociate through our smartphones, numb out with food, sex, shopping, binge watch on Netflix, or become addicted to fitness. We've bought into the lie: If we just don't let ourselves "go there," the feelings will eventually subside, and we'll remain in control—the ultimate goal being to avoid negative feelings and actively indulge the positive. Perhaps we worry that if we linger too long with big feelings they will overwhelm and engulf us. So, we become more anxious and depressed, while stuffing our systems full of opioids and various "cures" to chronic, toxic stress, and mismanaged dysregulation.

---

193 Freedman, "Integrated Emotions."
194 Freedman, "Integrated Emotions."
195 Freedman, "Integrated Emotions."

Why *Explain It*

It's one of the important parts of the Neighborhood, knowing that
feelings are all right. You know that you don't have to hide them and
that there are ways you can say how you feel that aren't going to
hurt you or anybody else. If there were a legacy that I would hope
for the Neighborhood passing on, that's certainly one of them.
—Fred Rogers

Children need a guide to walk alongside and model the way to safely engage big
emotions. They need someone to act as a container, like a net ready to catch an
acrobat who lets go. Our very presence says, *I'm here and I've got you.* When Mister
Rogers went to the gym to watch children practicing for the Special Olympics,
he stated to one of the children practicing, Alicia, "I was watching you the whole
time." A simple statement packed with meaning: "I enjoy watching you grow, I
see that you're working hard, I didn't take my eyes off of you in case you needed
me." As children grow, they need the net less, but the knowledge that it's there
gives them the confidence to focus on greater maneuvers.

****

To illustrate the *Name it. Claim it. Explain it. Strategy,* let's take a good look at
one of Rogers' songs, "What Do You Do with the Mad That You Feel?" Its lyrics
enamored US Senators as he read them to their subcommittee on communications
in May 1969. It addresses how children can recognize, explain, and manage big
feelings and, with a sense of connectivity, guides a child through safely engaging
the strong emotion of anger. As a child sings it, the words, the meaning becomes
their own, thus leading to what Rogers called "the good feeling of self-control":

> What do you do with the mad that you feel
> When you feel so mad you could bite?
> When the whole wide world seems oh, so wrong . . .
> And nothing you do seems very right?

What do you do? Do you punch a bag?
Do you pound some clay or some dough?
Do you round up friends for a game of tag?
Or see how fast you go?

It's great to be able to stop
When you've planned a thing that's wrong,
And be able to do something else instead
And think this song:

I can stop when I want to
Can stop when I wish
I can stop, stop, stop any time.
And what a good feeling to feel like this
And know that the feeling is really mine.
Know that there's something deep inside
That helps us become what we can.
For a girl can be someday a woman
And a boy can be someday a man.[196]

First, the song helps children to name it: "You feel mad. You feel so mad you could bite!"[197] Rogers said, "[It] was a question that a child really did ask a doctor one day. When I heard it, it reminded me how intense children's anger can be—and how hard for them to cope with and understand."

Anger is isolating and frightening to children. Rogers knew that "what children are really afraid of when they're angry is that they're going to hurt somebody, particularly somebody they love. And it's really scary because they just feel overcome with rage."

Next, the song helps children to claim it: "And know that the feeling is really mine." As we allow children to claim and voice their true emotions and feelings,

---

196 Fred Rogers, "What Do You Do with the Mad That You Feel?," Neighborhood Archive-All Things Mister Rogers, 1968, http://www.neighborhoodarchive.com/music/songs/what_do_you_do.html.

197 Rogers, "What Do You Do with the Mad That You Feel?"

we're establishing trust. It demonstrates that we deeply care about them as we look for ways for them to "express their real feelings and care enough to listen and talk with them."[198] Fred Rogers believed that "being supportive often means waiting and listening and more waiting until you're better able to understand the drama that a certain child is living through at the moment."[199]

And finally, Rogers' song helps children to explain it: "What do you do?" I often start to sing this song when children start to have conflict. It's funny how music engages their brain differently than words. They will stop and sing along, remembering Fred's suggestions for anger:

> What do you do? Do you punch a bag?
> Do you pound some clay or some dough?
> Do you round up friends for a game of tag?
> Or see how fast you go?

Ask a child for their input and refer to ways that have helped in the past. I try to make connections to the *Neighborhood* and books we've read in the classroom.

It's not uncommon for their peers to throw in ideas, too, from the sidelines: "Remember when Lady Elaine did that and she has to have a consequence?" The *Neighborhood* is alive and thriving in our room! Feelings come and go, putting children at ease. Nothing lasts forever, even anger, sadness, and loneliness, and everything is better when you have people who love you nearby. Always be sure to remind them of how they are growing, and validate each experience.

Another song I paraphrase to my kindergarteners is "Look and Listen," singing the last two lines to them:

> Look, look, look
> And listen.

They often jump in on the last "and listen." Do you see "talking" anywhere within that? We talk entirely too much when we need to listen to children. Stop

---

198 Rogers, *You Are Special.*
199 Rogers, *You Are Special.*

talking at them; listen. If we're trustworthy, children will tell us their truths. We'll witness miracles as they begin to trust their inner healthy controls. Don't be afraid to sit in silence. It's reassuring to them. It's often our willing presence that communicates the most.

Mentionable and Manageable

> We know everyone has lots of ways of feeling. And all those ways of feeling are fine. It's what we do with our feelings that matter in this life. I trust that you're growing in ways that will help you with whatever feelings you may have when you're a child and when you're grown up. I hope you're able to grow to respect whoever you are inside.
> **—Fred Rogers**

All behavior can be managed and understood. We want children to realize that all feelings—anger, jealousy, love, sadness, impatience, loneliness, for example—are part of the human experience. Fred Rogers used the Neighborhood of Make-Believe much like Christ told parables to his followers. A parable is an illustrative lesson with deep themes and lessons. Lady Elaine often is the mischief-maker whom Rogers used to illustrate when feelings go awry, while her neighbors come alongside to encourage and help her in making the right choices. Lady Aberlin and Chuck Aber act as surrogate parental figures, often listening, waiting, and witnessing the dramas of puppets like Daniel Tiger, Ana Platypus, and Prince Tuesday, the "children" of the neighborhood. Simply, they stop, listen, and connect, always offering their availability if more talking is needed.

"No child is born with self-discipline."[200] Guiding children toward self-control and the ability to regulate their arousal isn't done with "coaxing or cajoling or threats or punishments. Our reassuring presence may be enough to help them find inner resources of their own, and when they do, [teachers] and children can both feel proud."[201] As we hold space, we are fully present and curious with our

---

200 Rogers, *You Are Special.*
201 Rogers, *You Are Special.*

students, without judgment or attempting to change them, as they express their emotions and experiences. There have been many times I had no clue what to do next, so I sat down beside them and focused on my own breathing. In and out. It's a wonder, but they will begin to regulate to your nervous system as you aren't frantic or rushed. Sit quietly first, talk when necessary.

****

Gregory wants to be first all the time, to sit in a certain spot, and has difficulty disengaging from what he wants for many months this school year. It's clear he doesn't know how to label his feelings of disappointment and anger. We begin to talk about such words in relation to the *Neighborhood* and make connections to disappointment in other ways. Some days he's successful, other days he's not.

Much like waiting for a flower to bloom, we take it day by day. First, he stops throwing tantrums, then slowly begins to use his words with help and later voices them on his own. And on this day, Gregory reaches a small victory from within. Too many children had gathered to the front of the room for our dance break. For safety, I need a few to move, so I call out to Gregory, asking him to move to the back of the room. He smiles at me, says, "Okay, Mrs. Edwards," and moves there without incident.

"Whoa!" I exclaim. "Boys and girls, did you just see how awesome Gregory just listened and helped Mrs. Edwards?"

They nod and say yes.

"Have you been growing inside?" I ask him.

Gregory's face lights up. "Yes! I'm growing up. Just like Mister Rogers talked about."

Later that afternoon, during our time with the feelings lion, Gregory pulls out the yellow circle and proclaims, "Today, I feel proud because I'm growing inside."

Somewhere in Heaven, Fred Rogers smiles too.

Co-regulating: "I'm Right Here with You"

Children's behaviors and impulses are a mystery to them, as revealed by the lament of my former student Evelyn: "Why do I keep doing bad things?" Children are *present* oriented, although their brains and nervous systems could be reacting to previous traumas and old feelings. Until children can do so for themselves, adults are necessary to foster conversation, give explanations, offer comfort, and validate. This is called *co-regulation*. Co-regulation always proceeds self-regulation. As I touched on in chapter 6, in our discussion about developmental trauma, it's about reframing the way children view emotions and reminding them that they're growing and learning about their worlds. The message needs to be "It's okay, but let's figure out what we need to do next."

Co-regulating is an interaction or exchange between people that allows for safety and security to process a difficult and stressful situation.[202] For example, when a child falls and skins their knee while playing, they will run to their mother for comfort. If the mother uses a soothing, calm tone of voice while holding the child, simultaneously acknowledging the child's distress,[203] the child will eventually regulate, calm down, and come back to a neutral place. Because our energies and emotional states are transferrable, a child's nervous system will respond to that of their calm caregiver and release oxytocin, a bonding chemical in the brain. "The ability to co-regulate is established in childhood."[204] Children learn early from their home environments whether emotional states are safe or threatening. Insecure attachments leave children in a heightened state of stress/arousal, creating gaps in their ability to develop emotionally. Such children will have difficulty with certain tasks and skills:

- labeling basic feelings, such as anger, fear, sadness, happiness, disgust, surprise
- reading facial expressions and body language
- noticing a sensation in their body and connecting it to a feeling
- choosing a constructive way to control their emotional reactions
- responding in appropriate ways to others' emotions

Insecurely attached children become emotionally immature adults lacking the skills to co-regulate children and themselves.

---

202 LePera, *How to Do the Work*.
203 LePera, *How to Do the Work*.
204 LePera, *How to Do the Work*.

Over time, children become conditioned to what emotions are welcome or a threat to survival within their family structure. This is why the tone and cadence of *Mister Rogers' Neighborhood* is soothing and comforting to adults and children alike. As Rogers takes his time speaking, moving, and explaining, our sympathetic nervous systems downshift, causing our body to relax and become calm. Children often say, when they label their feelings for the day, "I feel calm inside because I watched Mister Rogers."

We All Need Bigger Emotion Vocabularies

Comforting our feelings and giving appropriate expression
always takes strength, not weakness. It takes strength to
acknowledge our anger, and sometimes more strength yet
to curb the aggressive urges anger may bring and to channel
them into nonviolent outlets. It takes strength to face our
sadness and to grieve, and to let our grief and anger flow
in tears when they need to. It takes strength to talk about our
feelings and to reach out for help and comfort when we need it.
—Fred Rogers

At the end of each day, my class and I sit in a circle with a stuffed lion. To increase their self-awareness, the children take turns pulling a colored shape from the pocket on his back, then sharing how they are feeling and why.

"I'm feeling _____ because _____."

Young children love to share how they feel, and we as adults can learn a lot by watching. If our schedule is altered, a student will often ask if we still have time for the lion. (We always make time for the lion and the *Neighborhood!*) At the beginning of the school year, children will use their primary feelings: happy, sad, mad, and calm. But quickly, they begin to incorporate the word *proud* into their sharing, as Mister Rogers often tells them how "proud" he is of their "growing."

Social problems that weren't resolved from recess will also pop up, giving me a chance to discuss options for the future. Never underestimate children solving problems. I'm continuously amazed. Although children may be defensive at first—and they can be brutal, as they haven't learned, as we have, to filter their feelings and annoyances—I've witnessed the power of children applying their compassion and forgiveness to generating solutions for the good of all. Increased self-awareness allows us—both children and adults—to understand how our behavior affects other people and our relationships.

****

"I hate her," Sadie says boldly as Cadence rushes to sit by her. Sadie moves her body away, scowling at Cadence, who hasn't yet noticed the annoyance. Sadie is usually an easygoing child who plays well with others, so her declaration is shocking.

"Come sit by me." I beckon, knowing that we will need to discuss it privately after the lesson.

Sadie scoots across the circle beside me, Cadence none the wiser. I brush my hand over her head, and she moves closer to my leg, never making eye contact.

I whisper down to her, "We need to talk after the story, because those were unkind words." She nods to me.

Our read-aloud for the day is *Personal Space Camp* by Julia Cook, a new text from my ever-growing collection of social and emotional books. In the story, the boy is obsessed with space and wants to move fast through the sky like a rocket while interfering with others' personal space. His principal sets up a "personal space camp" in her office and does several activities to help him. In the end, he learns how important it is to give people the space to feel emotionally and physically safe.

I haven't even opened my mouth to begin a discussion when Sadie blurts out, "Cadence, you are in my space bubble!" Cadence looks at her, confused.

"Honey, she's on the other side of the circle. Your space bubble is around your body," I reply, and then it hits me. "Has that been bothering you? When she sits too close at circle?"

"She sits on top of me," Sadie replies. "I'm smooshed!"

There it is! Sadie feels smothered. The real reason isn't that she hates Cadence, but Sadie has lacked the vocabulary to state what she needs. She's feeling smothered and needs her friend to move over.

Children need us to identify and name feelings until they can for themselves.

We All Struggle and That's Okay

Through music, Fred Rogers addressed the good/bad argument in the best way he knew how. In his song "Sometimes People Are Good," he looked deeper into the questions we ask ourselves throughout our lives: *Why do I do bad things? Can I be bad and still be good? Do my mistakes make me unworthy of love in the here and now?*

Sometimes people are good
And they do just what they should.
But the very same people who are good sometimes
Are the very same people who are bad sometimes.
It's funny, but it's true.
It's the same, isn't it, for
Me and . . .
Sometimes people get mad
And they feel like being bad.
But the very same people who are mad sometimes
Are the very same people who are glad sometimes.
It's funny, but it's true.
It's the same, isn't it, for
Me. . . . Isn't it the same for you?[205]

Our attuned responses, body language, facial expressions, tone, and use of silence all play a critical part in reaching dysregulated children. Feelings and emotions always tie into self-worth. When we are dysregulated, we need to be reminded that feelings are normal, communicate to us, won't last forever, and can be managed without hurting us or others. We need to be reminded that we are not a feeling, a choice, and that, above all else, we are loved.

My former student Evelyn, for example, didn't need another person freaking out over something she had done, but someone to listen to the bigger question she was asking: "Am I a bad person because I did a bad thing?" In the song "Sometimes I Wonder If I'm a Mistake," Fred Rogers created one of the most exquisite

---

205 Rogers and Flowers, "Sometimes People Are Good," *A Beautiful Day in the Neighborhood.*

moments in children's television during the week of episodes focused on making mistakes, which aired in 1987:

[Sung by Daniel Striped Tiger]
Sometimes I wonder if I'm a mistake
I'm not like anyone else I know
When I'm asleep or even awake
Sometimes I get to dreaming that I'm just a fake
I'm not like anyone else

Others I know are big and are wild
I'm very small and quite tame
Most of the time I'm weak and I'm mild
Do you suppose that's a shame

Often I wonder if I'm a mistake
I'm not supposed to be scared am I
Sometimes I cry and sometimes I shake
Wondering isn't it true that the strong never break
I'm not like anyone else I know
I'm not like anyone else

[Sung by Lady Aberlin]
I think you are just fine as you are
I really must tell you
I do like the person that you are becoming
When you are sleeping
When you are waking
You are my friend

It's really true
I like you
Crying or shaking or dreaming or breaking

There's no one mistaking it
You're my best friend

I think you are just fine as you are
I really must tell you
I do like the person that you are becoming
When you are sleeping
When you are waking
You're not a fake
You're no mistake
You are my friend[206]

Fred Rogers broke the vulnerability barrier with a tattered tiger puppet, as he dared to ask the deepest question of the human heart: Do I matter?

How we respond to big emotions and children's mistakes tells us a lot about our own heart's condition and where we still need healing. **Our inner child shows up, at times when we least expect them to.** Fred Rogers shared the following story:

> In my early training in child development, I often brought the puppets to the children. One four-year-old boy would intervene and actually prevent my being able to do much work. I remember how angry that made me. I was angry because of the frustration of my work; but I was angry at another level because when I was a little boy, I wasn't allowed to prevent adults' activities like that. It took quite a while to resolve that situation, and I came to realize that **one of the most important aspects of working with children is developing the capacity to differentiate between the inner child of our own past and the child we're working with in the present.**[207]

---

206 Rogers and Flowers, "Sometimes I Wonder If I'm a Mistake," *A Beautiful Day in the Neighborhood.*

207 Rogers, *You Are Special.* Emphasis added.

Our reactions are layered with old and new feelings. Clearly, Rogers was annoyed at the child for being less than helpful. Rogers noted that the child had actually taken X the Owl off his hand and hurled the puppet across the room! It makes sense Rogers would be annoyed with the child, but what was more telling is how he looked deeper within himself at his reactions of anger toward the boy. He experienced new feelings of annoyance toward the child for his lack of cooperation, but old feelings of resentment surfaced as his brain was wired about a child's place among adult activities. His old feelings intensified the anger toward the boy. Resentment is a form of envy, not anger, as we've been made to believe. In many ways, Rogers envied the young boy's ability to demonstrate such rage and not be worried about how it would be taken by the adults in the room, something Rogers was never allowed to do in his own childhood.

The same theme is interwoven into his song "It's You I Like" when he differentiates two types of feelings: old or new.

> But it's you I like.
> Every part of you
> Your skin, your eyes, **your feelings,**
> **Whether old or new.**[208]

What makes a feeling old or new? Old feelings are wired mindsets, narratives we've constructed about people and the world (internal working models), and the moments we felt ignored, exposed, mishandled, misunderstood or the thousands of moments we collected in our souls unvoiced. Old feelings are missed moments, stories, and heartaches we keep locked in our hearts as children.

Carl Jung said, "When an inner situation is not made conscious, it happens outside as fate." Fred Rogers believed that "everything in a child's development is connected—what has gone before, what is happening now, and what will happen in the future"—thus, we are always in the process of reworking the things from our own childhoods.[209]

---

208 Rogers and Flowers, "It's You I Like," *A Beautiful Day in the Neighborhood*. Emphasis added.
209 Rogers, *You Are Special*.

The good news is that we can, as adults, influence the future by acknowledging the past and the wounds it left in its wake. Each time we hold "emotional space" for a child, we're healing our own hearts, simultaneously. That's the beauty of it. Our stories, if studied, can illuminate our most profound resources, and we can offer the world things that others can't. "No one can lead the life you live." It's not about waiting until we have it perfect but offering it regardless of where we are. When we offer integration, it's because we're convinced it's right and have witnessed in our own lives what happens if children don't receive what they need. Rogers wrote: "It's true that we take a great deal of our own upbringing on into our adult lives and our lives as parents [caregivers, teachers]; but it's true, too, that we can change some of the things that we would like to change. It can be hard, but it can be done."[210]

When I saw Evelyn sitting alone in the office, I wanted to whisk her away from all the shame I knew she was feeling. Shame is what a child feels if they've had too much exposure to scorn or emotional neglect in their early years. It affects the essence of who they are at the core, in their self-esteem and self-worth. They don't simply *do* a bad thing; they *are* bad. Shame is only fought through the weapons of love and forgiveness.

Love reminds us that every person has infinite worth and value. When we have *secure attachment*, we understand through our caregiver's responsiveness that mistakes are part of learning but don't define us. Their engagement with each moment allows us the space to voice our fears, ask questions, and draw conclusions without the threat of abandonment or rejection. *Insecure attachments* keep children paralyzed by the threat of failure and abandonment, two brutal combinations when we want them to take risks and trust the outcomes.

This flip of their mindsets begins with the daily messages they ingest. Be aware that loving messages should be attached to any discipline or correction a child receives, as well. Affirmation and forgiveness are bookends for discipline and correction.

Insecurely attached children consistently have emotionally immature parents. Emotional immaturity is the inability to hold space for others' thoughts, opinions, feelings, or perspectives because of internal discomfort. Discomfort "results

---

210 Rogers and Rogers, *The World According to Mister Rogers.*

from a lack of emotional resilience, the ability to process emotions, communicate boundaries, and return our nervous systems to balance."[211] It will be up to us to help children in our classrooms learn the skills of healthy emotional regulation. And it will take some intervention, establishing "felt safety."

How to Establish Felt Safety

Old traumas need to meet new experiences to establish a felt safety for both ourselves and our students. Emotional *felt safety* can be divided into the following: safety in your body, safety in your emotions and thoughts, and safety in your environments and relationships.[212] Attachment trauma is activated in our interpersonal relationships with the students we teach, so we need adequate tools to defend ourselves from becoming dysregulated in both every day *and* overwhelming circumstances. By understanding what triggers us and our students emotionally, we set ourselves up for the good feeling of self-control.

In her revolutionary work with "children from hard places" the late Karyn Purvis coined the term *felt safety*. Felt safety is established when adults "arrange the environment and adjust their behavior so children can feel in a profound and basic way that they are truly safe in their home and with [those adults.]"[213]

Secure attachment is built within predictable, consistent environments, where a child's secure base (you, their teacher) isn't distracted or disengaged. Take note, there's a difference between "feeling safe" and "being safe." Traumatized children will need evidence of care many times over to *believe* that it will continue. Our goal is to communicate the messages of safety and reassurances in ways the child can understand. Use this sentence frame:

"I know _____, but [the child's name] _____ does not."

I know she will not go hungry again, but she does not.

I know I would never hurt him when he makes a mistake, but he does not.

I know the cut on her leg will heal after I tend to it, but she does not.

---

211 Rogers and Rogers, *The World According to Mister Rogers*.

212 Laura K. Kerr, "Live Within Your Window of Tolerance," laurakkerr.com, February 22, 2022, https://laurakkerr.com/wot-guide/.

213 Rachel Luttrull, "Felt Safety vs. Safe Environment," Adoption.com, January 15, 2022, https://adoption.com/felt-safety/.

Think of a recent interaction with a child where you could've given more reassurance as tangible evidence. The child needs to have tangible evidence that their needs *will be met*. **Actions speak louder than words.**

My student Amy had gone without nourishment on a consistent basis before being placed in foster care. Her new foster family ensured that healthy snacks—fruits, veggies, pretzels, etc.—were available and accessible anytime she felt hungry. It was clear evidence and communicated to her system "I will not be hungry again." Each day she delighted in opening her sparkly lunch box and choosing a snack for recess. Slowly, she began to trust and "feel safe."

Purvis developed *Trust-Based Relational Intervention (TBRI)*, a systematic approach to complex developmental trauma based on her work with foster children and their families. She identified that any good program designed to treat complex trauma in children must include three elements: (a) development of safety [physical and emotional], (b) promotion of healthy relationships, and (c) teaching of self-management and coping skills. Thus, she created the three principles of TBRI:[214]

- empowerment—attention to physical needs
- connection—attention to attachment needs
- correction—attention to behavioral needs

Let's take a closer look at each of the three pillars and how they can be used in the classroom.

Empowerment Principles

1. **Safe and Structured Environment:** The key is creating smooth transitions for the child, including daily transitions (what comes next—first this, then that), major life transitions (moving, divorce, new baby in the home, death of a grandparent, etc.), and developmental transitions (losing teeth, growing pains, learning to read, fine/gross motor, etc.). Everything is easier if we are with those we *believe* love us.

---

214 Karyn B. Purvis et al., "Trust-Based Relational Intervention (TBRI): A Systemic Approach to Complex Developmental Trauma," *Child & Youth Services* 34, no. 4 (2013): 360–386, https://doi.org/10.1080/0145935x.2013.859906.

2. **Sensory Needs/Nutrition:** Children with histories of hospitalization, trauma, adversity, or various forms of autism may have sensory processing deficits. Such deficits can be overcome with appropriate interventions that address the sensory systems, which may need to be implemented in the classroom setting with fidgets, special seating, picture exchange communication system (PECS) charts, and other forms of intervention. Proper nutrition and hydration are imperative, as many children have not had the care needed to thrive. As stated previously, regular snacks and meals will establish trust and stability. Let the children see you eating healthy foods and drinking more water than coffee or soda. Set an example for them through actions.

3. **Adequate Sleep:** Children from hard places tend to have dysregulated sleep patterns due to anxiety, abuse, hunger, and so forth. Speak to parents about the importance of quality sleep, routine, and rituals for their children. When necessary, I provide quilts and pillows for a child who simply needs to sleep. If a problem persists, document and loop in your school nurse and guidance counselor to empower parents and help the child succeed. Are you getting quality sleep? I signed up for an app that shuts down various parts of my phone at a designated time each night. Create a nighttime routine with rituals that help you disconnect easily. Your students need you fully present and alert to attune to their needs. Good self-care is your first step in helping them. Give to yourself first. No excuses.

4. **Physical Activity/Mindfulness Practices:** Fred Rogers promised himself in the 1980s that he would swim every day, and he stuck to it. His staff knew it was a priority for him and made sure there was always a pool everywhere he traveled. Physical activity improves cognitive, social, and emotional well-being. You need all of those to engage the hearts and minds of your students. Find a wellness routine that includes reflection and mindfulness. GoNoodle has many mindfulness and yoga practices and models deep-breathing exercises. My students are used to me saying things like "I'm feeling frustrated right now. I need to do some deep breathing. Will you join me?" Different types of breathing exercises are another wonderful transition routine.

Fred Rogers prayed for people by name and studied his Bible daily. I journal first thing in the morning to set my intentions, pray, and focus my energy. Listen to encouraging music and podcasts and drive to work in silence to get you focused on the day ahead. Getting to work early is important to me, and I'm often one of the first people in the parking lot. I'm not saying you need to do the same but be sure to find ways to help your mind and body. If you tend to run late, create a margin in your life with five minutes. Leave five minutes earlier. Go to bed five minutes earlier each night. Each day, spend five fewer minutes watching Netflix, scrolling Instagram, or doing whatever tends to make you late. Also, learn to say no. It's life changing.

Connecting Principles

This is the attachment repair component where we lean in and act as the "'external modem" for regulation of self-regulation, which includes awareness (of others and self), playful engagement, and attunement (see chapter 7). Many of these principles are detailed throughout this book through classroom illustrations, but I want you to see how they fit into the framework of healing insecure attachments and trauma.

1. **Observational Awareness:** Intentionally watch a child's behavioral and psychological responses during interactions to monitor anxiety and comfort levels. What are their signs of stress? Note what each child does when they aren't in their window of tolerance, which we will discuss later in the chapter.

2. **Self-Awareness:** Can you identify how your body feels if you are triggered? Do you become hyper or hypo aroused? This is when your attachment styles, unresolved childhood traumas, and maladaptive coping will surface. Also, any biases, prejudice, or rooted beliefs will influence our abilities to connect with a child. If it's unresolved, it's still hidden beneath the surface.

3. **Skills of Attachment:** How do you give and seek care? Do you feel comfortable with yourself? Secure attachment gives a child "voice" and cele-

brates autonomy each time they grow on the inside and on the outside. Can they negotiate or compromise to sustain relationships? Fred Rogers often sang about "taking good care" of others, including in "I Like to Take Care of You." It's about not only giving care but *taking delight* in it:

I like to take care of you
Yes I do.
Yes I do.
I like to take care of you.
Yes I do.
Yes I do.[215]

4. **Attunement:** Through verbal and nonverbal communications, we enter the experience of a child by matching behaviors, eye contact, voice (cadence, tone, pacing) and inflection, body positioning, and affectionate touch. "When [teachers] are taught to carefully, attentively [attune] to the child's physical and emotional space, a new foundation of trust begins to emerge, bringing with it behavioral and physiological gains."[216]

5. **Playful Engagement (see chapter 11):** Playful engagement was Fred Rogers' specialty. He wasn't afraid to be whimsical, silly, or childlike to demonstrate the importance of play. Watch his example when he creates a craft in the kitchen out of simple materials, the funny way Robert Troll speaks in the Neighborhood of Make-Believe, and Rogers' delight in playing hide-and-seek or peekaboo with the camera. Play generates trust and promotes healthy attachment. However, if a child has insecure attachment or complex trauma, they will have difficulty engaging in play and understanding humor/sarcasm, and they will struggle with appropriate arousal in their nervous system. Come alongside the child during purposeful playtime, modeling and encouraging them to take

---

215 Fred M. Rogers, "I Like to Take Care of You," The Mister Rogers Neighborhood Archive, 1990, http://www.neighborhoodarchive.com/music/songs/i_like_to_take_care_of_you.html.

216 Purvis et al., "Trust-Based Relational Intervention."

risks, scaffolding their learning, making connections, and cheering on their growth. Promote opportunities for silliness, laughter, and games.

Correcting Principles

What does a child need from us to socially engage with others? The objective of any discipline is an act of love. "I love you enough to help you be a good friend," I tell my students. "To have a friend, you need to be a friend." Once we give a child a firm foundation of connection and empowerment, correcting principles come easier. Whenever I need to correct a child, I start with "Does Mrs. Edwards love you? Is there anything you can do to lose my love?" I needed reassurance as a child, because of my ambivalent attachment, so I offer it to children. It's a staple of how I discipline children. Discipline is an opportunity for deeper connection and affirmation. We need to see "discipline" as a form of love.

Here are some of the things Fred Rogers indicated in his notes on discipline from the early 1980s:

- Discipline has to do with boundaries (self/others/property).
- To love a child, we often tell them "no."
- Discipline needs to be immediate.
- Be honest. It's okay to tell them, "You made me mad when you _____."
- Remind them that even people who love each other get mad sometimes, as Rogers notes in "The People You Like the Most":

  It's the people you like the most
  Who can make you feel maddest.
  It's the people you like the most
  Who manage to make you feel baddest. [217]

- Children aren't born with self-control, and it must be taught. If teachers don't give them healthy direction, the child remains "lost."

---

217 Fred M. Rogers, "The People You Like the Most," The Mister Rogers Neighborhood Archive, 2022, http://www.neighborhoodarchive.com/music/songs/people_like_most.html.

- A lack of consistent discipline/boundaries adds more chaos and insecurity to a young child.
- If a child's behavior is taking away from learning or "your right to teach," there will be added anger.
- Always execute loving discretion.
- Allow children to give their input in setting the rules for healthy/safe learning.
- Let children help choose their consequences for infractions to the above rules.
- Discipline is a growing thing, responsive to a specific child. Often our first instinct is a reaction, not what we ought to do to sustain the relationship and facilitate their growth as human beings.

We must be proactive, not reactive, always looking and listening for opportunities to teach all children they are significant, important, and loved enough that you will step in when needed. Share social stories, read trade books that pose a genuine problem and solution, role-play with puppets and stuffies, or have children model specific behaviors. On the *Neighborhood*, Fred Rogers often allowed a problem or misunderstanding to grow throughout the week in the Neighborhood of Make-Believe to illustrate the many ways adults and children can work together, talk about hard things, and accept their similarities and differences.

Our Fancy Nervous System

To give good, attentive care, we must have received good, attentive care. A grateful receiver is a grateful giver. Likewise, a grateful giver is a gracious receiver. If we did not receive adequate care, we will be unable to establish the felt safety children need to thrive.

A child responds to *our* nervous system, so it's up to us to do the work to remain within our own window of tolerance. What is a *window of tolerance*?

Let's take a look at this concept, along with two other terms that are key to understanding our own and our students' stress response systems.

Window of Tolerance

Our window of tolerance is our individual zone of arousal in which we are able to function most effectively. When we're within this zone, we're able to readily receive, process, and integrate information and otherwise respond to the demands of everyday life without much difficulty.[218] It's the place where we thrive, create, are at peace, and adequately communicate without feeling overwhelmed or frantic. When in our window, we're able to play and relate well to ourselves and others. However, if we move out of our window of tolerance, we experience dysregulated hyperarousal or hypoarousal states.[219]

Hyperarousal

This stress response system is characterized by excessive energy/activation. Words to describe hyperarousal include: flight or fight (moving away from threat/moving toward threat), fearful, worried, furious, panicked, nervous, frustrated, or angry.

Hypoarousal

This stress response system includes freeze/flop/fawn, where there is a sense of shutting down or disassociating. This can present as exhaustion, depression, flat affect, numbness, and disconnection. Words to describe hypoarousal include: depressed, collapse/immobilize the threat, shameful, trapped, stuck, sad, shut down, and helpless.

A person's stress response system—hyperarousal or hypoarousal—can be tricky to pinpoint, as anxiety can mask itself in other ways. Although most people think of worried being communicated by a "worried face," as we learned from the studies of infants, that was not always the case. *Avoidantly attached* children, for example, are typically good at showing little to no emotion on their faces. According to research, anxiety can also look like the following in a child: many alterations to their voice, flinching or jumping, increased tension/rigidity in the body, telling stories, looking startled, "spacing out," rocking back and forth, picking things off the carpet to fiddle with, clowning around, humming or singing at inappropriate times, tears in their eyes, and becoming increasingly active.[220]

---

218 "Window of Tolerance," GoodTherapy.org Therapy Blog, August 8, 2016, https://www.goodtherapy.org/blog/psychpedia/window-of-tolerance.

219 "The Window of Tolerance," Jersey Psychology and Wellbeing Service, Government of New Jersey, May 2020, https://www.gov.je/SiteCollectionDocuments/Education/ID%20The%20Window%20of%20Tolerance%2020%2006%2016.pdf.

220 Bombèr, *Inside I'm Hurting*.

Anxiety—particularly for a dysregulated nervous system—can be triggered by the following:

- surprises
- an unexpected change of plans to the routine
- not understanding something
- insensitivity from staff
- a sudden noise
- a visitor to the class
- an assembly
- an emotive topic being discussed or read about in class
- conversations on the playground
- exclusion by peers/perceived exclusion
- autobiographical activities
- someone brushing past them or bumping into them accidentally
- sharing materials/waiting their turn
- sitting for long periods of time
- not getting called on to answer
- overpraise/attention
- not winning at a game
- a substitute teacher
- raised voices, harsh tone
- crying students
- sarcasm
- perceived chaos in environment
- smells
- sudden movements
- atmospheres (moving to a new classroom or special class: art, PE, music, etc.)
- touch
- mannerisms/facial expressions

Remember—and this is key—the toxic stress in our childhood causes our *own* nervous systems to get stuck in a dysregulated state as well. Our *own* window of tolerance needs to be addressed, and the focus is not isolated to the needs of a student. If toxic stress was part of your childhood like mine, then dysregulation feels "normal" to our brains and bodies. As I healed my ambivalent attachment, my brain reshaped from a hyperaroused state into my window of tolerance. Do you know what I noticed first? Life felt a lot slower. Hypervigilance is exhausting to our systems. In adverse circumstances, the brain's chemistry actually changes, and as Mister Rogers suggests, it will take practice to learn to take our time.

One thing that many teachers are often unaware of is that, often, some children are working to regulate even in the calm environments they're providing. It's the calm that's triggering their systems. Your predictability is terrifying to their nervous system. Remember, our stress responses are meant to keep us alive. For instance, you don't lay down on a savanna or desert, or something will eat you! You have no time to relax when you're busy trying to survive.

When children have been conditioned to feel that dysregulation is normal, when they're used to people screaming at them, making them feel unsafe, and never knowing what's around the corner, their bodies think it's normal that there's no peace, rest, or silence. If you, like a student, have trouble sitting in silence or struggle with inactivity, it's your body speaking to you. One of my students, Isaiah, was telling me with his choices that he was in pain. His brain was craving calm and stability, but he needed time to understand and trust it. And he needed me to help him practice living in it. I understood his journey.

****

Our goal, then, is to first learn to live within *our* window of tolerance. Otherwise, helping children will never be a reality. We can't pour from an empty bucket. "A dysregulated adult cannot regulate a dysregulated child."[221] We are ultimately responsible for developing greater peace and emotional regulation within ourselves. Regardless of your past, your future is your responsibility. If you didn't have good models, it's not an excuse for being a crappy one for the kids you interact with. The world doesn't need more jerks, period. Your window of tolerance *will*

---

221 "The Window of Tolerance."

grow larger with intentional focus and mindfulness practices as you become aware of your triggers.

Who, me?

Yes. *You* have triggers.

What Bugs You? Identifying Your Triggers

When we love a person, we accept him or her exactly as is:
the lovely with the unlovely, the strong along with the fearful,
the true mixed in with the façade, and of course, the only way
we can do it is by accepting ourselves that way.
—Fred Rogers

What bugs you? Where do you get emotionally and/or physically flooded? By identifying what feelings, emotions, sensations, thoughts, and stimuli trigger us, we can become more aware of when *we* are the problem and step back. It will likely be vastly different for everyone, even children growing up in the same home. That's why it's essential that we engage our individual stories of harm and heartache to get to the root of why we react the way we do. Your body is giving you all the clues you need—if you stop and listen. And as you learn how to do this for yourself, it will become easier to engage a dysregulated child in their moments of distress and find solutions using care and wisdom. Although it's hard work to examine the younger parts of ourselves, the excavation leads to greater love and compassion for the child within—both ours and our students'—who's waiting to experience "felt safety."

Have you ever noticed that when you're super angry or sad you exhibit child-like characteristics? It's because your brain is functioning from its primal state, at the brain stem. And the stem's only function is to keep us alive, so it will never help us make cognitive decisions.

Thus, it's important to identify your triggers and create a game plan. A *trigger* is a stimulus—such as a person, place, smell, sound, situation, or thing—that contributes to an unwanted emotional or behavioral response. For instance, I hate the smell of coffee on someone's breath because my fifth-grade teacher smelled like it when he'd yell at me for not understanding fractions, and the sound of an NFL game on TV because it represents being ignored by my dad when I was little. Consistent, repetitive, unnecessary noises people make, like clicking their pen in a meeting or shaking their legs in my peripheral vision, drive me to distraction, as do the smell of cigars and the shame of being told I'm "so emotional."

Did any come to mind? Look closely, as we rarely ask ourselves why things bug us. I had a colleague who treated me with annoyance and disdain for no apparent reason, and I was baffled as to why she hated me so intensely. One night she and her husband joined three other couples for a drink at a wine bar. She treated me the way she always did, with snotty remarks, rolling her eyes, cutting me off, and so on. The next morning, I was surprised to see her enter my classroom.

"Mark [her husband] called me out last night after we left on how I treat you," she remarked.

"Oh?" I replied cautiously.

"I've been thinking about why I have such a hard time with you."

"Okay," I said. What could I say, honestly?

To my amazement, she started to sob.

I froze. Should I try to comfort her? She didn't like to be touched, so I opted to hand her a box of tissues instead.

"You remind me of my mother. She is always floating and flittering around, always talking, driving me crazy."

"I see," I responded.

"But you're not my mom. I've been unfair to you, and I'm sorry."

Without waiting for my reply, she walked out. Looking back, I can see how brave it was for her to look within herself and ask, "What is triggering me?" Of course, I'm not her mother, but her automatic reactions from her nervous system responded to a "potential threat." We worked amicably together for the next year, even becoming friends. There's always room for more understanding.

****

I am still discovering the truth about me.

—Fred Rogers

Everything in this neighborhood is obnoxiously scrunched together. Cars are parked on both sides of a street initially made for horses at the turn of the century, and there's nowhere to turn around. Big cities adapt to whatever is necessary, and Seattle is no different. What a mess! I'm thankful I don't live here, on top of people like this, and I'm ready to leave.

Although the house with the Airbnb is level with the street, the entrance is down a driveway that dips drastically at a forty-five-degree angle, only to level out at a carport, fence, and back deck. It snowed yesterday, and I never left the house, as Seattle drivers are scarier than driving in the elements. The incline makes it challenging to jump into my car, and I turn on the defroster to warm it up. Noticing the retaining wall on my driver's side, I see the homeowner's car parked to the right of the driveway under a carport. I'm surprised how hard I must push the gas to get my car to move in reverse due to the angle of the driveway. "Come on," I mutter, annoyed, and gradually, my car moves up the hill.

That retaining wall looks a bit closer than I thought. Stopping, I inch forward a bit. Reversing again, I am almost to the other owner's car in my mirror (it's parked right at the edge of the driveway), but will I be able to clear it? I stop again, pausing to think. I look side to side. I can barely make out his windshield. *How close am I to his bumper?* Thinking back to our conversation yesterday, I recall that he told me he's completing his residency at a hospital in Tacoma, home only every four days. The last thing he needs is for me to crash into his car. I need to just get out and look.

Near the top of the hill, the little wagon inside my car rolls backward and hits the hatch with a thud. Startled, I hit my brakes with force. My body whips forward as adrenaline shoots through me. *That's it. I need to get out and check before that sound is his car!* It's better to just check than have to knock on the door and tell him I crunched his vehicle.

Catching my breath, I open the door and walk around my car to investigate. Suddenly, my car rolls forward and down the driveway like a roller coaster. I run to the driver's side just in time to barely touch the steering wheel but lose my grip as it moves faster.

Helpless, I watch as my car picks up speed and heads toward the bottom of the driveway.

There can only be a bad outcome: hitting the carport with the owner's car parked inside or smashing through the back fence and crashing over the cliff. I'm keenly aware of the quiet as I brace for the inevitable sound of impact. At the last minute, the wheels pivot toward the carport. *Crash!* Rapidly, two poles bend out of place; the first bends backward, while the second jams up into the roof and back down into my windshield. It shatters into a webbed mess.

Silence. And for a split second, like a child, I think, *Maybe they didn't hear it.*

"What are you doing?" yells the owner, coming out of the house.

"I didn't do it on purpose," I retort like a child.

Humiliation covers me like a blanket, and I'm alone, looking at the damage I've done. What started out as fear that I'd hit another car has ended with me hitting a house!

The owner says he knows a contractor who will head over to inspect the damage. I sit shivering in my car.

"Wystie, I love you more than a car," my husband reassures me over the phone. "I'm just thankful you didn't go over the cliff."

The owner says I should wait inside where it's warmer as several men, presumably the contractors, arrive to survey my damage. I watch them through the window.

My phone rings. I had texted my friend I was meeting that I'd just had an accident.

"Wystie, it's a car, and it can be fixed. At least you're okay."

I cry harder, unable to catch my breath. What if I can't get my car home to my kindergarteners tomorrow? Jazlynn was so worried about me being gone, and now I'd done something so dumb. I'll have to be gone longer!

"This is trauma. You know that."

Oh, yeah, trauma, that topic I've been writing about all weekend. One of the contractors moves closer to my car, throws a comment over his shoulder, and all begin to laugh.

"They're looking at what I did and laughing at me!"

"Who cares! Let 'em laugh," he says.

Then it hits me.

"I'm just like Evelyn and the water bottle," I say.

Instantly, I'm flooded with peace. Of course, I'd been transported back to childhood without realizing I'd made the trip. Inside, we're all still waiting to be found in our complex and confusing moments. I needed comfort the same way Evelyn did sitting in the office, alone and humiliated. Emotions reveal the truths about where our identities are bound to the challenging moments in our past—moments when we felt isolated or vulnerable.

The estimation is more than eleven thousand dollars' worth of damage to my car and the carport. My humiliation is only eased by the fact that I'm eager to use the experience for good.

I see Evelyn enter the cafeteria and make her way toward me. Although she's wearing her COVID mask, her eyes tell me she is smiling. I hug her as my students grab their lunch cards and file past. Moving her toward the wall, I slide down, and she mimics me.

"I did a bad thing this weekend," I say.

Evelyn's eyes get bigger above her mask. "You did?"

"Yep. Do you remember the hand sanitizer and the water bottle?" I ask.

Her eyes dart to the ground for a split second but then shoot back to mine. She nods.

"I wrote about that in my book about Mister Rogers this weekend."

"I'm in your book a lot, huh?"

"Yes, you've given me lots of material. So, I was at the top of this big hill that was someone's driveway, and my car rolled into their house!"

"Whoa! That's bad."

"I guess I'm my mistake," I bait her.

"No, you're not. You aren't your mistake. Remember?"

I grab her into a hug she gladly receives.

"You're so stinking right. I knew you'd tell me the truth. In the middle of it, I said to my friend, 'Everyone is looking at me.'"

"Hey, just like me. You're just like me!"

"Yes, I'm just like you," I say.

****

We live in a culture that only wants to talk about what's going
well. Anything that's not going well is positioned as a detour from
the main road. The truth is that pain is not a detour from the main
road. Pain is part of the road we walk as human beings.

—Susan Cain

Caden is in crisis. No doubt about it. He's been diagnosed with severe ADHD,
but that's just the tip of the iceberg. His mother and father chose to divorce three
and a half years ago but remained in the same house, "for his sake," while dating
other people. No judgment here, just facts. When his father introduced a new
girlfriend into the picture last year, Caden's mother welcomed her and her three
children into the home too.

As an only child, Caden appreciated and enjoyed having other children to
play with; his mother had begun to date, leaving her distracted and emotionally
unavailable. When his mother discovered she was pregnant, his father and girlfriend and surrogate siblings moved out, leaving Caden with a new adult male in
the home. Their loss was palpable, leaving his heart orphaned and wounded.

The month before school started, Caden's mother found out that the baby
she was carrying would need emergency surgery in utero and immediately upon
birth. This threw her into a panic and whisked her away to Seattle to induce the
labor of her unborn baby girl.

Caden was left with his distracted father and shuffled off between various rela-
tives for an unknown period. As school begins, his mother communicates her sadness over missing the first days and asks how she can help him transition from afar.
I encourage her, telling her that I "have him" and that we can remain in contact.

During Meet the Teacher Night, his father hobbles up to me, having recently
had knee surgery, and promises to help with Caden's transition too. Caden is a
beautiful boy with natural curls and olive skin. He clings to his father's side, not
speaking but wanting to take a look inside the bucket of school supplies others
dropped off. Children rarely let you meet the real version of themselves when
their parents are around. They're often holding out until they have assessed you
as trustworthy and safe. Parents are equally nervous, as if it's a "dating situation"
where they're hoping and praying we "like" their child.

Caden doesn't stand out from the rest that night, but I place the need for attunement in his folder so I can be aware to sit him closer to me during the *Neighborhood* and offer any extra support.

Disconnect Distractions

Distraction is a chief thief in our desire to have an authentic connection with children. Where we give our attention demonstrates what we value. There are two types of distractions: outer and internal. Internal distractions keep us from emotionally showing up and interfere with our ability to see, read, and stay with a conversation at the moment. We get distracted by our internal distress, especially when it triggers a stress response or attachment wound. Most of us don't like to look or feel weak. We have bought into the lie that there is perfection to be reached. If we had unpredictable, dismissive, or terrifying caregivers, it would be easy to respond similarly to children seeking our comfort.

The typical cellphone user touches their phone 2,617 times every day![222] Want to see how much? Turn on your screen time feature on your phone and see how often you're checking Instagram or Facebook each day. I had a sore thumb once from "pinning" on Pinterest too much, so I'm guilty too. We must remember what it was like to not have our cell phones to constantly distract and help us to numb out. When I consciously chose to show my kindergarteners *Mister Rogers' Neighborhood*, my phone had to go. It was much more challenging than you'd expect. If we have a free moment, we check our phones. Yes, I know that one or two of you reading this will triumphantly tell me, "I can go days without looking at my phone." Fabulous. You will use *something* else to distract you, I promise.

When I place my phone on my desk each day, it becomes an outward sign that I chose my students over myself. Attunement signals our awareness of another person's needs. What could I do to set the stage for them to fully receive what Fred Rogers intended for each episode? I became keenly aware of why Rogers had loved the Quaker adage "attitudes are caught, not taught." I used my body, eyes, hands, and heart to attune to Mister Rogers and them. Every moment matters.

---

222 Julia Naftulin, "Here's How Many Times We Touch Our Phones Every Day," *Business Insider*, July 13, 2016, https://www.businessinsider.com/dscout-research-people-touch-cell-phones-2617-times-a-day-2016-7.

Becoming childlike is a vulnerable choice. It's about allowing yourself the freedom of staring at the screen with wonder, allowing authentic reactions and excitement, and emptying yourself of adult notions and expectations. There is freedom in breathing slowly and stopping to enjoy something, just because we can. Stopping doesn't come as easy for us, as we live in an age of constant distraction and noise. But I trust in Mister Rogers. He never failed me as a child, and my students needed him more than ever. Although I had not had deep peace and rest as a child, I craved it for them. I would push past guilt, uneasiness, helplessness, and insecurity to lead them to security. As I slowed down to look and listen, my heart was healing too.

Fred Rogers said, "It's true that we take a great deal of our own upbringing into our adult lives and lives as parents, but it's true, too, that we can change some of the things that we would like to change. It can be hard, but it can be done."[223]

There's a Block

What happens when there seems to be a block in loving a child? Caden needs constant reminders:

"We need to keep the chair legs on the floor."

"Swinging our backpack and sweatshirt in the line is unsafe."

"Please, sit correctly on the carpet."

"People feel unsafe when you _____ with your body near them." It could be kicking, hitting, rolling, karate-chopping, and so forth.

There are redirections at every transition and one after he does the behavior *again*! It reminds me of trying to train my basset hound puppy, who, unlike my obedient German shepherd, couldn't care less. It's exhausting! Never mind that we're still teaching in pandemic compliances: desks a mandated three feet apart, masks covering up expressions and adequate phonics instruction, no Mister Rogers fish tank/library calm-down area, block station, Maker Space, art/painting area, or dramatic play. I hate it. Every day I wait for a sign that we might go back to some semblance of normal. As a revolt, I've kept apple crafts on my windows, now faded from the sun, made by the children I had in March 2020, when COVID-19 shut us down for "at least six weeks." I'm angry that they're now second graders, and

---

223 Rogers, *You Are Special*.

that somehow I hadn't kept my word that we would be back together.

Watching *Mister Rogers' Neighborhood* after lunch is becoming my only solace. It's Fred who comes through the door, whether we're online, in a hybrid model, or in-person, sitting alone at six-foot tables, to welcome us into attunement and secure attachment. My most significant achievement teaching in a pandemic? Watching the *Neighborhood* 180 days in a row, in order. On the hybrid days, two times! David Newell (a.k.a. Mr. McFeely) was impressed at this news and sent me a text: "Quite an achievement. Not sure how many people could say that."

What was once a nonnegotiable is now a lifeline. I knew Fred would be the only normalcy we would have with the constant shifting in numbers, contact cases, and new mandates. I needed him. His presence helped me remember who I was as a teacher, as one whose love changed those around me. I was losing my way.

I make a choice to move Caden in front of my teaching station, where I can model, encourage, and modify lessons to foster his success. But every movement, chair tip, flinch, and "naughty behavior" catches my eye and frankly makes me irate. *What is it about that child that makes me so angry?* I find myself fixated on his every move, breath, and gesture. It's as though catching him being naughty is my mission. Where has my love gone? Sometimes children catapult our faces flat into the wall of our own humanity. *Smack!* I'm not okay! Still, I know that spending time with Mister Rogers will be the key for Caden. It's worked with Blue Eyes and countless others over the last three years.

I put him to my right, next to the chair, and wait to let Mister Rogers soothe his pain. But this time it's not working. He can't sit still—and then there's the poking, physical and emotional.

C: Mrs. Edwards, why are we watching this? (*spins in spot and falls over*)

Me: We watch Mister Rogers every day because it's good for our hearts and he teaches us new things. Let's listen carefully.

C: When is lunch?

Me: Caden, we don't talk during Mister Rogers.

C: (*makes a slurping sound that causes another child to glare and move away*)

Me: Caden, look here, please. We need you to sit quietly and watch Mister Rogers, please. Do you remember how we practiced? (*he nods*) Be kind and quiet, please.

C: Do you like this show? (*POKE!!!*)

I choose to shake my head no and point at the screen. *All I want to do is watch Mister Rogers.* This kid is driving me crazy. It's like his chaos has transferred to my body, and I'm getting angrier and angrier. What I'm feeling is helplessness.

We don't like to feel like we aren't successful or capable when it comes to young children. I'd been an educator for twenty-two years, and it wasn't like he was the first child who didn't understand boundaries or need reminders. Even writing out this story I'm thinking about you reading it, the reader who has multiple ways *you* would handle the situation better or differently. But we can't know how a child will trigger something deeper within us if we aren't honest about what is really going on. Is it that I just wanted Mister Rogers? Could it be that Caden was activating helplessness that was attached to a deeper pain I was hiding? Yes. Remember, every child that drives you crazy is a gift. They're revealing something to you if you're brave enough to enter in and attune to your own heart.

How's Your Heart?

This summer I became an empty nester. What should've been a time of celebration has left me in a state of deep sadness. I understand that millions of others have gone before me into this stage of life, but my story is laced with triumph and regret. My older son was accepted to an elite technological institute, near Seattle, Washington, and my younger to Belmont University in Nashville, Tennessee. We couldn't be prouder of their accomplishments, and yet I have deep, deep regret over the years I lost to distraction and behavior addiction.

Where most parents can remember their child's life in vibrant detail, I have large chunks of time I was physically present but emotionally absent and checked out. In many ways, I feel like I just got my kids and life back, and now they're gone. I can't bring myself to enter their rooms, and I often find myself listening for their sounds, voices, smells, and presence. Our new normal consists of watching the BBC, eating cereal for dinner, and saying, "I don't know. What do you want to do?" The struggle is real. It's the death of what was and the newness of what might be. Even FaceTimes with my children bring me little relief, as the ache is so profound, and my identity feels like a tangled mess. Yet I'm still teaching in a pandemic and writing this book. And Mister Rogers still comes in the door to give me sweet relief.

But it's not working, and that terrifies me.

As I sit at my writing desk, pouring out my thoughts into my journal and praying for guidance, it finally hits hard. The words flood my brain, and I feel their truth. *Caden's chaos is reminding me that I am sad.*

I open up my laptop and the following letter spills out:

Dear Mister Rogers,

My boys just left for college, and I have all these big feelings inside. I look at their rooms and feel like I died inside. I made bad choices that kept me sick for a long time, and now that I'm better they are gone. I miss them.

I bring my kindergarteners to the *Neighborhood* each day to find love, comfort, and care. But I need you too. I know that you wouldn't chastise me for getting frustrated when I don't have all the answers. You'd tell me that you're proud of me for all the times I try, show up, fail, and try again. Loving children is a big responsibility, and teachers hold the keys to giving life or more emotional pain. I'm learning to tell the truth that makes me free. I'm sad. I am tired of teaching in a pandemic. I need relief, support, and kindness that can only be found in something greater than myself: faith, hope, and love. You continue to teach me that love changes people, but it is intentional and harder than reacting to things I can only see. You would remind me of all the times where I took a step toward love when it was hard and found freedom.

I'm part of Caden's story. I'm his teacher. That is my daily glimpse of glory. He'll think of me and remember how I made him feel. You said the greatest gift we can give the world is our honest self. Here I am, a beautiful disaster and a woman who loves children. I'm telling the truth that I am sad but believe love still works. Whether my feelings are old or new, love has me. Love has Caden. You're still helping me teach them that they matter. There's only one me, and that is enough for the children in my care.

Love,

Wystie

Have you ever had a moment where you finally admitted the truth to yourself?

I'm not okay!
I'm sad!
I'm angry!
In fact, I'm downright livid!
That's freedom.

****

Repairing Emotional Ruptures with Children

Forgiveness is a strange thing. It can sometimes be easier to forgive our enemies than our friends. It can be hardest of all to forgive people we love. Like all of life's important coping skills, the ability to forgive and the capacity to let go of resentments most likely take root very early in our lives.
—Fred Rogers

When I say the word *forgiveness*, what do you think of? For me, I instantly think of my faith and my husband, Matthew. If you have trauma surrounding church or organized religion, it might be a trigger word for you. In the case of attachment, it's about an upset or disconnect in a relationship followed by the restoration and positive affirmation of that same relationship.

Children get mad at us, and we get frustrated with them. That's what doing life together is like in a school setting. Honestly, the more I love children, the angrier I can get with them. "Why can't you see why that would be a bad choice?" I want to yell—because I love them so stinking much.

When there is a conflict, it is a disconnect, a rupture. In a secure relationship, I could go to the child, offer nurturing and explanation, and with time, the connection is repaired. Repairs give our nervous systems tremendous relief. If you've ever conflicted with someone you love and then make peace, the relief is one of the sweetest feelings. It feels nasty to be at odds with someone, misunderstood, angry, betrayed, or sad. Children with insecure attachments didn't receive adequate repairs to recalibrate their systems. Repeatedly, their truths, emotions, and feelings were dismissed, ignored, berated, or threatened. Little to no relief came.

Conflict sends children with broken connection into a tailspin. Jade thinks I'm disappointed in her, and she starts to sob: *avoidant attachment.* Casen is told "no" about tipping in his chair, and he asks if I still love him: *ambivalent attachment.* Blue Eyes comes back from the principal's office after fighting and ignores me when I ask what happened: *disorganized attachment.* I can't stress enough the importance of repairing emotional ruptures with children. We cause these ruptures frequently when we snap at them, don't really listen, disengage with our distractions, and misunderstand their behaviors. Ruptures happen when we least expect them to. But here's the beauty of working with children: **Children are much more forgiving than adults.**

****

"Mrs. Edwards! The ceiling is raining again!" Quinn calls out from the classroom library. Two months earlier I had come into the biggest mess imaginable as the ceiling was leaking water from the air conditioning system. My beautiful art center and filing cabinets were in large puddles, and the damage was creeping further into the center of the room.

I panicked, calling maintenance and administration, and my room was covered with black garbage bags for several weeks while they located the various leaks. It had finally been addressed after a month of school, much to our delight, but I was always checking every morning, due to PTSD.

"I felt it hit my arm," she says. "Oh, but it's green."

Getting up from the reading table, I make my way to the library and see green paint dripping off the dollhouse at the end. I glance back to see Diego and Coleson channeling their inner Jackson Pollock. Both boys are having a competition on who can fling more paint on their saturated papers.

I erupt. "Nooooooo! Boys! Stop, right now! There's paint *everywhere!*"

They stop dead in their tracks. None of the children has ever seen me this mad. They stop playing and watch. Hot rage boils inside me, and I feel the urge to punish the boys with words, let them know exactly how mad I am. Still, I recognize that this is old trauma from my own life bubbling to the surface.

I manage to take a deep breath and hand them the wet wipes. "Get down and clean all of it. Now!"

They work fast and efficiently.

My conscience is already working on me: *Wystie, that was over the top. It's freaking paint. It's cleaning up, and look, you really upset them.*

"It's just paint. But we still need to get it off the floor," I manage to spit out.

There, I apologized, I tell myself—knowing it's not what they needed. Why am I so mad? I honestly don't know. Is it because the leaky ceiling was traumatic? I remember how helpless I felt, knowing that the space I'd created for them was compromised, how long it took to be fixed, and the emotional toll it had every morning when the trash bags were still there.

We end the day normally with our feelings lion, and Coleson says he's sad because he "made a mess with the paint." Do I respond well? I don't remember.

It's not until I'm journaling the next morning that I feel like God hits me in the heart. The message is palpable: *You need to make that better with Coleson. He's not okay.*

I think about Coleson and his mother, who often stirs the pot with parent volunteers and always seems angry about something. Coleson is an avoidantly attached child to the core, but super affectionate, often giving me extra hugs and love notes. He loves pleasing me and prides himself on following the rules. I feel terrible. The rupture would've felt horrendous to him, as I'm his only safe place.

When I go to make copies, I'm in luck. There he is walking toward me to go out to the line. "Hey, you. Good morning."

When he would've usually grinned and run to hug me, he diverts his eyes to the ground and shrugs. I think, *That's my fault.*

"I need to talk to you about what happened yesterday with the paint."

He looks miserable, and I get on my knees in front of him, in the middle of the hall, and take his hands in mine.

"Coleson, I need your eyes."

He looks up at me, and the tears are close to falling.

"Buddy, I totally failed you yesterday, big-time. I was so mad, and it wasn't okay to yell at you. I need to ask for your forgiveness. Will you please forgive me for working out my mad at you?"

He nods his head yes.

"Can you tell me with your words?"

"I forgive you," he mutters, falling against my neck. Without thinking about it, I start to cry, too, out of relief.

I don't know if his mother has ever repaired the countless times I've witnessed her hurting him with her words, but I made a choice that day that Coleson would get an apology from at least *one* grown-up. We can get spun up about things that are fleeting. His forgiveness was one of the best gifts he gave me that year, as I've told this story to educators all over. Most of them cry, because they remember having to forgive an apology that was never spoken. If that was you, you are brave. Are there children in need of your repair?

Fred Rogers said: "Even good people sometimes do bad things. Errors might mean corrections, apologies, repairs, but they didn't mean that we, as a person, were a bad person in the sight of those we loved. The second thing we learned (if we were fortunate) is that having someone we loved get mad at us did not mean that person had stopped loving us; we had their *unconditional* love, and that meant we would have their forgiveness, too."

****

Garrett's mom is frantic as they sit down for conferences. "I need to discuss some things with you. Recently, he has started to say that he 'wants to die' and we are totally freaked out."

I look over at Garrett, surprised. This isn't like the little boy I teach every day, and I'm concerned. "Really, buddy? Did you say that to your mommy?"

"Yes. But I didn't mean it." Looking caught, he starts twisting his fingers.

"Those are super serious words to say, Garrett. I can see why Mommy is worried about them. Can you tell me why you're saying that? Are you sad inside?"

"No," he says and starts to smile. He's not getting the seriousness of the subject.

"Has something changed at home?" I ask her, still baffled with the whole thing.

"We took away all the TV and video games and are spending as much time as we can as a family outside."

"That's great. But I meant before he said that to you."

"I started a new job. It's tough because it's seven to seven, so I'm gone when he gets up and home right before he goes to bed."

"Wow, that's got to be hard. What's the new job?"

"I'm a hospice care worker." *Ding-ding!* There it was plain as day.

"Garrett, did you say you wanted to die to get Mommy's attention?" She turns in her chair and looks at him.

"Yes," he mumbles. "I hate that she's working, and I want to see her."

"Ah, like when Prince Tuesday didn't want his parents to go to work," I remind him.

"Yeah, like that."

"Garrett, look at your mommy and tell her the real truth: 'I don't want to die. I just want to be with you.'"

She starts to cry out of relief when he says it so easily.

Of course, I document the conversation, but it's clear from all I know about him that he used the most extreme language he could to explain the big feelings inside. Oftentimes, ruptures are repaired when we ask the right questions or look for the most logical answers.

This is one of my favorites of Fred Rogers' stories:

> So many people have asked me, "Do you ever get mad?" And, of course, I answer, "Well, yes, everyone gets mad sometimes. The important thing is what we do with the mad that we feel in life."
>
> A few weeks ago, on my way home from a particularly tough day at work, I stopped to see my two grandsons. Their mom and dad weren't there, but the boys were there with the babysitter in the backyard, squirting water with hoses. I could see that they were really having fun, but I felt I needed to let them know that I didn't want to be squirted, so I told them so, and little by little, I could feel that the older boy, Alexander, was testing the limit until finally, his hose was squirting very close to where I

was standing. I said to him in my harshest voice, "Okay, that's it, Alexander, turn off the water. You've had it!" He did as I told him, said he was sorry, and looked very sad.

The more I thought about it, the sadder I got. I realized that Alexander had not squirted me and that I had stepped into his and his brother's play with a lot of feelings leftover from work, so when I got home, I just called Alexander on the phone. I told him I felt awful about my visit with him, and the more I thought about it, the more I realized that I was taking out my anger from work on him. I told him I was really sorry.

Do you know how he answered me? He said, "Oh Bubba"— he calls me Bubba—"Oh Bubba, everybody makes mistakes sometimes." I nearly cried. I was so touched by his naturally generous heart, and I realized that if I hadn't called him, I might not have ever received that wonderful gift of Alexander's sweet forgiveness.[224]

---

224 Fred M. Rogers, "Mr. Rogers Asked About When He Gets Angry," December 29, 2020, YouTube video, https://www.youtube.com/watch?v=dp7mE0_8VP4.

Lynn Johnson Collection.

Chapter 9:
Routines and Rituals

"I'll Be Back When the Day Is New"

Children feel far more comfortable and secure when things happen
predictably—with routines, rituals, and traditions. Those traditions,
big or small, create anchors of stability, especially in rough seas.

—Fred Rogers

Our principal gathered us outside to celebrate the last day of school after teaching in a pandemic, virtually, hybrid, and in-person (separated by masks and mandates). She asked us to go around and share what we were most proud of after such a horrible year. I listened to my colleagues share remarkable things, like how much their students had grown academically, what they'd learned about teaching with technology, and spending time with their families. I was proudest that my class and I watched the *Neighborhood* 180 times without missing a day! In fact, I'd watched the *Neighborhood* twice a day while we were in a hybrid (Group A/Group B) model.

Because COVID-19 was traumatic for us all, the simple routine of watching Mister Rogers entering the door every day saved *my* heart. The grief was palpable and just below the surface for me. I was angry and grieving over all I'd lost the school year before and the uncertainties surrounding our world. I felt "far more comfortable and secure" when Mister Rogers predictably showed up with his rou-

239

tines, rituals, and traditions. Those traditions, big and small, created anchors for *my* stability, especially in the rough seas of sadness and uncertainty. Fred Rogers' face, voice, and love partnered with me in carrying our children through a pandemic. My goal wasn't to teach them to read, write, or count (which they learned too) but to let them know that they were loved and to connect their hearts to an anchor of hope: "Mister Rogers and Mrs. Edwards will be here daily because we love you. You can count on us." The peace of genuine presence. Never underestimate its power.

How you structure your day is a tangible way to influence rhythm and set the scene for deeper interactions. Routines and rituals create a natural, calming rhythm to the emotional atmosphere of your classroom. Children crave boundaries and order; if they can't find a boundary, they will push until they find it. Be aware.

Boundaries and Discipline

All good discipline involves solid boundaries, both emotional and physical. These boundaries are established through our rituals, routines, and rhythms each day in our classrooms. The pendulum swings back and forth on the best ways to "discipline" children. Each school district adopts what they believe is the best system to ensure student success while facilitating support for children struggling in the areas of behavior. But here's something I believe we miss all the time—that is, all behavior is a bid for connection.

Fred Rogers' notes on discipline from 1980 to 1981 were some of the favorites I read in the archive because they confirmed what I've always known about working with children. Discipline is a form of love. **We discipline children because we love them and want to keep them safe.** Whenever my students misbehave, my explanations always come back to safety, physical and emotional: "My job is to keep you safe and help you grow into an incredible human being. If you make unsafe choices for yourself or others, I promise I will help you."

I recall taking little Isaiah's sweet, chubby face in my hands one afternoon and saying, "I love you so very much, enough to send you to the principal's office for doing that." He grinned, exposing the missing teeth that had popped out in a fall, and bounced away down the hall.

Then there were two boys I taught in seventh grade, Tanner and Luke. Tanner had spent the better part of the semester flirting with the girls beside him, attending football, and avoiding all his assignments. After we dove deeper into comprehension strategies, he was empowered and determined to do well. Unfortunately, there were only three weeks left in the semester before summer break, and he squeaked by with a D. As I picked up materials in my classroom during summer school, Tanner called out to me, "Hey, Mrs. Edwards! Thanks for giving me a D instead of an F."

"Tanner, you just started to care when it was close to being too late."

"It's okay. I'm learning a lot." It made me laugh.

Luke was an ACEs kid if I ever met one. He was notorious at the middle school when I took my job, and the students warned me that he'd physically assaulted people. *Great.* The only thing I could get him to talk to me about was movies. He couldn't get enough of dark comedies and horror films. Still, I made a point of asking him about them and giving him suggestions based upon his interests in aliens and lore. Some days he was interested in talking, others he'd cover his head with a hoodie and melt into the chair in the back of the room.

One day he came in spun up. Another teacher had said something that set him off, and no matter what I did, he got louder and more belligerent. "Luke, I need you to lower your voice, please. I don't like being yelled at," I said calmly. He leaped onto his desk and walked across the rows, to my surprise. Kids scrambled to get out of the way.

"You're just like the rest of them!" he screamed at me. Students looked at me in horror. All I felt was sadness, as if the months of intentional connection were for nothing. When I sent him to the office, the classroom breathed a sigh of relief, but I was devastated. Was he beyond my reach, after all?

Later, my principal stuck his head inside the door and said he's sent Luke home.

"I have to tell you something, though. He didn't care about the suspension. He was more worried about you."

"Me?" I asked.

"Before he left, he said, 'I need to go back and tell Mrs. Edwards that I don't think she's like the rest of them.'"

I smiled. It was the best thing I'd heard in a long time.

Organize the Space

In college, my friend Lydia had an alarm clock with various nature sounds. It would initially begin softly and gradually build in volume if you didn't shut it off. What started as the soft patter of rain could eventually be a full-blown thunderstorm in a short time. That's how behavior works in children. When a child doesn't receive the attunement and care they need for security, they enter our classrooms ravenously hungry for affection, validation, and someone's full attention. In this way, it's an extreme privilege to create boundaries through consistent routines and rhythms for children. Many may have never felt the kindness of a limit.

Our set limits help them learn predictability, loving correction, and guidance. Our learning spaces need to create safety inside their bodies, and chaos and mess don't help. Take note of how your learning space would feel to a child who needs order and peace. I can't tell you how messy some classrooms are. It may be fine for you, but I'm thinking of the children you teach. As we think about the children, it may be time to get more organized. Think of it as a way of taking good care of them. Fred Rogers often sang:

> I'm taking care of you
> Taking good care of you
> For once I was very little too
> Now I take care of you.[225]

Set Limits and Rules

One of the ways that we take good care of children is by having firm limits. My students are taught the rules and then expected to obey them after some practice. Remember, our brains find rest and peace in the familiar and predictable. During the *Neighborhood's* week on discipline, Lady Elaine Fairchilde, the classic mischief-maker and boundary pusher, makes some unkind choices, jealous that Cornflake S. Pecially isn't making dolls that look like her instead of King Friday XIII. Later, she paints her face on all the dolls, causing King Friday XIII to summon the chief of discipline for her "misdemeanor."

---

225 Fred M. Rogers, "I'm Taking Care of You," The Mister Rogers Neighborhood Archive, 1975, http://www.neighborhoodarchive.com/music/songs/im_taking_care_of_you.html.

One of the best parts of how Rogers discussed the topic of punishment is having Lady Elaine part of the conversation. He believed that when children are part of the process, it makes learning more meaningful. In the end, Lady Elaine makes amends by helping in the factory for several days and learns she's actually good at it.

He reminds us that learning to follow rules and limits is difficult when we are young, but they help us grow inside. Children who've never had a secure foundation will need more reassurance that we don't find them any less valuable or less wanted, although they are making mistakes.

Transitions Prevent Surprises

Surprises and transitions often provoke a compromised nervous system that is healing from being on high alert. Children from hard places have brains and bodies that have grown accustomed to understanding that change equals threat. And threats equal danger and loss. For example, a simple transition to PE after recess can throw them into a tailspin even if they enjoy PE. Observe a classroom of kindergarteners when a substitute teacher barely has control, and they're like a herd of feral cats. Our brains love novelty but crave order. Knowing what to expect next, or having certainty that they can ask questions, puts their nervous systems at ease. Children from hard places can only heal when they sense there is no longer a threat. Routines and rituals are the surest way to empower children to trust your guidance and protection. Fred Rogers addressed this concept regularly in the *Neighborhood*, expressing the importance of being told what to expect and the sense of predictability and rhythm.

In music, rhythm is a strong, regular, repeated sound measurement. The rhythm of a piece creates the foundation for the other melodies to move and sound beautiful. This is much like how attunement fosters a healthy, secure attachment in a child. A rhythm is predictable, even when it speeds up or slows down, and it's always present, offering value, security, and safety. Within the classroom environment and activities, rhythm means routines, regulation, and responsiveness.

We adjust our speed (rhythm) to theirs with moments of exuberance and moments of calm containment. Therapist and neurodevelopmental specialist Tricia Klassen writes:

One of the best ways we can help children develop calm and regulated nervous systems is through activities that expose them to an alteration between settled and aroused states. When children can move into activated states for a short time and then back into a calm state, they are teaching their bodies to naturally move out of the fight or flight alarm state. Think about *Duck, Duck, Goose,* [*Simon Says, Red Light, Green Light,*] and *Charades.* . . . Anything children or adults do that allows the nervous system to experience pattern and pendulation between being settled and activated teaches the body to regulate itself.[226]

****

We watch *Mister Rogers' Neighborhood* every day, in order, after lunch recess. Before we go to lunch, I pull three names of children to sit beside me, two to flank my chair, and the other for the "hot spot." When Blue Eyes was in my class, I often placed him in the hot spot to attune to him through touch. If I struggle to have affection for a child based on their behaviors that morning, I'll sit them next to me while watching the *Neighborhood.* As I place my hand on their head or their back while we watch, I remind myself of their value, age, and how precious they are. It's easy to forget they are five and six when you tame dragons all day. **This routine never changes.**

I recently glued into my journal at home a picture of them I took the first day they weren't wearing COVID masks. Slowly, I looked at each small face smiling with genuine love and happiness back at their teacher. "They're so little," I heard myself say. Sometimes I lose sight of that when I'm in the thick of the wilderness, fighting for them in every encounter. Just like a garden, flowers don't bloom because we pull the petals open with force. They bloom in their own time, at their own rate.

---

226 Tricia Klassen, "Childhood Resilience and the Role of Rhythm," Crisis and Trauma Resource Institute, May 5, 2020, https://ca.ctrinstitute.com/blog/childhood-resilience-rythym/.

Before they return from lunch recess, I dim the lights, place my chair in front of the screen, set down my phone, and cue the episode. They are encouraged to get cozy to receive the gift that Mister Rogers is about to give them.

We sit together, cloistered in a community of neighbors waiting for Mister Rogers to enter through a wooden door, wave, and smile.

When I viewed the *Mister Rogers' Neighborhood* set, located at the Heinz Museum in Pittsburgh, Pennsylvania, I shot David Newell (a.k.a. Mr. McFeely) a text saying, "It's amazing how one door can change your life."

He replied, "I walked through that door thousands of times."

It's just an ordinary door with a few stairs to step down, but it represents intention. What do you do with intention? I liken it to turning on the lights in my classroom each morning. Lamps surround my space to make it feel like a home, a cozy place where we can "take off our shoes" and be honest with one another. It's made up of a thousand moments. "Success doesn't come from what we do occasionally. It comes from what you do consistently."[227]

The Routines and Rituals of *Mister Rogers' Neighborhood*

From the moment Mister Rogers enters, it's real time. He comes through the door, welcoming us with "Won't you be my neighbor?" Then he takes the time to walk to the closet, methodically taking off his jacket and hanging it up, putting on his sweater and sneakers—all before he starts talking with us. With that ritual, he's giving us time to settle in before our "visit" officially begins.

For this same reason, I never skip the intro for any episode (we currently watch them all on the paid PBS Kids Channel on Amazon). I also paid to have advertisements removed from YouTube just in case a substitute had to look for the *Neighborhood* there. Fred Rogers didn't believe in marketing to children, so I had a visceral reaction when toy advertisements would pop up. Most people won't ask me why I paid to remove ads, assuming I thought they were annoying, but it goes deeper. I want to love my students as Fred Rogers believed was developmentally appropriate and necessary. (Always have a reason behind everything you do; he did.)

---

227 Marie Forleo, "20 Business Motivation Quotes to Get Inspired By," Lovely Impact, August 26, 2021, https://lovelyimpact.com/business-motivation-quotes/.

Here's a quick review of Mister Rogers' routines and rituals (he covers a lot of ground): Fred, smiling and singing, walks through the door and brings only one thing; changes into a sweater from a jacket; changes shoes; begins with a question/observation; visits with Mr. McFeely and neighbors, and always introduces his television neighbors to visitors; feeds the fish (and says so, because a child who was blind wrote in once to say they needed reassurance); picks up his toys and materials; signals the beginning of make-believe using the trolley, as it ventures into the tunnel (cuing the transition from reality to fantasy, then back again); gives a bit of explanation/lecture afterward; sings to neighbors; demonstrates a new way to play, speak, think, make music, move, pretend, wonder, create, or be silly; and shows how things are made with Picture-Picture. He also shakes people's hands, waves hello and goodbye, always shows gratitude, tries new things, gets in closer to get a better view, tells the truth, asks questions and makes connections, sings the same goodbye sequence, snaps his fingers in the same place, promises to come back, tells us we matter and are loved, and then exits the door. All in less than twenty-eight minutes!

A routine is a predictable activity done at the same time or in the same way each day. Mister Rogers never missed a beat in his opening segment for thirty-five years. That's commitment! (I thought I was sick of counting to one hundred every day.) Children *need* those routines we are sick of, especially if we work to repair inconsistent attunement and insecure attachments. Mister Rogers is trustworthy because he is predictable, which generates trust in their nervous systems. In fact, if there were ever a major change on the set of Mister Rogers, like painting the room blue or the porch swing yellow, he did it right in front of the children. No surprises. Society would make us believe the opposite, that children enjoy surprises. Still, any disruption to routine can make the average kindergarten class act like a wolf pack under a full moon.

Children with *insecure attachments* are particularly sensitive to changes in schedule, transitions, surprises, chaotic social situations, and any new situation in general. Busy and unique social situations, even if they are pleasant, will overwhelm them. Birthday parties, sleepovers, holidays, family trips, the start of the school year, and the end of the school year . . . all can be disorganizing for these children. Because of this, any efforts that can be made to be consistent, predictable, and repetitive will be very important in making these children experience *felt safety* and security. When they feel safe and secure, they can benefit from the nurturing and enriching emotional and social experiences you provide. If they are anxious or fearful, they cannot benefit from your nurturing in the same ways.[228]

Because attachment systems are activated in interpersonal relationships, insecure children will struggle in social situations. Be proactive in your approach to preparing your students in advance, if possible, by telling them what to expect. "Uncertainty can be felt as overwhelming anxiety, and tolerating the uncertainty of not knowing becomes an unbearable threat."[229] We all struggle with various forms of ambiguity, and the unknown is often worse than the truth. Fred Rogers understood this about children when he composed "I Like to Be Told." In an interview two years before his death, he attributed people's gratitude to their longing "to be in touch with honesty . . . that we want to be honest with them [on the program]."

He said: "I've told children . . . this might hurt, if you go to the doctor and the doctor gives you an injection, it might hurt at first, but it won't hurt for long. I mean, we're not going to fudge stuff. We're going to tell them the truth, and we're not going to dance around and say how happy things are when they're not."[230] Children crave honesty.

Clear is kind, unclear is unkind. Knowing what to expect next, or at least having certainty that we can ask questions, puts our nervous systems at ease. Children from hard places can heal only when they sense there is no longer a threat, and routines and rituals are the surest way to empower children into trusting your guidance and protection.

As you read the following lyrics, look at them through the eyes of a child needing reassurance and the power your simple explanations will bring:

> I like to be told
> When you're going away,
> When you're going to come back,

---

228 Perry, "Bonding and Attachment."
229 Geddes, *Attachment in the Classroom.*
230 John Donvan, "Mr. Rogers . . . Cool Dude," Nightline: There Goes the Neighborhood, 2001, YouTube video, https://www.youtube.com/watch?v=bYAXD-Z-ztE.

And how long you'll stay,
How long you will stay,
I like to be told.

I like to be told
If it's going to hurt,
If it's going to be hard,
If it's not going to hurt.
I like to be told.
I like to be told.

It helps me to get ready for all those things,
All those things that are new.
I trust you more and more
Each time that I'm
Finding those things to be true.

I like to be told
'Cause I'm trying to grow,
'Cause I'm trying to learn
And I'm trying to know.
I like to be told.
I like to be told.[231]

****

I'll be back when the day is new.
—Fred Rogers

I'm going to be absent for three days to write this book. As I speak to the class about my upcoming absence, Jazlynn looks like she is in visible pain. She hugs her

---

231 Fred M. Rogers, "I Like to Be Told," The Mister Rogers Neighborhood Archive, 1968.
   http://www.neighborhoodarchive.com/music/songs/i_like_to_be_told.html.

legs tight and buries her head in her arms. I can see the news flooding her system, making her feel out of control, overwhelmed with uncertainty and the loss at my absence; I am her secure base.

Aware that transitions and changes need to be explained and truthful, I take out an Expo marker, turn toward the calendar, and point to the Thursday I will be leaving.

"Tomorrow is Wednesday, which is our early release," I explain.

They nod understanding.

Next, I write the word *sub* on Thursday and Friday. "So, you'll have a sub on Thursday and Friday."

I place a smiley face on the Monday I will return. "This is when Mrs. Edwards will be back. Why will I come back?"

This is one of my favorite messages Fred Rogers taught me to say.

"Because you love us, and you want to," they say all together.

"Yes, because I want to. I love you, but I need to have time to write the book about why we love Mister Rogers so much and how other children can receive the love that we have every day. You are helping me by allowing me to take the time to write. Thank you for doing hard things."

I can see Jazlynn is still not okay. As we line up to leave, she comes to hug me, but this time I can hear her breath is shallow and quickened. Her little body begins to shake, but she's not crying; instead her eyes are glossy and fearful. Is she having a panic attack?

Even though I'd tried to give her a sense of what she could expect and therefore an element of control, it's not enough. Slowly the shaking turns into a moan, then a sniffle, then a sob.

"What's wrong with her?" Hannah asks looking concerned. I begin to use nonverbal cues to children to clean up and find their places while I hold her tightly to my chest. She needs to feel my heartbeat as I begin to breathe louder so she can hear it.

"I'm right here, baby girl. You're safe. I'm right here, Jazlynn. I love you."

I rock her side to side as I watch my kids motioning to each other, and Hannah points to Jazlynn while shaking her head to the boys. They begin to self-monitor each other, aware that she needs all my attention. I couldn't be prouder of them. It's like time slowed down, and we have all the time in the world. Although those few minutes feel like an eternity, she eventually calms, breathing deeper and slower. At last, her body regulates, and she stills in my arms.

"Those were some big feelings, huh?" I speak.

"I hate it when you leave," she grumbles into my chest.

"I know. You're my brave girl and will have all your friends with you. And I will come back right here." I point to the next Monday where I've drawn the smiley face.

This time it's enough. She moves away and gets on her "sticky spot" to line up. She's lived a thousand years already. It's unfair. But at least she'll always be safe in my love. Before I leave for the day, I take a marker and write the words *I love you. Be brave!* above her name tag left for the substitute.

When I return, as promised, the following Monday, her face lights up as she comes in through the door. She opens her arms wide and says, "I knew you'd come back!"

****

A Checklist of Classroom Routines and Rituals

- Post schedules with pictures if possible.
- Use music or nonabrasive sounds/timers.
- Incorporate movements and gestures.
- Affirm that the end of something is the beginning of something new.
- Explain what is going to happen/could happen.
- Teach routines as a way of "growing on the inside."
- Celebrate when children remember what is happening next and prepare.
- Ask children for input if you need to change the schedule so they have a voice.
- Give reminders when a transition will occur and how to cope with disappointment.
- Empathize with the sadness, anger, or disappointment *before* giving an explanation.
- Predict when children will have difficulty with new routines, giving extra time and consideration.

- Make transitions smooth by having them follow the same pattern each time.
- Speak simply, repeat yourself, if necessary, then check for understanding.
- Follow through on your promises.
- Be calm and patient.
- Watch for sensory overload—too much, too soon, too fast?
- Explain what is safe/unsafe regarding moving from one place to the other in the room, ways to act appropriately in common areas, how to ask for help, and ways to communicate.

Lynn Johnson Collection. Used with permission.

Chapter 10:

The Words We Use Matter

"It's You I Like"

It's you I like.

—Fred Rogers

I f there's one adjective that could describe Fred Rogers' commitment to word choice, it's *careful*. No word was uttered on the *Neighborhood* without considering how a child *could* perceive it. So unwavering in his attention to detail was Rogers that his staff created a parody entitled "Let's Talk About Freddish."[232] He'd stop production and speak with his mentor, Dr. Margaret McFarland, when he was unsure of things. Just because he said things in simple ways didn't mean that those words weren't chosen with the utmost care. "[What] Fred understood and was very direct and articulate about was that the inner life of children was deadly serious to them."[233] His wife, Joanne, recalls, "Whether he was working on a script for the *Neighborhood* programs or on a speech, he fretted over the words, attempting to make the content meaningful. I can remember him saying over and over again, as he worked on the fourth or fifth draft of whatever he happened to be writing, 'Simple is better.'"[234]

---

232 King, *The Good Neighbor.*
233 King, *The Good Neighbor.*
234 Rogers and Rogers, *The World According to Mister Rogers.*

Say What You Really Mean

Fred Rogers believed that "honesty is closely related to freedom." Have you ever stopped to think about word choice in your classroom? As I began to live in "the world of Fred Rogers" daily, this was one of the first areas I saw a change in me. I noticed it in the cafeteria one day as a student ran past me to use the restroom. Without thinking, I blurted out, "Are you on fire?" Instantly, I felt a pause inside and remembered Fred's stance on words. I turned to my kindergarteners sitting at the table and asked, "You don't think he was really on fire, do you?"

"He's not supposed to run," Ellie said, eating her hamburger.

"I just didn't want you to think that he was really on fire."

They looked at me, smiling, but I decided that I needed to be more mindful of my words.

Many called Fred Rogers a perfectionist, a trait often found when someone grew up with avoidant attachment. Still, he gained tremendous insight in observing children being "in the moment." "Rogers knew how to conceive of, and anticipate, the concerns of his young viewers. . . . How the young audience might misunderstand information mattered to him."[235] A classic example of this is when he "halted a taping of a show when a cast member told the puppet Henrietta not to cry. Rogers came out from behind the puppet set to make clear that his show would never suggest to children that they not cry."[236]

In his book *Mister Rogers' How Families Grow*, he spoke about misunderstandings and the need for clarification:

> There must be thousands of times during childhood when children misunderstand what they hear. Our mind has a way of making sense—any kind of sense out of what our ears and eyes bring to it. When what comes in is new or unfamiliar, or undefined, the mind will do its best to match that information with something it already knows. . . . But there's also another frequent source of children's misunderstandings, and that's their tendency to take what we say literally. How can they do otherwise when

235 King, *The Good Neighbor.*
236 King, *The Good Neighbor.*

they're just beginning to put words together [or connect to their preexisting experiences]? At the same time, as their parents [teachers/caregivers] may be telling them, "Say what you mean," those parents [teachers/caregivers] themselves aren't saying what they mean at all. [237]

Tell the Truth

How our words are understood doesn't depend just on how someone receives what we're saying. I think the most important part about communicating is the listening we do beforehand. When we can truly respect what someone brings to what we're offering, it makes the communication all the more meaningful.

—Fred Rogers

"Is Mister Rogers dead?" Violet asks me from her desk. The question halts all movement as several children look up from their math books, horrified.

I have a choice to make at that moment as it's vital for healthy development. After all, I'd never had to worry about such things growing up; Mister Rogers was alive and well. But now, years after his death, we spend time with his programs every day. And I'm reminded of when I spoke with people who knew him in Latrobe, Pennsylvania: "Fred was a television friend. He can't see children and never wanted them to be persuaded otherwise." He told the truth.

"Yes," I say simply. "Mister Rogers died in 2003, and he's no longer alive."

"How did that happen?!" Gabe wails in disbelief. "We just saw him yesterday!"

"Have you ever heard the word *cancer* before?" I ask. Many nod their heads.

"My grandma had cancer, and she died," Kayla adds.

Looking around at their sweet faces, I know math is essentially over. "Come sit with me on the carpet." They move quickly to take their seats.

Violet sits down and starts talking right away, "My mommy said Mister Rogers is dead, and I told her that wasn't true."

---

237 Fred Rogers, Barry Head, and Jim Prokell, *Mister Rogers' How Families Grow* (New York: Berkley Books, 1988).

"It's true," I say. "Mister Rogers had cancer in his tummy and died."

"Do we all have cancer in our tummies?" Chase asks, concerned.

"No. We don't all have cancer in our tummies, and they aren't sure what causes cancer. But they are working on that problem in many places right now. Maybe you'll grow up and help solve that problem."

"So my mommy was right?" Violet says, her eyes filling with tears.

"Yes," I say. "But I want to tell you something wonderful. Ask me 'What?'"

"What?" they echo.

"Mister Rogers loved children like you so much that he left us almost nine hundred episodes to watch and learn from."

"Whoa!" several exclaim (counting to one hundred in kindergarten is a big deal).

"He will look the same today when we watch?" Liam says.

"Yes. Mister Rogers will come through the door and have another television visit with us. Isn't that wonderful?" They nod their heads.

****

Could I have lied for my own comfort? Yes. Just like years ago when I'd tell my students that the sprinklers for fire on the ceiling were cameras and that elves on the shelf were watching them for Santa Claus. But I learned that although it's fun to pretend, children desperately crave honesty. If I wanted to be like Mister Rogers, I needed to tell children the truth and listen to their questions. The unknown is more frightening.

When a child asked Fred Rogers if he "liked being famous," this was his reply: "I don't think of myself as somebody who's famous. I'm just a neighbor who comes and visits children; [I] happen to be on television. But I've always been myself. I never took a course in acting. I just figured that the best gift you could offer anybody is your honest self, and that's what I've done for lots of years. And thanks for accepting me exactly as I am."[238]

---

238 Hollingsworth, *The Simple Faith of Mister Rogers*.

Telling the truth, and being seen as reliable, is one of the easiest ways to participate in attachment repair. Violet brought her question to me as a sign of trust. Without telling me, her question said, "I'll ask my teacher because I know she'll tell me the truth." What an honor to be counted as a truth-teller in a child's life. Remember that insecure attachment is broken trust. We set children free when they find us to be a safe harbor they can run to with their questions and concerns.

I was only in second grade on January 28, 1986. Tears streamed down my teacher's face as we watched the *Challenger* explode in the skies above Cape Canaveral, Florida. Seven astronauts, including teacher Christa McAuliffe, were gone right before our eyes.

"Boys and girls, something very sad just happened," my beloved teacher told us. The feelings from that moment are deeply etched into me, so much so that the *Challenger* disaster became the backdrop to my most successful play to date, *Mrs. Murphy's Porch.*

Fred Rogers said, "Being a giver grows out of the experience of having been a receiver—a receiver who has been lovingly given to."[239] I deeply believe that my teacher wouldn't have been able to comfort a classroom of second graders so beautifully had she not had others who "loved her into being." Her ability to remain present and calm is what my body remembers most. A feeling of sadness, yes, but also a deliberate pause, an opportunity to feel whatever we needed to feel at that moment. She understood that even young children feel tremendous grief, and her job was to give the comfort she had received in her own life. Someone had taken the time in her growing years to tell her the truth, and now she was giving us the same gift.

I remember watching the five o'clock news with my parents when President Reagan addressed the nation:

> And I want to say something to the schoolchildren of America who were watching the live coverage of the shuttle's takeoff. I know it is hard to understand, but sometimes painful things like this happen. It's all part of the process of exploration and discovery. It's all part of taking a chance and expanding man's horizons.

239 Rogers, *Many Ways to Say I Love You.*

The future doesn't belong to the fainthearted; it belongs to the brave. The Challenger crew was pulling us into the future, and we'll continue to follow them. I've always had great faith in and respect for our space program, and what happened today does nothing to diminish it. We don't hide our space program. We don't keep secrets and cover things up. We do it all up front and in public. That's the way freedom is, and we wouldn't change it for a minute. . . . The crew of the space shuttle Challenger honored us by the manner in which they lived their lives. We will never forget them, nor the last time we saw them, this morning, as they prepared for their journey and waved goodbye and "slipped the surly bonds of earth" to "touch the face of God."[240]

Embrace Radical Acceptance

"I don't think anyone can grow unless he's loved exactly as he is now, appreciated for who he is rather than what he will be."[241] Children can't grow if they don't feel loved. Through radical acceptance, the love of Fred Rogers changed the world. To be accepted, no one had to clean themselves up or do anything more than be.

In his book *I'm Proud of You: My Friendship with Fred Rogers*, Tim Madigan tells the story of his life-changing friendship with Rogers near the end of his life. Fred was delighted when Madigan, a journalist, accepted his invitation to attend church with him. He shares this memory of that morning:

> I remember consciously trying to freeze each surreal moment as I stood next to Fred and sang hymns and watched him wrestle with his fidgety grandchildren in the pew. I can attest that even Mister Rogers became exasperated with little kids in church.
>
> It was midway through the service when the pastor asked if anyone wished to publicly share their joys or concerns. . . . The

---

240 Ronald Reagan, "President Ronald Reagan's Speech on Space Shuttle Challenger," September 25, 2015, YouTube video, https://youtu.be/DqilE4AAa-M.

241 Fred M. Rogers, *Life's Journeys According to Mister Rogers: Things to Remember Along the Way* (London, England: Hachette Books, 2019).

old woman behind us at the back of the church spoke last. She began with a vague complaint about the Gulf War, then took up against Vietnam, and the president, and members of Congress and generals, and anyone else who, in her mind, might have had something to do with the death of American soldiers. The diatribe went on for at least five minutes. People throughout the church began to squirm in the pews. At the pulpit, the pastor shifted from foot to foot and stared at his notes in embarrassment. I stifled an impulse to turn and look back at the woman, who, as the minutes passed, began to seem deranged. When her long rant was finally ended, there was an audible sigh of relief in the church. Most of the congregation were clearly mortified, but not the man sitting beside me. The moment the old woman finished and the service resumed, Fred leaned over and whispered in my ear.

"The poor dear," he said. "You can be sure that at some point in her past, she suffered a great personal loss because of war."

After the service, Fred hurried from his pew, found the old woman, where she stood alone in the back of the church, said a few tender words, and gave her a hug.[242]

In this same way, it is up to us to respect the child every day as they enter our classrooms. Let us "treat him as a person. The best thing a person can feel is to be accepted as he is, not as he will be when he grows up, but as he is now, right this very minute."[243]

Our words and reactions can bring life or emotional death. In our phone conversation, Madigan relayed his first conversation with Fred Rogers, realizing that he was in the presence of someone who tried being fully present to people's needs and feelings.

---

242 Tim Madigan, *I'm Proud of You: My Friendship with Fred Rogers* (Los Angeles: Ubuntu Press, 2012).
243 Rogers, *Many Ways to Say I Love You.*

"Do you know the most important thing in the world to me right now?" Fred asked me that day.

"No," I said.

"Talking to Tim Madigan on the telephone."

I'm sure I blushed, incredulous and skeptical. But somehow, in the way he said it, in that famous, gentle, oh-so-slow voice, I knew that the famous man was speaking the truth.[244]

Show and Tell Your Students They Are Special

The world needs a sense of worth, and it will achieve it
only by its people feeling that they are worthwhile.
—Fred Rogers

We all have infinite value. We are beautiful and unique, giving the world different expressions of who we are. While teaching virtually during the pandemic, I chose to sing the song "You Are Special" to my kindergarteners a cappella at the closing of our time together. I took the time to look into their eyes through the screen and connect with their personhood. As I sang, I saw Bailey, Selena, and Lucas—children with names, not just kindergarteners.

> You are my friend
> You are special
> You are my friend
> You're special to me.
> You are the only one like you.
> Like you, my friend, I like you.
>
> In the daytime
> In the nighttime
> Any time that you feel's the right time

---

244 Madigan, *I'm Proud of You.*

For a friendship with me, you see
F-R-I-E-N-D special
You are my friend
You're special to me.
There's only one in this wonderful world
You are special.[245]

It's easy to look out at the classroom of children and see "my class." But what if you slowed down your gaze and really looked carefully at each face? What is their story? Attachment style? Fears and worries about the world? Do they have a secure base at home where they can share about their day and their conflicts on the playground? When they look at you, what do they feel? Do they know you love them?

Each year, I fall wholeheartedly in love with my students. They are mine, and I'm theirs. I grow to love their little quirks, their mannerisms, the smell of their hair when they hug me, the nicknames that come from something endearing (this year I call one of mine "bean" because she's a little bean sprout). I pull their loose teeth, wipe their noses, tie their shoes, and hold them when they fall down outside. I listen to their hopes, dreams, and fears while giving them encouragement and smiling at their enthusiasm. Many mornings I put hair into pigtails, listen to a child read a book independently, double-check for Mom that they're in one piece emotionally after a hard morning, and ask questions about scratches, bumps, or a black eye.

The thing about loving children is they get inside you, they change you and strengthen your resolve to be better at reaching them—that is, if you let yourself be affected by them, if you enter in and embrace what they have to teach you. If you could ask my students, "Does your teacher love you?" I guarantee they would say, "Yes." How do they know?

I tell them. I show them. I live it out in front of them, real and raw. As Rogers said:

---

245 Fred M. Rogers, "You Are Special," The Mister Rogers Neighborhood Archive, 1968, http://www.neighborhoodarchive.com/music/songs/you_are_special.html.

Learning and loving go hand in hand. My grandfather was one of those people who loved to live and loved to teach. Every time I was with him, he'd show me something about the world or something about myself that I hadn't even thought of yet. He'd help me find something wonderful in the smallest of things, and ever so carefully, he helped me understand the enormous worth of *every* human being. My grandfather was not a professional teacher, but the way he treated me, the way he *loved* me and the things he did with me, served me as well as any teacher I've ever known.[246]

****

How I wish that all children in this world could have at least one person who could embrace them and encourage them.
I wish that all children could have somebody who would let them know that the outsides of people are insignificant compared with the insides: to show them that no matter what, they'll always have somebody who believes in them.
—Fred Rogers

Those who knew and worked with Fred Rogers consistently spoke about his ability to take the spotlight off himself and shine it on others. As I mentioned back in chapter 7, this made him super annoying to interview, and I heard many firsthand accounts of this very thing happening. What's remarkable was his "other-centered" approach toward people. It wasn't unhealthy, or to hide who he was, but a deep and genuine curiosity about people and who they were on the inside.

He called out the good in others, the piece of divinity in us all. He saw everyone he met as his "neighbor." Rogers often commented that the exchange between two people was hallowed ground, or a bit of what Heaven must be like. There are

---

246 Rogers, *Life's Journeys According to Mister Rogers.*

times when I couldn't agree more. Those encounters happen when I take my mind off myself and focus on what a child is teaching *me*.

But life gets busy and frantic sometimes, and it's easy to lose sight of the glory when we're knee-deep in the gross. For those of you who teach kindergarten, you totally understand. If you teach older kids, I'll spare you the details. I've been halfway through my day and realized, *I haven't looked at them once*. Not to worry—yes, I've looked at them, but I mean *really* looked at them and remembered to slow down, take time, and be present.

> The world needs a sense of worth, and it will achieve it
> only by its people feeling that they are worthwhile.
> **—Fred Rogers**

Affirmations to Use in the Classroom

- I appreciate you.
- I can count on you.
- I delight in you.
- I enjoy you.
- I like the person you're becoming.
- I know that things take time, and you'll get there.
- I know that you tried your best.
- I know there's no one else like you in the whole world.
- I like how you see the world.
- I like how you solve problems.
- I like to be told things too.
- I love how you listen to others.
- I love you.
- I love your curiosity.
- I need your help.
- I like your stories.
- I'm glad you're the way you are.
- I'm learning from you.

- I'm proud of you.
- If it matters to you, it matters to me.
- It's you I like.
- I like you exactly as you are.
- People can like you exactly as you are.
- Thank you for _____.
- You are a great friend.
- You are a helper.
- You're a _____ (reader, illustrator, inventor, engineer, scientist, etc.).
- You're a great listener.
- You're a problem solver.
- You are brave.
- You are forgiving.
- You are generous.
- You are growing inside.
- You are kind.
- You are more than your outsides.
- You are my friend.
- You are responsible.
- You are safe with me.
- You are special.
- You are the only one like you.
- You are unique.
- You can make mistakes.
- You have a great imagination.
- You make me happy.
- You take your time.
- You tried hard.
- You'll solve problems someday.
- You're exactly where you need to be right now.
- You're full of wonder.
- You're such a hard worker.

- You've got to do it, and I know you can.
- Your big feelings matter to me.
- Your heart is full of love.
- You can never lose my love.

Lynn Johnson, 1992.

Lynn Johnson, 1992.

Fred Rogers with Lady Elaine Fairchilde puppet on *Mister Rogers' Neighborhood*
at WQED studio. 1992. Lynn Johnson Collection.

Chapter 11:

The Good Hard Work of Play

"You can try out many things by pretending"

Play is often talked about as if it were a relief from serious learning. But for children, play is a way to cope with life and to prepare for adulthood. Playing is a way to solve problems and to express feelings. In fact, play is the real work of childhood.
—Fred Rogers

Why Is Play Essential?

- Play helps us cope with old and new experiences.
- Play fosters independence and autonomy.
- Play brings relaxation and peace to our nervous system.
- Play develops friendship skills.
- Play distinguishes the differences between real and make-believe.
- Play develops responsibility as we maintain toys and clean up our messes.
- Play encourages self-expression (self-esteem), creativity, and problem-solving.
- Play cultivates appreciation and understanding.
- Play invites whimsy and nonsense.
- Play teaches competition and fairness.
- Play uses the imagination.

- Play can be simple.
- Play bonds children to a caring adult who takes the time to stop and engage.
- Play establishes authority/boundaries (what are the rules? who makes them?).
- Play teaches cause and effect.
- Play allows the expression of feelings and fears.
- Play is the beginning of the creative/artistic expression for later in life.

Fred Rogers had a fantastic sense of humor and whimsy that came through in various forms on the *Neighborhood*: in his play with words (Robert Troll, King Friday XIII speeches, and his use of the French he acquired while studying abroad in college), but also in his storytelling operas in Bubbleland and on top of Spoon Mountain, or looking for a grandfather for Daniel Striped Tiger. Always incorporating all the learning for the week, each episode is packed with imagination and engagement. We can still learn how to play well from *Mister Rogers' Neighborhood*.

Play and Curiosity Naturally Build Attachment

Rogers understood that play is natural and key to building attachment. He brought everyday objects with him on each television visit to prompt children's imaginations and playfully foster their curiosity. He'd ask questions like "What do you suppose this is? When do we use one of these? Have you ever seen/heard/ smelled one of these?" Sometimes he'd let us know about upcoming visitors, like children's performer and musician Ella Jenkins, a star basketball player, a blind saxophonist, and a dance troupe, or about an upcoming visit to a factory. Whatever it was, he piqued a child's interest, their curiosity, right away.

Although it seemed like it wouldn't hold my students' interests, one of my greatest discoveries is their love of peekaboo with Mister Rogers. When he drops the towel and says, "Peekaboo," they giggle and love it. Then I realized it was strengthening their attachment systems, like mirroring does with infants. When a mother attunes to her infant, mimicking their facial expressions, it builds attachment in the brain. As Mister Rogers makes a funny face, my kindergarteners begin to mimic him, and like magic, they are attuning to him. They are captivated by his facial expressions, his attention to the camera, and how he includes them in his discoveries, such as bird whistles, farting balloons, and cars rolling down tubes. No wonder they love copying him so much.

Use Puppets

All the kids in our school love popcorn day, when their fifty cents can get them a bag of the coveted snack. But due to allergies in kindergarten, it's only distributed to grades one through five, and Blue Eyes is irate. He comes in from recess, quarters in hand, mad at the world. He crashes into his chair, throwing his arm across the table, knocking everything over to make a scene.

"What's up?" I ask, although I had an idea after reading my morning emails.

"It's stupid!" he yells.

As I get the students started on their next activity, I call him up to my desk.

"Wanna talk about it?" I ask him, but he turns his back on me and stares at the wall. *Fabulous. This is emotional regulation at its finest*, I think. Then I get an idea. Reaching into my cupboard, I retrieve my X the Owl puppet I grabbed on eBay for a steal. In my best southern drawl X voice, I tap him on the shoulder.

He turns around and looks at X on my hand.

"What seems to be the problem there, Blue Eyes?" I drawl.

"Well, X, they won't let me buy any popcorn outside, and that makes me really mad."

I can't believe it. He's totally telling the puppet how he feels. "It's always good to talk about your big feelings with a friend or grown-up," I say as X.

Blue Eyes rolls his eyes. "That's why I'm talking to *you*!"

I start to laugh, and he actually smiles.

"Can I give you a hug? Maybe that will make you feel better."

Taking my hand with the puppet into his chest, he hugs it hard, closing his eyes. And to my amazement, I see his whole body calm down. He doesn't say another word but walks back to his desk and takes out his math book.

Encourage Escape

In play, a child isn't responsible for the cares of this world but is free to imagine, dream, and make sense of what's inside their heart. What do they want to understand? Encourage escape. Let them play. Where do they need to make sense of the people in their life, the situations, or the new baby? Let them play. There are no limits in play, no rules, except to keep each other safe and clean up our messes (Mister Rogers takes time to clean up the toys too).

Foster Make-Believe

"Let's have some make-believe," Fred says as he turns the switch. As Trolley makes its way through the tunnel, we enter a world where puppets talk, kings and queens rule the land, purple pandas stop by for a visit, reindeers create inclusive teams, flying aliens hang out, large seeds grow and change, and tame tigers learn that family is all the neighbors who love you. Mistakes are part of learning, and no one is forgotten. Feelings are mentionable, and we can talk about them as long as necessary.

Why are there no hands on Daniel's clock? Because there's no time in make-believe. Anything is possible here. Towels fly, dolls come to life, a cow can be the teacher, and a platypus plays the bagpipes.

There's freedom for every child who enters into make-believe, but often, when they're wounded, they need the invitation over and over again. Mister Rogers invites them every time. We can encourage a child, "If it's hard, just watch us play. But come along, join in when you're ready. It won't take much time before you'll want to play too."

And it's up to us to give children permission to explore their imaginations.

"What do I draw?" Anything you'd like.

"What should I write about?" All the things you can dream up.

We've grown accustomed to shoving facts into children, hoping that quality people will come out, but we're missing the essential. That which is essential is invisible to the eye—childhood is about play. We've been too busy making it about us, our agendas and ideas of what will help them be successful. A child will learn more in a thirty-minute block of play than hours of direct instruction. Fred Rogers was right all along. Time is never wasted in play.

Play Is Necessary

Children who have suffered prolonged, continuous developmental traumas find play difficult. Fred Rogers believed wholeheartedly that play is the work of childhood. It's not a relief but a necessity—ever more essential when a child lacks the connection to a constant secure base of loving comfort and care. Through play, we can facilitate immeasurable growth in our students and return to a renewed understanding of our own childhoods.

How do *you* feel about play? Do you believe it's essential in the life of a child? In what ways can we come alongside our students to deepen their understanding of their natural world?

In her book *Attachment Play*, Swiss/American developmental psychologist Aletha Solter poses the following questions regarding your own childhood play:

1. What was your favorite toy as a child? What did you enjoy doing with it? With whom?

2. Is there a specific toy that you wanted but never received? What was it? Where did you see it?

3. What was your favorite game as a child? Who did you play it with? How did it make you feel?

4. Recall a time when your mother or father played with you. What game? How did you feel about it? Was it pleasant or disagreeable? Do you wish that they had played more with you?

5. What memories do you have associated with competition? How did you feel when you won a game? When you lost a game?

6. Did anybody ever criticize you for the way you played or for the toys you chose to play with?[247]

In his book *Mister Rogers' Playbook: Insights and Activities for Parents and Children*, Rogers said,

> It seems probable that every one of us has buried some painful events—and the feelings that went with them—so deeply that they're hard for us to find again. At the other extreme, some of us may still be so shaken by the aftershocks of a past event—

247 Aletha J. Solter, *Attachment Play: How to Solve Children's Behavior Problems with Play, Laughter, and Connection* (Goleta, CA: Shining Star Press, 2016).

even one long past—that we can't get any distance from it at all and can't seem to move beyond it. I think what we'd all like is for these crises, after a time, to blend into the landscape of our lives so that they no longer jump out at us when we look back at where we've been.[248]

Play Makes Sense of a Child's World

By understanding the difference between reality and make-believe, children make sense of their world. They learn that wishing doesn't make something happen, drains are too small to swallow people, and our worst fears are usually not as bad when we talk about them. Make-believe gives children the freedom to work out their big feelings without the fears that they are responsible for having a thought, wish, or impulse. Their anger didn't cause a divorce, for instance, and wanting the new baby not to come is part of learning and growing. Being able to make sense of their world brings order and peace.

A child with a broken connection can learn to play again. It's as natural as breathing, but they must first remember the freedom of taking air into their lungs. I've often said, "I've got you. You just work on being five and I'll take care of the grown-up stuff." When I see them trying to step into my shoes, I say, "Can I have the teacher back, please?" They will pretend to hand it back to me.

It's important that we give every child permission to stop carrying the burdens of others, to be little again, and to play.

---

248 Fred Rogers and Barry Head, *Mister Rogers' Playbook: Insights and Activities for Parents and Children* (Pittsburgh, PA: Family Communications, Inc., 1986).

Fred Rogers made time for rest, rejuvenation, and reflection
during the summers in his beloved Nantucket.
1992. Lynn Johnson Collection.

Chapter 12:

Peace and Quiet

"We all want peace"

Peace and quiet, peace, peace, peace . . . we all want peace.
—Fred Rogers

F red Rogers was a man of discipline and reflection. To understand our profession as educators, we need time to reflect, receive revelation, and renew
our vision. Teaching is a monumental task where we are asked to empty
ourselves into little neighbors. We are their hope and guide, regardless of all that
has come before. Although we can't change their past, we influence their outcome,
but we can't do it without true peace and rest.

Fred wrote:

> In the long, long trip of growing . . . there are stops along the
> way. It's an important moment when we need to stop, reflect,
> and receive. In our competitive world, that might be called a
> waste of time. I've learned that those times can be a preamble
> to periods of enormous growth. Recently, I declared a day to be
> alone with myself. I took a long drive and played a tape. When
> I got to the mountains, I read and played and listened and slept.
> In fact, I can't remember having a calmer sleep in a long, long

time. The next day I went to work and did more than I usually get done in three days.[249]

How Do We Enter Silence and Rest?

Taking time off to rest is selfish. Behold the greatest myth teachers believe and therefore end up at burnout. Fred Rogers said, "You rarely have time for everything you want in this life, so you need to make choices. And hopefully those choices can come from a deep sense of who you are."[250]

Discovering our personal boundaries is worthy work. There's that dreaded word, *boundaries*. Some of you may have just rolled your eyes, but I am a living testimony of learning to make my mental, emotional, and physical health a priority. It's annoyed some teammates, administrators, and classroom parents, but I can't reach my own personal standard saying yes to everyone but myself. We've bought into the lie that as teachers we're supposed to be all things for all people, then go home and do the same for our families. Don't forget to post it all on social media too. The pressure is intense if we don't guard ourselves and our boundaries.

What's a boundary? It's where you stop and someone else starts. I liken it to the fences we erect between properties. I mow my grass, pull my weeds, and water my lawn on the schedule I choose; you do the same. But perhaps you decide you don't like my water schedule and think I need a flower bed in the center of my lawn, so you hoist yourself over the fence and begin doing what you deem is important. You just crossed my boundary. Insecure attachments damage boundaries. We feel guilty for erecting them or don't understand why others have limitations as we barrel through life. Most conflicts come from unmet expectations and boundary crossing.

Setting Boundaries at Work

Schedule Time Off

Sick time is for mental and emotional health, and for physical ailments. Each summer I take an honest look at the calendar and ask myself some questions:

---

249 Rogers, *You Are Special.*
250 Rogers, *You Are Special.*

Where did I struggle the most last year? What times of year could I have chosen more rest but didn't? I choose at least four days to sprinkle throughout the school year that I consider "mental health days."

When the day comes up, have sub plans prepared, and spend the day doing what replenishes your soul. Go tech free, get out in nature, sleep in, go for a walk, journal, pray, do yoga, get a massage, do a guided meditation, read a book for pleasure, take a hike or run, take yourself on an ice cream date, get a pedicure, listen to music or a podcast of your choice, work in your garden, or take your pups to the dog park. **Don't work on anything related to school.** Each time you find yourself wondering about your students or thinking about texting a colleague, don't go there. Fill your rest days with little, quiet moments that will give life extra meaning.

Let "No" Be a Gift

When we say yes to something, we're saying no to something else. It's the nature of all decisions. If we want to attune and teach with intention, we must love ourselves enough to recognize we are not the solution to every problem. I often tell myself, *Wystie, just because there's a need doesn't mean you have to fill it.* This even goes for the things like Kinder Camp that others would assume I would be a part of. But saying yes to that would mean this book wouldn't be in your hands today. I had a deadline, so I erected a boundary. The previous summer I was taking my children to college and understood I would need the emotional space to grieve. This hasn't been a quick journey but has ushered in more peace than you could ever imagine each time a new opportunity presents itself. (Many thanks to the ladies who continue to do Kinder Camp.)

As teachers, we love to be helpful and needed, at our own expense. Brené Brown states, "Boundaries are the distance at which I can love you [my students/colleagues/district, job] and me simultaneously."[251] When I deny what I need for the sake of everyone else, I am not living in my truth. It also guards your peace. A major indicator of not being true to yourself and a personal boundary is guilt, condemnation, bitterness, resentment, boredom, and compassion fatigue. If they

---

251 Brown, *Atlas of the Heart.*

show up, ask yourself, *What do I really need to say or do to usher in more peace?* Not to make them happy, but to have deep peace and contentment.

Communicate Your Boundaries to Yourself and Others

Brown calls this the "what's okay and what's not okay."

It's okay to want me to be part of that committee, but it's not okay to guilt me into it.

It's okay for you to take extra work home, but it's not okay to apply that same expectation to me or other teammates.

Think of a recent conflict or boundary snatching at work. Use this sentence frame: "It's okay to _____. It's not okay to _____."

I'd suggest writing them out in a journal and keeping them in your phone or on a Post-it note on your desk. I surrounded myself with good ideas until they made their way from my head down to my heart. Please know that saying no is going to feel like a small death to those of us desperate to please and keep the love and admiration of others. Some people will get mad when you stop hustling and allow yourself to "just be." It has more to do with them than you. Be patient with yourself as you learn the art of saying no. It's a journey. Slowing down to enjoy our life and gain more peace and self-awareness is the only way we can participate in the divine. People's expectations aren't more important than your inner peace.

Get Proper Sleep, Hydration, and Nutrition

What's Your Bedtime?

Do you know that it's not the quantity of sleep that is important but the quality? Recently, I began using an app that taught me more about the importance of quality sleep. I choose how many hours of sleep I want, and it sets a timer on my phone when I need to start getting ready, turns off various apps, and gives options for guided meditations, soothing sounds, and stories to lure me into sleep. There are tons of apps for such things, but it's all about follow-through. Going to sleep around the same time every night helps me feel refreshed and rested in the morning. But as Mister Rogers often sang, "You've got to do it." It's the little choices we make that matter.

Don't just take my word for it. Scientists have proven that sleep is essential to a healthy and productive lifestyle. Lack of sufficient sleep may increase your risk of developing concerns such as

- cognitive, memory, and performance deficits
- increased stress and irritability
- depression and anxiety
- hypertension, high cholesterol, heart disease, and stroke
- weight gain and obesity
- immune system issues
- diabetes and insulin resistance[252]

Nutrition/Hydration

If you have unhealed developmental trauma, it will show up in the various ways you care for yourself: physically, emotionally, and mentally. Much like the children in our care who are healing from traumas and broken trust, we also need to take the time to care for our basic needs of healthy nutrition and hydration. Have you ever worked through your lunch? Be honest. Instead of sitting down to eat a meal, are you guilty of pulling a Snickers Mini out of the cabinet, opening a Diet Coke, and coasting on fumes? I've seen you, girl, walking in every morning with your Starbucks and nothing else. That's not healthy. Be sure to eat a balanced meal packed full of what you need to be as effective in the afternoon as the morning.

Each day I set an intention for how much water I will drink. Make a point of only drinking water at work. I find that I drink it more frequently through a straw, but you may like something different. Keep the water bottle at work, and fill it first thing in the morning. If you have a mini-fridge in your classroom, stock it full of healthy choices and make a point of stopping for lunch. When I was writing this book, at lunchtime I would deliberately focus on reading what I'd written or looking through Fred's work to disengage my brain from the masses.

---

252 Michael Breus, "Sleep Quality vs. Sleep Quantity," The Sleep Doctor, June 30, 2022, https://thesleepdoctor.com/how-sleep-works/sleep-quality/.

Lunchtime Nonnegotiables

- I set up *Mister Rogers' Neighborhood*: Place my chair in the center of the room and cue the episode.
- I don't answer my phone during my lunchtime. If it's an emergency, they will come tell me or send someone.
- I turn off the overhead lights to illuminate the room with only lamps, listen to quiet music (Yo-Yo Ma is my favorite), and focus on slowing down my breathing. I mindfully check in with myself.
- During lunch, I take care to chew slowly and drink only water.
- I check my email at certain times during the day and turn off the notifications that will interfere with instruction/focus. I took my work email off my cell phone, as it stole my joy, peace, and focus at home.
- I send my boys texts to tell them I love them, as one is in Nashville, Tennessee.
- If a colleague chooses to join me, I deliberately steer the conversation away from work.
- If I feel dysregulated, I will often lie down with my back on the floor and stretch. I allow my breathing to regulate to a place where I can remember my best intentions of connecting with children. In the presence of big feelings, I've used this time to cry it out or call my husband, who is my safe place. If you're worried about people interrupting you, I have gone behind my desk or sat in my car. Do what you can to find your silence and peace.
- I make it a point to sit or stand for a few minutes in silence before bringing my students in from recess.

Silence, peace, and stillness are friends you invite in.

Sometime in your day today, try to turn off all the noises you can around you, and give yourself some "quiet time." In the silence, let yourself think about something. Or if possible . . . think about nothing.

—Fred Rogers

Mister Rogers' Gift of Silence/Slowing Down

We are teaching our children in our homes and classrooms that silence is not the norm. Each time we've entered *Mister Rogers' Neighborhood*, I've become increasingly aware of the power of silence as he watches his fish swim, observes a bubble float or water move, or cuts out a piece of paper. According to former *Neighborhood* director, Paul Lally, he and Rogers had a bet on how long the show's jazz pianist, Johnny Costa, could remain silent after famous cellist Yo-Yo Ma finished his concerto. They were both surprised. **Fred Rogers loved silence.** In fact, he would deliberately pause throughout his program to allow his young viewers time to think and ponder new ideas.

While speaking with Charlie Rose in an interview conducted for his book *You Are Special* in 1994, Rogers shared, "I'm very concerned that our society is much more interested in information than wonder, in noise rather than silence. . . . **Real revelation comes through silence.**"[253]

I am not talking about the all-famous teacher wait time but intentionally allowing our students the time they need to wonder, synthesize, predict, reset, and rest. Rogers embraced this concept wholeheartedly through creating his own peaceful rhythm of intentionality fostering amazement and curious joy. In 1983, Rogers wrote, "One thing is certain: Children need lots of free, quiet time to get used to all that's developing within them. Have you noticed that an unhurried time by yourself or with someone you really trust can be the best setting for your own personal growth? It's no different for children."[254]

What replenishes your soul? Where do you find power to do the impossible? Is it your faith in God? What are you doing when you feel most alive? Schedule time to do that. Really do it. Don't spend time envying others who choose to rest. It builds resentment. Love yourself. Enjoy your own company. That is where you learn to listen well, love deeper, and come back another day to do the work of teaching. We all crave and want peace, regardless of whether we have the courage to admit it. Rogers penned this desire in his song "Peace and Quiet" written in 1968:

---

253 Charlie Rose, "Remembering Mr. Rogers (1994/1997)," February 27, 2016, YouTube video, https://www.youtube.com/watch?v=djoyd46TVVc.

254 Fred Rogers and Barry Head, *Mister Rogers Talks with Parents* (New York: Berkley Books, 1983).

Peace and quiet.
Peace, peace, peace.
Peace and quiet.
Peace, peace, peace.

Peace and quiet.
Peace, peace, peace.
We all want peace;
We all want peace.[255]

****

"What do I do now?" Austin calls out to me, always the first to finish his math page. Computation comes easily for him, unlike Kaitlyn sitting beside him. I notice her instant anxiety. She is only halfway done and will begin to rush if I do nothing. I am instantly transported to the sounds of my peers finishing tests, as I was just getting started in third grade. There was always that one child who would loudly slam their pencil down upon completion, and my blood pressure and heart rate would hit the roof.

I smile and quietly whisper to Austin, "Try sitting and doing nothing so your brain can rest and grow." He nods with acceptance and places his head down on the table willingly. I have created a culture that values the in-between moments. We have spoken about the necessity of choosing silence as a gift.

Please understand, I am all for the buzz of children cooperatively learning. After all, I teach kindergarten in a STEM (science, technology, engineering, and mathematics) elementary. But if we do not give our brains the chance to breathe and rest, it can work against us. Does Austin need to be in constant motion? Must he be engaged and entertained every moment he is in my care? No. Austin will learn to self-regulate quicker if he is not always in motion. I try to let my students know that there is a time and place for everything, even silence. He may place his head down to rest, look out the window, stretch, and take deep breaths. The

---

255 Fred M. Rogers, "Peace and Quiet," The Mister Rogers Neighborhood Archive, 1968, http://www.neighborhoodarchive.com/music/songs/peace_quiet.html.

less he does, the better. Brain breaks should be a break from intense learning. I have books available, which some students peruse, while others draw a picture on the back of their work. They are learning to be comfortable in their own skin, empathetic to each other's needs for a quiet work environment and to the need to replenish. Just like our physical bodies need food, air, and water, our brains need silence. Silence grows and restores our brains!

****

In 2012, my family took a road trip to Yellowstone National Park, stopping at whatever we found interesting or beautiful. After a brief pause on a dirt road to watch a mama bear and cub bounding into the woods, we parked and walked down to a meadow. It was a moment I will never forget, and words will never do it justice. The sky was free of clouds, and the breeze was just enough to tickle the hairs on my arms and brush wisps of hair off my face.

I walked over to the creek that rushed between myself and a herd of bison and their calves. Peeling off my shoes and socks, I sat upon the bank and dipped my feet into the cool water. To say that the moment felt perfect and holy would be an understatement. I was content beyond words. Over the next thirty minutes, I did not utter a word, as I wanted to soak in every sensation, memorizing that place so I could return whenever I needed to in the future.

When we find moments of shalom, I consider them to be a view of what Heaven will feel like. The renewal it gave my weary spirit was indescribable. Speaking in that moment would have lessened the impact. We each need quiet places in our souls we can retreat to. Places that are not full of expectations and responsibilities but just silence that replenishes and restores. Children must be given moments where they are able to simply rest. We model the power of intentional pause to them and ourselves. Try watching water, fire, or the face of a newborn child. Wind dancing through the trees or the majesty in a bird hatching out of an egg.

Fred Rogers gave us the tools to be lifelong learners—a sense of wonder, a curiosity about the world around us, the willingness to ask questions. His genuine interest in the world was infectious. Whatever he showed us, he encouraged us to look and listen carefully, to keep trying, and to see the world as a wondrous place. Fred Rogers believed that although children's "outsides" may have changed a lot, their inner needs have remained very much the same. They still need to fall in love with the beauty of being alive and savor being part of the interconnectedness of all people.

Conclusion

I hope you're proud of yourself for the times you've said
"yes" when all it meant was extra work for you and
was seemingly helpful only to somebody else.

—Fred Rogers

D o you remember the story of Katie from the introduction of this book? I'd love to share the end of her story with you now.

After a short drive I finally pulled into Katie's driveway. I made my way inside and was met by her frazzled, distracted grandparents. They were given the task of looking out for the three other children, as Bailey had been life-flighted to Seattle. Their grandma wanted me to know all she had done to help but was overwhelmed. I took her hand and said, "I'm here to help. Where's Katie?" She and her younger brother were outside playing in their swimming pool. As I opened the sliding door, I called out to her, "Somebody told me you might need a hug?" Her face lit up and she came running, soaking wet, and jumped into my arms.

"I have so many big feelings we need to talk about!" I held her tight, her swimming suit soaking my T-shirt and shorts. Her younger brother crawled up beside us, as I wrapped a towel around him. "Bailey was blue and spitting out of her mouth, then she went away."

"Do you know why she turned blue?"

She shook her head no.

"It's called a seizure. When our brain isn't getting oxygen, our body sends out messages to let people know we need help. The spit was because she was having trouble breathing."

"She used to not be blue," she said.

"Katie, she's not blue anymore," I reassured her. "People are taking care of her right now, but they have tubes inside her nose and mouth to help her breathe. She needs time to rest."

"To rest?" She looked puzzled, and then it hit me. She thought Bailey was dead. No one had told her that she wasn't. In all the fuss and chaos, Katie didn't get the message.

I took her face in my hands. "Bailey is alive. She's not dead, Katie. That's why Mommy went in the helicopter with her. They could only take one other person so they could get there quick."

"That's why she left me here?"

My heart ached for her. She felt left behind. "Yes. Mommy knows that you and your brother and sister are safe here at home."

"Oh, okay. And Bailey is alive."

"Yes. And I came to answer any questions you have. Because when I heard the news, I came to find *you*. I thought of you and wanted to know that you were okay."

"Because you're my teacher," she said, nuzzling her face into my neck and hugging tight.

I began to rock her and affirmed the truth. "Because I'm your teacher."

I would like to tell you what I often told you when you were much younger. I like you just the way you are. And what's more, I'm so grateful to you for helping the children in your life to know that you'll do everything you can to keep them safe. And to help them express their feelings in ways that will bring healing in many different neighborhoods.

—Fred Rogers

****

Amy enters our class bow-legged, wearing clothes too big for her gaunt body. A foster-care placement, she now lives with her uncle and aunt after surviving horrific conditions. The final straw was when her mother overdosed on meth in front of her, and the state intervened. The home she had occupied with her mother was condemned due to hoarding, infestation, and neglect, and social services reported dead animal carcasses and rodent activity. Food was rare and Amy noted that it wasn't "healthy or good" when it was offered. After consuming a meal, she was forced to do jumping jacks so she wouldn't "get fat." Although her foster placement is with family members, life is still chaotic. There are younger children, too many pets, a screaming, unstable aunt, and mounting debts. Amy begins to act out, causing the family to tell her they will be surrendering her back to the state.

This Monday morning, Amy arrives at my desk with the news that "a stranger is going to pick me up after school and take me away." Her tiny body trembles with fear, and I wrap my arms around her.

"I won't let that happen," I promise her, and I then quickly confirm the truth. Yes, they've had enough and are waiting on a new placement. Hurriedly, I call her caseworker and say I, along with her best friend Chelsea's family, will be willing to act as an emergency placement for her in the interim. Supposedly her parents are "clean" and trying to work on getting visitation and custody. The last thing she needs is to be terrified and going home with people she doesn't know. To my surprise, they state that we can have her the next day and that they'll start the paperwork.

Amy isn't in class the following morning, but I try not to panic. Ten minutes after we begin instruction, the secretary calls me. "There's a little girl in the office needing your help." It's Amy.

As I open the door, there she is, tearstained, sitting next to her aunt, who is in a dysregulated state. "She's violent. I can't handle it anymore!" It's clear Amy has been living in an environment that isn't healthy, and it's time to move on.

"Just take care of you. I've got her now." After she leaves, I move Amy to the bench beside the office to tell her the news. She's going home with either Chelsea or me.

"Really?" She looks amazed. My heart floods with relief for her. "How long will I live there? Forever?"

"No, not forever. But until Mommy and Daddy are well, and your heart is better. I want you to be ready and feel safe. I want you to not have so much anger and sadness in your heart."

"Not forever," she repeats. Just then, Blue Eyes walks up from his third-grade classroom to check in for his morning behavior.

"Hey! I need you. Come here for a minute," I call over to him.

He sits on the other side of Amy.

"Amy, this is Blue Eyes. He was in my class when he was in kindergarten, and he's my success story." He looks up at me surprised, but then back at Amy.

"Do you remember when you had all that anger and sadness in your heart?" I ask him. He nods. "Amy can't see her mommy and daddy right now because they need to get better."

"My daddy had to get better. He was sick for a long time."

"And he was angry and sad," I explain.

"You know what you need? A friend," Blue Eyes says.

"Chelsea is my friend," she says.

"Cool." He looks up at me. "Can I go now?"

"No, not yet. I need you," I tell him. We sit for a minute, and I hold Amy's hand in silence.

"How about this, Amy." He places his hand on her shoulder. "I'll come by at my lunch and check on you to see how you're doing?" I smile at him.

"Okay," she says. He stands up and walks off.

Two hours later, while we're doing our playdough/brain break, the door opens and Blue Eyes enters, but he's not alone. Behind him walks a group of third graders. He's rounded up as many of the kids who were in his kindergarten class as he could find and brought them with him. There they are, those once-tiny faces for whom I turned on the *Neighborhood*, in hopes of reaching a little boy in need of connection and love.

"I'm here to check on Amy, Mrs. Edwards, and I brought the gang with me."

As I hug each one of them, telling them thank you, he makes his way over to Amy.

"You doing okay?" he asks her.

"Yep," she says sweetly, continuing to roll out her playdough.

"Good. I'll keep checking in on you," he says and waves at me as they leave.

My memory floats back to the day a visitor came from the Fred Rogers Center. As we passed around a Daniel Tiger puppet, they each spoke about what they loved most about Mister Rogers.

As the puppet reached Blue Eyes, he took it in his hands, looked me straight in the eyes, and said, "When we watch Mister Rogers, my teacher loves me."

Author's Note

I've come to learn that creating is a vulnerable, gut-wrenching process. We often find the truth that sets us free at the end of pretense, where we lack complete control and are forced to trust. In the wilderness, we learn who we are, what matters, and where we won't bend, regardless of popularity or understanding. Writing this book has been a walk into the wilderness.

My greatest hope and prayer for you, the reader, is that you have been challenged and have laid down some of your armor reading these words. Fred Rogers believed in radical authenticity and embraced his humanness while entertaining the divine, trusting goodness would come if we leaned in and loved.

Humbly, I acknowledge those who've loved this book into being:

To my Matthew, "the only one who makes me lonely simply leaving the room," you are my greatest choice, my best friend, and your love is my landing place.

To my sons, Jonathan and Benjamin, you are my heart walking around outside of my body. May you know that your love and forgiveness gave me the strength to fight for freedom.

To Morgan James Publishing, thank you for welcoming me into your family.

To acquisitions editor W. Terry Whalin, your unrelenting pursuit of this work made it a reality.

Thanks to my developmental editor, Kathleen Becker Blease, for your insight, kindness, and humility. You organized my chaos and affirmed me, repeatedly writing notes taped beside my laptop: "I'm positive you can do this!"

Copyeditor Rachael Clements, your attention to detail put me at ease and fixed my "comma problem."

Jenny TeGrotenhuis, LMHC, CCTP, you witnessed my stories and contained my ache with grace and wisdom. You offered the attunement my little girl needed all along, naming my wounds and pointing out the road to freedom. You were there as God slowly revealed this vision. Thank you.

K.G., "You are loved." Every morning you leave me the same message because you know, see, and hear me.

Lydia Reid, my dearest "Luv Luv," you are my heart's home, my remedy in dark places, and always enough for me. You loved me while I was "chasing myself in the skies."

Bekkah, my forever unicorn, you get me. I love you.

Phyllis Ferguson, you have mothered my heart, calling out my best, molding my life more than you ever know.

David "Mr. McFeely" Newell, thank you. Fred Rogers used you from Heaven each time I was discouraged; I'd open my mailbox and find a care package from Pittsburgh with pictures, shoelaces, stickers, signed photos for my students, and handwritten letters. *Speedy Deliveries* arrived in my classroom, and each year we reach one hundred days in the *Neighborhood*, your texts come back quickly like a familiar knock on Mister Rogers' door. May you know that you and Fred were right all these years.

Jim Okonak, from our first meeting at the McFeely-Rogers Foundation that fall morning, your kindness and presence reminded me I was on the right track. You contained my tears of disappointment just like Fred would have and encouraged me to keep writing. Thank you for helping me see Fred through your eyes and sharing your family's history in Latrobe, Pennsylvania.

Tim Madigan, thank you for sharing your stories of friendship with Fred and your willingness to lead me to the answers I sought. I'm grateful to you. I asked you once, "When I get to Heaven, will you introduce me to Fred?" to which you replied, "You two are already acquainted."

Photographer Jim Judkas, your interactions with Fred gave me a deeper insight into his simple beauty and how he interacted with children in your presence. My "friend in Fred," your work is the closest I will ever get to sitting in the presence of Fred Rogers. The world has no idea how much your photographs have defined the legacy of Mister Rogers.

Photographer Lynn Johnson, from the moment I saw your work, your reverence and delight in spending time with Fred were evident. Thank you for getting up close like a child, showcasing his humanity and intention. Including pieces of your collection in this work is a tremendous honor. "You two really are connected," you texted as I couldn't stop crying, looking through your moments of Fred.

Maxwell King, you helped make Fred Rogers' last dream a reality and gave the world a lasting masterpiece in *The Good Neighbor: The Life and Work of Fred Rogers*. You guided my research in the archive through phone calls and emails and believed in this book.

To those at the Fred Rogers Institute: archivist Emily Uhrin, for your patience, knowledge, and time that rainy week in 2019. Hedda Sharapan, thank you for your insight and memories and for reassuring me to simply "tell your stories." Dana Winters, for your understanding of Simple Interactions and for inviting me to visit the institute and research. Lastly, Theresa Noel, your enthusiasm and acceptance were like a welcome-home hug.

I'm indebted to the countless others whose work continues to bring light to healing developmental trauma, especially those at the Allender Center.

My parents, Dan Johnston and Nancy Gaffney, for your love and support of all my creative endeavors.

To the countless children I've been privileged to teach over my career thus far, I have learned *everything* from you.

Fred M. Rogers, the best of prophets are voices of consciousness in an age that cries out for righteous leadership. You led the way and invited me into the stream of your intentions. I am humbled and honored to have my name in some small way attached to yours. May these words bring deeper revelation and set hearts free. Someday, I will sit in your presence and tell you that you were right all along. Thank you for your unrelenting dedication to your service for children and their families.

Jesus, you are enough. May this be a tribute to your goodness in my life.

About the Author

Wysteria Edwards, BA, Ed.M., is setting a new standard for how to teach with attachment, attunement, and intention. As a Kindergarten teacher in Eastern WA, she specializes in creating a classroom environment of care, hope, and healing. Her unwavering attention to attachment repair in the classroom is changing how teachers and parents engage their own stories of harm and heartache while applying the simple and deep principles of Fred McFeeley Rogers. To learn more about Wysteria and her work, visit wysteriaedwards.com.

A free ebook edition is available with the purchase of this book.

To claim your free ebook edition:

1. Visit MorganJamesBOGO.com
2. Sign your name CLEARLY in the space
3. Complete the form and submit a photo of the entire copyright page
4. You or your friend can download the ebook to your preferred device

Morgan James BOGO™

A **FREE** ebook edition is available for you or a friend with the purchase of this print book.

CLEARLY SIGN YOUR NAME ABOVE

Instructions to claim your free ebook edition:
1. Visit MorganJamesBOGO.com
2. Sign your name CLEARLY in the space above
3. Complete the form and submit a photo of this entire page
4. You or your friend can download the ebook to your preferred device

Print & Digital Together Forever.

Snap a photo   Free ebook   Read anywhere

Printed in the USA
CPSIA information can be obtained
at www.ICGtesting.com
JSHW022246250823
47256JS00005B/6

9 781636 981031